INTERRUPTING VIOLENCE

INTERRUPTING VIOLENCE

One Man's Journey to Heal the Streets and Redeem Himself

Cobe Williams and Josh Gryniewicz

ROWMAN & LITTLEFIELD

Lanham • Boulder • New York • London

Published by Rowman & Littlefield
An imprint of The Rowman & Littlefield Publishing Group, Inc.
4501 Forbes Boulevard, Suite 200, Lanham, Maryland 20706
www.rowman.com

86-90 Paul Street, London EC2A 4NE

British Library Cataloguing in Publication Information Available

Library of Congress Cataloging-in-Publication Data

Names: Williams, Cobe, author. | Gryniewicz, Josh, author.
Title: Interrupting violence : one man's journey to heal the streets and
    redeem himself / Cobe Williams and Josh Gryniewicz.
Description: Lanham : Rowman & Littlefield, [2024] | Includes
    bibliographical references and index.
Identifiers: LCCN 2023035748 (print) | LCCN 2023035749 (ebook) | ISBN
    9781538166871 (cloth) | ISBN 9781538166888 (ebook)
Subjects: LCSH: Williams, Cobe. | Urban violence—United
    States—Prevention. | Violence—United States—Prevention. |
    Violence—Social aspects—United States. | Crime—United States.
Classification: LCC HN90.V5 W55 2024 (print) | LCC HN90.V5 (ebook) | DDC
    363.32/16092 [B]—dc23/eng/20231212
LC record available at https://lccn.loc.gov/2023035748
LC ebook record available at https://lccn.loc.gov/2023035749

CONTENTS

FOREWORD

Alex Kotlowitz

I'm not sure of the exact moment I first met Cobe. It feels like he's always been present in my life—or at least that's how I imagine it. Honestly, now I can't imagine a world *without* Cobe. His naturally buoyant nature regularly lifts my spirit. His tell-it-like-it-is attitude guides me. His loyalty gives me comfort.

Although we had met earlier, I came to know Cobe well while working on the documentary film *The Interrupters*, which featured him and two other extraordinary individuals who, like Cobe, worked as violence interrupters. We spent fourteen months filming, and it quickly became clear how much respect Cobe had on the street, especially among younger people. He'd walk in a neighborhood, and we could hear his teasing and his laughter from a block away. He has this uncanny ability to make people laugh along with him—even in the tensest of situations. I once saw him talk down a young man who had a pistol tucked into his waistband, ready to seek revenge. This young man was so angry that he punched a hole through the wall of his home's vestibule. Cobe didn't flinch. "What can you do for me?" the young man challenged Cobe. "What can you do for me, right now?!" Cobe instinctually replied, "We could get lunch." It was such a simple but profound gesture. And so Cobe took him to lunch, and in the weeks and months to come, Cobe nurtured him, listened to his story, shared meals and conversations and wisdom. Cobe became his friend, his mentor—and once Cobe gets a hold of you, he doesn't let go.

   This is Cobe. Generous to a fault. He can be playful—which puts people at ease—but he's always thinking to himself, *What can I do to help?* He makes people feel like they're the most important person in the world.

For over thirty years, I've been writing about the intersection of race and poverty, and in my reporting, I've come to write a good deal about the violence in our cities. Make no mistake about it: the disputes that erupt into something more are a direct consequence of the traumas of growing up poor and Black or Latino in cities like Chicago, which are still deeply segregated. Look at a map of the murders and shootings in Chicago, and it creates a swath through the city's South Side and West Side, like a thunderstorm barreling through the city. How can there not be a link between a loss of hope and the ease with which spats explode into something more? Cobe knows this. It's why, for him, being a violence interrupter is more than just acting as a mediator. He recognizes the need to lend a hand, to help widen that narrowing window of opportunity, and to provide care for those who have suffered trauma. It's why he sees the need to fortify the human spirit as well as fortify a sense of community. Cobe has been a part of a revolution in the way we view the violence in our cities—and a part of a revolution in how we try to defuse it. For so long, we've simply called for more police and longer prison sentences. Cobe is a part of this exciting national effort to treat people with a sense of dignity and respect, a national effort that is, in effect, reclaiming ownership of community. It's formally known as community violence intervention, but that doesn't begin to capture the scope of what Cobe and others do as they walk their communities with an open heart and a quiet fury stemming from their belief that things need not be this way. I feel so fortunate to count Cobe as a dear friend. Over the years, I've leaned on him for advice and for guidance. We've traveled together and shared meals, stories, and so many laughs. We talk regularly about family, about work, and about life. I've come to count on him—and I like to think he's come to count on me.

   I don't want to give away Cobe's story, but suffice it to say I marvel at his journey and revel in his companionship. His personal journey is one of heartbreak and loss but also one of an abundance of joy and redemption. I hope in these pages you, like I, will come to treasure his company, that you will come to understand the true capacity of the human heart, that you will get at least a taste of what it means to have Cobe by your side.

FOREWORD

Joakim Noah

Cobe Williams is the real deal.

The first time I met him at a P.F. Chang's in the suburbs of Chicago, I knew it. These events appear in this book, but it is important that I express how I experienced them. We met for lunch to talk about how I could help my adopted city over egg rolls. More than a decade later, we are still working together. In that time, I have had opportunities and experienced things that would have never happened if not for that lunch meeting. In many ways, my life is one of the many Cobe has impacted and improved. I am better for knowing him.

I was playing for the Bulls in Chicago, a city that already has a kind of mythic quality. Obviously, the team itself was legendary, but also there are some aspects of Chicago culture that just embody everything about America for better or worse. The violence, racism, separation, and segregation there were unlike anything I had encountered growing up or witnessed anywhere else.

Throughout my life, I was raised around social work. My grandmother built a school in Africa. My father, even though he was a very successful tennis player, always looked for ways to give back. His mother raised him to see his position as a vehicle to help others. So, when I came to Chicago as a basketball player, I knew I had a responsibility to use my position to be able to give a helping hand.

I knew that I wanted to do something in the city. I knew I wanted to use my platform to do something good, and I thought it was worth exploring that with Cobe. I had just watched *The Interrupters*, a documentary by Alex Kotlowitz and Steve James about violence prevention, which featured Cobe doing his thing: mediating conflicts. This was something positive and powerful happening in my backyard. I wanted to help. I tweeted something endorsing the film. Cobe reached out immediately in what I would come to know as the signature Cobe way: "I am glad you liked my movie."

Chicago is a deeply divided city. It is divided by race, economics, gang territory, and on and on. They practically invented modern segregation there. As Cobe talks about in these pages, Chicago is one of the prominent American cities that has been dramatically segregated. Even today, you have a "Black Chicago" that is cut off from the rest of the city.

On top of these divisions of race, Chicago communities are further divided by gangs. Boundaries virtually invisible to an outsider dictate where you can go, what you can do, who you can connect with, and so on. It is no wonder that so many kids growing up on the South Side and West Side never venture too far off the block.

Cobe moved between these divides effortlessly. I was impressed by how he navigated these divisions as if they didn't exist, especially knowing what I knew about how he grew up and what his life had been like before as a default enforcer of some of these divides. I couldn't believe he could just enter a space designed to box him out and win everyone over. In part, this is his sense of humor (I don't know that I have ever laughed as hard as I have driving around with him), but more so, I think it is his authenticity. He is so genuine as a person.

That's what I mean by the real deal. He makes connections with people everywhere he goes in deep and meaningful ways. It's impressive.

When he showed up at the restaurant, he came in without an agenda. Cobe talks about how impressed he was with me that I didn't just want a photo op, but I was just as impressed that he didn't just ask me for a donation.

In fact, he didn't even mention money.

We just sat down for eggrolls, started talking, and didn't stop. We talked and talked and talked and talked. It was just a cool conversation. A really cool, honest conversation. By the end of it, we had a bond. I felt like this is my brother. Cobe was my big brother.

The following week, he brought out kids from the neighborhood to hang out in our practice space.

Again, no agenda.

He wasn't pushing to create a program. There were no strings attached. He wasn't angling for something else. This was just an opportunity to bring some kids off the block and show them a bigger world. They were wide-eyed and excited to play on the same court where Michael Jordan played. We opened up possibilities for them. That was something special. It wasn't about trying to do anything other than give these kids an amazing experience.

After that, Cobe invited me out into the neighborhood. Now, when I say this man brought me out in the community, I do not mean that we gathered up some kids at a local rec center gymnasium to shoot hoops and pose for pictures. This was not a highly curated, media-managed, tailored experience philanthropists will sometimes get.

None of that.

No.

I mean, this man took me to his grandmother's house! I met his mother, brother, sister, aunties, uncles, family, and friends. He didn't just introduce me to his family; he welcomed me into it. He made me feel that I belonged.

That is a part of Cobe's charm. It is all love. He wants everyone to feel the same sense of connection. I know it is what has made him so successful at what he does working with high-risk kids. It makes me proud to call him a friend. People come up to me sometimes to tell me how much I inspire them. Well, Cobe inspires me. Truth. His passion, his work, his integrity. It is inspiring.

At first, it was just getting a few tickets here and a few tickets there. Just bringing the kids out to games, maybe bringing them out on the court afterward. This wasn't much effort for me, but it had a real impact on some of these children.

After that, it just built and built organically. I kept wanting to do more. I wrote a series of op-eds about violence in the paper. Cobe and I started working together on peace tournaments with Duce, Father Pfleger, and others documented in this book. I got some of my teammates involved, Derrick Rose and others, but we didn't really have too much of a structure to it at the time. It started with something as simple as getting these kids together from different neighborhoods in different parts of the city and letting them ball together. There was something extraordinary about using the game that had given me so much to truly give back, but beyond that, it wasn't all that complicated at first.

It kept building.

We planned a whole season, bringing these kids together to play over nineteen weeks or so to learn skills they could take back into the neighborhood. We weren't doing anything formal. There was no playbook or curriculum, but we were teaching skills around meditation, conflict resolution, collaboration, cooperation, teamwork, and so on. Even in those early days, we saw results. I remember seeing kids would straighten up and act right just to stay in the program.

Then, as the seasons passed, we started innovating. We began to mix the players up so that kids from one street organization played alongside teammates from a competing street organization.

Guys who were literally shooting at one another on a Monday could be playing on the same team, passing the ball to one another on a Wednesday.

It was truly remarkable to see this game connect young people, who hours earlier truly wanted each other dead, now embracing each other over a win just before the final buzzer went off. There are few things in my life as awe-inspiring as witnessing that firsthand.

In a matter of a few seasons back-to-back, we went from being an after-school program to an initiative that was truly healing the community. In the same spirit of building, building, building, we asked ourselves what can we do next to make an even more profound impact. We started using the games as a way to bring opposing groups together to sign peace treaties.

It was powerful.

As Cobe writes about, groups that were into it with each other from all over the city, who had inherited a war from their older siblings, parents, and grandparents lasting decades longer than they'd even been alive, now had the space to resolve that conflict.

That was a far cry from bringing some kids down to the United Center. It was a far cry from even just playing the game throughout the season. These events were remarkable, but to actually establish peace treaties over conflicts that had been raging in neighborhoods for years, claiming lives— seemed nothing short of a miracle.

It kept building.

Once we had a few seasons under our belt, we began replicating in New York, Baltimore, and Philadelphia. Similar tournaments with similar results throughout the country. We kept this up for seven years. Even after I'd left the Bulls, we kept supporting the work. I can honestly say it changed my life. I experienced things I'd have had no other way of experiencing, met people I would have no other way of meeting, and impacted lives I would have no other way of impacting if it weren't for Cobe.

He helped me find my purpose.

When we'd meet up in New York or Los Angeles, I used to tell him that after basketball, we are doing violence prevention full time.

And I meant it.

Today, I am making good on that promise. This work is a huge part of my life.

Noah's Arc Foundation, my organization, leads citywide basketball tournaments for peace on a scale much larger than anything we've done before, working in collaboration with Cobe. The One City events formalized many of the processes and practices we stumbled on organically, developing art programs, workshops, training, and more, providing young people with access to opportunities they aren't getting through more conventional channels. We bring youth, many who have never been off the block before, to Africa.

Cobe is the real deal.

It has been a great honor working alongside my brother to make the world a better place. I am a better person for knowing him, and I believe the world is a better place as a result. I hope in reading this book, you are as inspired by Cobe as I have been and, more important, that you are moved to take action.

INTRODUCTION

Interrupting Violence is the story of my personal transformation. It is my journey from gang member to peacemaker. It is my journey from being a "shot caller" in the Black Disciples to becoming a leader in a national movement of community violence intervention, a revolution in the way we look at violence and how to solve it. It is my journey from being part of the problem to becoming part of the solution.

I was born into one of America's most notorious street gangs. My father was an influential member. He was a big-time drug dealer, making a lot of money, driving Cadillac cars, rocking sharp suits, and wearing expensive jewelry. I grew up wanting to be like him. When I was eleven, my father was murdered by his so-called friends. It flipped my world upside down.

I rose through the ranks as a drug dealer, hustler, and leader. I learned the code of the street before I even learned to ride a bike. I ran wild and didn't give a fuck. I knew right from wrong. I just didn't care. My time in the streets was spent fighting a war I inherited decades before I was born that claimed bodies on both sides. By the time I was eighteen, I caught my first case. Before I was twenty-two, I went to prison for aggravated battery and drug possession.

Gun violence is a leading cause of death for children and adolescents. Communities of color are disproportionately affected. Young Black Americans (ages fifteen to thirty-four) experience the highest rates of gun homicides across all demographics. Black children are eight times as likely as other children to die by gunfire. They represent two-thirds of gun homicides while making up only about 15 percent of children in America.

It often claims the life of the shooter as well as the victim, sending one to jail and the other to the grave. It leaves families devastated and communities destroyed. It locks entire generations away, creating a culture of violence and a climate of pain. It leaves a wake of trauma, economic disadvantage, and ruin.

Behind bars, I began to see for the first time the full impact of these actions. I promised not only to turn my life around when I got out but also to dedicate it to helping others. I have spent nearly two decades working to reverse this epidemic. First, mediating conflicts in the street. Working with the men most likely to kill or be killed. I walked into situations others were running from to keep the peace.

Then, as a national leader, having crisscrossed America more times than I can count to establish programs. I logged thousands of frequent-flier miles to help set up hundreds of community violence intervention sites across the country in the most violence-impacted communities, training thousands of violence prevention workers in the process. I have been an activist, outreach worker, violence interrupter, national director, community engagement expert, public safety consultant, trainer, educator, public speaker, and now an author.

Community violence intervention is a growing public safety movement that stops shootings and killings on the front end. It uses formerly incarcerated gang members as "credible messengers" to interrupt violence. More important, it is a model of community self-reliance working in the most violence-impacted neighborhoods, with those at the highest risk of being shooters or victims. It helps communities to govern themselves without feeling an occupying force has overrun them.

This book is my story. It is also the story of two families, interconnected, coping with the impact of trauma across generations and the racist history of Black Chicago. It is about surviving hardship and coming out stronger on the other side. It is about finding ways to resolve this pain transmitted, parent to child, to resolve the cycle of intergenerational trauma for a hopeful future.

This book is my story. It is also the story of a movement that has come of age. It is the story of community activists, often formerly incarcerated individuals, working to undo the harm they've done. It is the story of ragtag groups of organizers working out of community-based storefronts in ramshackle strip malls to keep tenuous peace on mean streets. Others like me who have left behind gang life to convene peace talks in church basements on borrowed time to save lives. This is the story of connecting those groups from the Bronx and Brooklyn to Cherry Hill, Baltimore, syncing Englewood, Chicago, and Inglewood, California, with movements in Minneapolis and St. Louis, Oakland, and Los Angeles to form a cohesive revolution in violence prevention. A movement that went from unlit, hardscrabble alleyways all the way to the White House.

This book is my story. It is also a guide for what cities need to know to set up a community violence intervention in their neighborhoods. It is about the nuts-and-bolts logistics of creating a program. The challenges faced from laying the groundwork to launching the site. It is my story, but it is also a call to action for leaders looking for a new way forward in public health for some of the nation's most violence-impacted communities.

Much of the purpose of writing this book is to move the conversation about justice further upstream. When we talk about justice in this country, we often get focused on courts and prison, leaving what happens on the streets and in the community out of the conversation. I want us to begin thinking big picture when looking for ways to transform the justice system. From adopting community violence initiatives to manage safety on the street to reimagining the community conditions that support a program, I am inviting you to reimagine with me.

In revisiting my story, I look at the role that systems play in influencing my experience. I share what decades of disinvestment do to Black and Brown communities across the country, disadvantaging residents from the start, and the inability of families to take part in a formal economy, get steady employment, access reliable job opportunities with living wages, buy homes, start businesses, and create intergenerational wealth.

I look at the role of education in contributing to mass incarceration. By default, the school system is often converted to warehousing rather than educating and training young people to contribute to society. This leads to the school-to-prison pipeline, where young people are moved from one system into another without broader opportunities.

If we are going to transform justice, we must focus on more than the legal system and the policies that contribute to it. For years, the "solutions" put forward have involved more cops on the street and longer sentencing behind bars. These have only created more problems. I also look at other forms of intervention that provide a map for healing from trauma rather than doing further harm. We need to expand our tool kit: restorative justice, peace circles, reconciliation, and trauma-informed care.

Throughout this book, I try to show what mediation actually looks like from the inside. There is a lot of professional literature on the topic in social work and psychology that shows clean models of an individual working through a mediation, which I will share when necessary. I aim to bring you into the process so you can see it ain't all flowcharts and logic models. It can be messy, filled with rage, confusion, trauma, and pain. I bring readers into that experience so that they can see it for themselves.

I also show how the usual dynamic of street interactions goes when police get involved. Law enforcement is trained to approach these issues differently and can often create more pain and hardship in the community. Based on my own experience and the experiences of others, I try to show how the mediations covered in this book would have gone differently if it were police responding instead of a violence interrupter.

Finally, a quick note on some of the events included in this book. In order to protect the identity and respect the privacy of program participants involved in violence featured here, we have opted for street names when necessary. These stories have been retold with permission and are shared with the utmost respect. Our hope is that their experiences can provide valuable insight to readers and future conflict mediators. King Shorty Freeman, rest his soul, the founder of the Black Disciples and my mentor in violence prevention, had an encyclopedic knowledge of gang history and events. Sometimes, when we worked together, it was like being in school. Many of the conversations reflected here were fact-checked with historical references or interview sources for accuracy.

Memory is a funny thing, especially when trauma is involved, so certain events are reflected as I recollect them. In many instances, we checked with others involved. We conducted more than twenty interviews with family, friends, coworkers, colleagues, and fellow travelers on this journey. We talked to guys I came up with on the streets—friends and family—who knew me back then. We spoke to activists who were doing community organizing in cities where I would eventually help set up sites on what happened before we began our work together. We spoke with organizers who were instrumental in bringing me to their city. We also spoke with coworkers who traveled and trained with me. If there were ever any discrepancy between how we each saw certain events, we would go with my version because, you know, it is my story.

As a result, this being my story, how I talk is how I talk. As most Black Americans know, a lot of code-switching happens when you go back and forth between social situations. I will sound different with my boys on the corner in the hood in anywhere USA than I will sound presenting in the oak-paneled conference room in the mayor's office in that same city. The writing reflects that here. If the grammar is "incorrect," it is only so by certain standards and not others. Wherever possible, we erred on the side of authenticity so that the conversation sounds the way it does in any given scene or setting.

I

BORN INTO IT

❶

ONE CHICAGO SUMMER

Englewood/Auburn Gresham, Chicago, July 2015

A scorching midsummer afternoon on Chicago's South Side. On 77th and Aberdeen, the block runs hot. A black Caprice opens fire on a mob of corner boys. Shooters miss all six marks. The guys arm up in response.

In this neighborhood, shootouts are as much a part of summer as open hydrants and BBQs. As the temperature climbs into the nineties, the body count pushes toward five hundred homicides—shootings in the thousands. I'm a violence interrupter, a highly trained conflict resolution specialist, so I take these numbers personally. I am responsible for talking these guys down before they add to those statistics or join them.

"What up, Cobe?" D-Boy calls as I pull to the curb. He looks more California surfer than Chicago hustla. A fluorescent T-shirt with matching cargo shorts, bright orange, and beige camo. Close-cropped hair bleached blonde.

Where this went down, it is a short sprint from my Granny's house. Most of my childhood took place on or around this corner. Mom had her first home on Carpenter, right behind Granny's place, where the yard runs up to the back gate via the alleyway. I bounced around between houses as a child, visiting in on aunties and Granny, all within a few blocks of this spot, whenever the mood struck. I park my car within eyesight of Granny's Dutch Colonial, the centerpiece of my family's orbit.

"You look like you fixing to go on safari with Sponge Bob Squarepants," I rib.

Despite the tension, perhaps because of it, D laughs.

His boy, Lil' B, laughs along with us.

I reach out my hand, coming around the front of the car as he and Lil' B step over to greet me. I sync up with D-Boy first, shaking his hand as he scans the block, back and forth, with an unsteady gaze. Hypervigilant. He looks like a bobblehead at the moment.

I've known him and his family for years. His dad is a bit older than me, but I know him from way back. D-Boy can't quite settle enough to fix on me yet. He holds a residual smile from laughing out loud but is still rattled.

Air smells of gun smoke and motor speedway: adrenaline and fear. An electric charge hangs over the street still vibrating with danger—the static discharge of a storm. Shell casings litter a lawn sprinkled with broken glass that shimmers like diamonds in sunlight.

A couple guys, amped up, pace the opposite corner. Fresh scorch marks from burnt tire treads. Fresh pockmarks on the brick facade.

Police likely won't come around for a shooting without a body. You've heard it, probably before most of these guys were born: *9-1-1 is a joke in our town.*

And here's the punchline: if the cops did show, they'd have D-Boy, Lil' B, and the crew seated on this curb. They'd spend their time rounding up these guys instead of learning the specifics of the event. An interrogation of victims would follow. The logic that *"they must've done something to deserve it"* dominates. Some of these guys might be dragged down to the station for the crime of being shot at.

Punish them all. These victims are just as guilty. Charged with being on the wrong corner at the wrong time. Charged with being young and Black. Charged with living in this zip code. Because they all gangbangers anyway—*ain't that the case?* Victims and perpetrators, opposite sides of the same coin, must be punished equally.

Lil' B reaches past his friend in a greeting. Nods to me, then up the street. He is as round-faced as the Gerber baby. Even with a Tar Heels cap pulled low over his close-shaved head, Lil' B looks younger than his sixteen years. He is wearing a sleeveless white undershirt and a pair of shorts, powder blue, the color of Carolina, the Knicks, the Jazz, or a baby boy's bedroom.

He is younger than my sons. That observation can feel heavy sometimes, it weighs on me. Lil' B, better suited for the classroom than the corner, offers an easy smile.

"Vice Lord, just come through—pop, pop, pop—open fire," Lil' B says, motioning in the direction of the tire marks lead, "then race off just like nothing."

"It's random, man. We ain't even into it with them, not like that, right now," D-Boy adds. Nodding in the same direction as Lil' B confusedly. "I don't get why they'd want to start something now."

I offer skepticism with a look and a smirk but believe what they're saying. I haven't heard anything about them beefing any more than usual. At least, nothing that would provoke this level of action.

"At least no one was hit," I offer.

'True. True." D-Boy responds. "Still messed up, though."

"Soon as we get some wheels, we're going hunting," Lil' B says, smacking a balled fist into an open palm like a little league catcher signaling a pitcher on the mound. "Already arming up and everything."

I describe violence interrupters as firefighters. They're called into a burning building as everyone else is rushing out. They have the equipment and the training to put out the flames before it gets out of control. In the same way, an interrupter runs toward the gunfire. We try to get an incident, like this one, under control before it escalates.

Years ago, visiting the UN headquarters in New York, we got compared to Blue Helmets a lot. They are seen as a global peacekeeping force sent into conflict countries to mediate. There are similarities. We try to act like neutral noncombatants, the same as the Blue Helmets, so as to not take any one side over the other. In some neighborhoods, police are looked at as an occupying force in the same way a foreign military might be viewed.[1] Whereas we are regarded as an indigenous presence, a homegrown part of the community. Our aim is to broker peace by whatever means possible.

We intentionally try not to use gang names—opting for Group A or Group B rather than Black Disciples or Vice Lord—so we can toe that line of neutrality. We operate from a place of diplomacy. What is it going to take to de-escalate? How are we going to find a win-win that keeps the peace? What really kicks off an incident? How can we resolve that? How can we maintain a sense of justice and resolution without resorting to retaliation or retribution?

There are differences, though. We aren't armed soldiers marching into a battle zone. Our only equipment is our cell phones, our charisma, and jokes for days. We focus on stability, but we're not on the rule of law. We aren't policing. We aren't placeholders for power. And we are rarely mistaken for Smurfs.

Interruption exists between street outreach and activism, community health work, and social work. That is where we operate. If you want to get technical, we use conflict resolution theory, crisis response tactics, and cognitive behavioral skills. We meet these kids where they are at, on the corner and in life, without judgment. We use harm reduction to decrease their level of risk—to explore safer options and alternative strategies.

Actually, if you want to get really technical, there is no other job in the world like violence interruption.

"Why would they make a move on us now?" D-Boy asks out loud.

"Got to be curious, right?" I ask.

Just pulling that thread can help us discourage retaliation. I'll use what I can to talk something out. Get them thinking about their kids or their family: Mom, Grandma, aunties, or uncles, and so on—*how are they going to feel if you get hit?*—or get them talking through how they feel. Processing. Hitting pause. Buying time. Often, that's the whole mission.

"I don't know if it matters much the *why,* being as they did what they did," D-Boy shrugs in response and rocks his hand back and forth, gesturing ambivalence.

"Fact is they got to get got," Lil' B chimes in, "that's the only way to settle this, really."

"What happens if you let this slide?" I ask coyly.

B looks like I just boxed his ears.

"Stand down?"

"I'm not suggesting, just asking."

"Going to make us out to be punks, I'd figure." Lil' B answers.

D-Boy scratches his chin. Leans forward. "Maybe not, though."

"At least to get a handle on *why,*" I offer. "Seems this could have been something rogue. Maybe you don't have to handle it."

"It'd be good to know," D-Boy conceits.

"What's Big Folks' take on everything?" I ask, referring to the leader of the crew.

He is going to have to say the same things Lil' B has been saying. It's his crew, his responsibility. He will have to go on defense. Big Folks doesn't want to be made out a punk. He doesn't want his guys branded punks either. This is the code of the streets.

If you get seen as a punk, you make yourself an even bigger target, inviting even more attacks.[2] You are marked. Easy pickings for a robbery, a fight, a takeover, or a takedown. Big Folks needs to protect his reputation. This isn't an ego thing. It isn't just about status or identity. Reputation is life or death. A protective spell cast over you and your crew. A solid rep makes someone think twice before they move on you. Not taking action can undo years of building a position.

D-Boy and Lil' B are foot soldiers. Big Folks calls the shots for the clique: his corner, his boys. If I manage to get through to these guys, they are going to need Big Folks' blessing not to take action. Having all the players in the conversation is easier when you push toward standing down. Bringing him in on the discussion now saves us all precious time.

AN ANTIDOTE FOR THE CODE OF THE STREETS

Big Folks stands sentry a few feet away, arms folded across his chest. He leans against the wall. He holds a scowl as I smile over at him. No bad blood between us, but there is a piece tucked in his waistband that he's fixing to use, and he knows I am there to stop him.

The same graffiti that tags the wall around Big Folks is tattooed across his massive chest, neck, and folded forearms. It is as if Big Folks and the wall are part of the same mural. It's a mural that I was a part of for years, some time ago.

Black Disciples run this area. They rule this corner. It's a background that I share with Big Folks, D-Boy, Lil' B, and the rest of the guys. A large part of an interrupter's success is that we come from the same world as these guys. It is not just the neighborhood but the lifestyle that makes us effective. Our rep can be legendary. They came up hearing our stories and knowing our deeds. If we encourage them to stand down from a fight, it helps them save face. We are an antidote to the code of the streets.

ARITHMETIC OF INTERRUPTION

Here is the basic arithmetic of interruption. A conflict of this type requires a minimum of two parties involved. That's your starting point. You stand your best chance of finding a peaceful resolution if you can get everyone on their own at first. One-on-one. Away from friends and family. You want to isolate against anyone who is going to have some sway. If someone else has their ear, then big talk, fear, anger, concern, or hurt can push someone into action. Someone always gonna be *"if I'd been there,"* that makes those who actually were second-guess their actions. If it is a group like this one, you work in stages. Same principles different setup. It takes as long as it takes. Your focus is on creating space and claiming time. Time in tiny increments. Minutes. Moments. Days. Any measure that can create distance between the incident and the emotion is a win. If you can add up enough days between an event and a response, they become weeks. The answer is less likely to be violent. The desire for revenge and retaliation fades. You work from foot soldiers to shot callers with discussion and debate. Buy time. Influence.

That's all I am trying to do with Big Folks right now. Buy some time. Try to get cooler heads to prevail.

Big Folks is having none of it: "I don't even want to hear what you have to say." He shakes his head.

I smile. Nod. Let out a deep laugh.

"Just like that?"

"I don't want to hear any of that peace shit."

"D-Boy said you guys aren't even into it with them like that."

"True."

"You got an idea who did this, though?"

"Some."

"What are you thinking?"

"I'm telling you, Big Homie, I don't even want to go there with you," Big Folks tells me.

"Y'all still waiting on a car, right? You can chat while we wait. You ain't doing nothing but holding up this wall, right?"

Big Folks gives a solemn nod. Encourages me to continue.

"You have to have some idea who you're going to hit."

"Some."

"Who you thinking?"

"I'm telling you, I don't want to go there with you."

"Okay. Okay. Can you play it through for me, though? You know where this leads, so play it out for me."

"How you mean?"

"Let's say this thing is rogue. Something that has been done independently. How long is it going to stay that way?"

"I don't want to hear it, Cobe. I don't."

"You feeling blessed y'all spared? That's got to be some kind of miracle, isn't it?"

"Sure."

"So, this thing is rogue, like we figure. They just come through, and you hit them back without knowing what's behind it. What do they got to do?"

Big Folks goes stoic. I don't know if I have him, but he seems to be chewing on it. I push.

I tell him, "Maybe now they crew up. What was an independent act they'd get violated for becomes official business, so now you're risking your guys over something that was just shortsighted stupidity?"

"I can't let this shit slide."

"I'm not even suggesting that just yet," I tell him honestly. "I'm just asking that you know who you moving on before you make a move. I'm suggesting that you get clear on who did this to you in the first place."

Big Folks squints, biting his lip.

"Every minute I don't do something puts us in danger."

"I get that," I tell him, "But if you give me some time to figure out who and what is behind this, at least you know you ain't starting a war over a joyride."

"I don't like being used as target practice."

"I hear you. It's crazy stupid they'd even try something on you. That's why I figure it has to be rogue. It doesn't make sense for anyone to come at you for no reason. I'm not even saying stand down," I tell him. "I'm just asking for a day or so to find out what's what. If you are going to go at them, wouldn't you rather know who you are going at?"

Big Folks stares off in the direction of his crew. He brings a vape pen to his mouth and pulls a drag.

"My boy, T, isn't going to have a car here until after he gets off work tonight, so maybe I give you that. I give you the rest of the day to do what you got to do, but then, you know, I got to do what I got to do."

"You gimme your word that neither you or your guys are going to respond until this evening, and I will leave you alone."

"You got until tonight, you got my word, but then I got to do something."

That was good enough for me. We shake on it. I head to the car. The clock is ticking. I have until the streetlights come on until Big Folks and his crew are out for blood.

2

CADILLAC GOALPOSTS

Englewood/Auburn Gresham, Chicago, 1980

"Whoa! Whoa! Whoa! Here comes Cobe Baba," shouts Ms. Simmons, my next-door neighbor, shuffling out of my way as I run past. Across her front lawn, hugging the ball to my chest, making for the street. Moving so fast I barely hear her.

On a sunny Saturday morning in Auburn Gresham, we are playing football on the street in the middle of an endless childhood summer. I am Lynn Swann, Pittsburgh Steelers wide receiver at this moment, a four-time Super Bowl champion, all before my ninth birthday. Days filled with mischief and games until the streetlamps come on at dusk. Even then, a little bit longer if we can find an excuse to stretch out the time.

Football, baseball, basketball on rotation.

"And, here comes his forty thieves, too," my granny replies from our porch next door, gesturing up the block with a spray of her garden hose in the direction of my friends—Terrell, Antoine, Edward, and AV—chasing after me.

Fields spanned the front yards, breaking for the through traffic on the one-way street. Makeshift goalposts moved for incoming cars. Messy versions of time-honored traditions played by grade-schoolers the world over. Front lawns and sidewalks, beyond the curbside rows of parked vehicles, inbound; front porches, walkways, gardens, marked foul, out-of-bounds. These versions of football navigate shrubs, trees, and garden trestles between the maroon Monte Carlo and gray Cadillac goalposts, set away from the green Pontiac and brown Oldsmobile of the opposing team.

Obstacles became a part of the game—an ever-changing landscape, not league-approved. If a neighbor had to drive a "goalpost" to work, we changed the shape of the field. When Granny declared the game needed to move three houses down because she was sick of footprints in the flower garden, the whole game moved three houses down. That's how football is played in neighborhoods throughout the West Side and the South before the age of peewee leagues and uniforms and teams with real names.

Chicago is notoriously divided along racial lines.[1] Urban planning in this city invented the contemporary American apartheid. Over half of the Black population lives in twenty of the city's seventy-seven communities, a so-called Black Belt chain of neighborhoods—at one time the largest contiguous area of African American settlement in the country.[2] The city is one of the most segregated in the nation.

Segregation by structure physically divides Black Chicago from the rest of the city. The built environment of highways, byways, railways, industrial parks, and bridges split one Chicago from the next. It really is two cities. Underlying these structural divisions are racist redlining policies, discriminatory banking, and unfair housing practices. A third of the city, encompassing mainly Black neighborhoods, was deemed undesirable by the Federal Housing Administration at one time, with residents from these neighborhoods being denied bank loans and insurance. The result is limited access to education, employment, economic mobility, and intergenerational wealth.

Now, stretching more than one hundred blocks from 35th to 138th at the city limits, situated between Western Avenue and the lake, a narrower belt, ever tightening, is still separated, segregated, and ignored by the rest of the city.

For many growing up there, it becomes your entire cultural experience. You know nothing beyond the blocks that surround your home. Even if you can traverse the geography, you are trapped by the social divide. It might as well be on the other side of the world, not just the other side of the city.

By design and default, Englewood was my world for nearly the first quarter of my life.

I was born Ricardo Williams, but I mostly go by Cobe. How that came to be is Granny's shortening my name to Cardo, which became Cardy. Eventually, Cardy became Cobe, Co-billa, Cobester, Cobes, Co-bey, Cobi, Cardi, or King Cobe. Alternately, I was called Lil' Rick or Lil' Silk after my father, who went by Rick, Ricky, Slick Rick, Silky, Silky Smooth, and Fly. His given name was Arthur Hoover Jones, so those pseudonyms give you an idea of what he was all about.

On 77th and Aberdeen, I raced for the end zone, crossing Ms. Simmons's lawn with my Forty Thieves closing in for the takedown. Terrell's fingers outstretched, grabbing for my collar. At least for the block, I was about to make my name ring out for a game-winning touchdown as the Lynn Swann of streetball.

Streetball, a version of the game as all-American as anything endorsed by the NFL, has its rules. Messy but consistent. Teams between six and eleven guys, depending on who is available on a given day, running the ball one hundred yards, give or take a dozen, on either end. There is no clock. Offense and defense are fluid and negotiable. Grabbing clothes; takedowns on curb and concrete; occasional jabs, elbows, hip checks: all fair play and encouraged.

The harder the takedowns, the more likely the entire game morphs into a melee, dissolving into my favorite game, "Killa Man." More than basketball, baseball, softball, or running bases, my number one "sport" as a kid was always "Killa Man." The last pieces of the structure falling away from streetball devolved into a free-for-all of tackling, grappling, and wrestling. That's "killa man."

One player holding the ball becomes a team unto themselves. Everyone else, offense and defense, merge into an opposition together. The only objective: throw the guy with the ball to the ground.

Our version of streetball breaks down quickly to its most aggressive parts. We Lost Boys and Lords of the Fly, seemingly fatherless children, drawn together in negative space. Ain't none of us got to toss a football back and forth with Dad. An entire generation from adolescence to middle age vanished completely from our hood. One in three Black males in the United States will go to prison at some point in their lifetimes.[3] Most everyone in this game is on that list. They disappear from daily life as if, in a single instant, with the flip of a switch.

Mass incarceration started in the 1970s.[4] By the time we were throwing each other around playing "Killa Man" on 77th, the number of Blacks locked up had grown from two hundred thousand to almost double that rate by the end of the decade. This was the result of a sustained "law and order" rhetoric that started with the founding of this country and ramped up nearly every decade since. Stories of crime wave after crime wave bound with race crashed into our communities one election cycle after the next until they'd built into a tsunami sweeping away our fathers, brothers, uncles, and sons.

Campaign rhetoric caught in one-upmanship on both sides of the aisle promoted tough-on-crime solutions from street level to sentencing. Political pressure ratcheted up. Pressure on law enforcement to increase arrests, pressure on prosecutors to seek harsher penalties, pressure on courts to impose longer sentences, and so on. All of these policies were weighted with racial undertones that made the color of crime consistently Black. It would continue an even more aggressive climb in the decades that followed, until reaching the nearly 2.3 million behind bars today.

On that sunny summer day, these facts were far from my mind. The realities of our daily existence are often invisible, like water to a fish. Forces that shape the trajectory of our lives run like an electrical current—powerful yet invisible—behind the scenes, surrounding and influencing us all the time. As a result, it seems like they are unavoidable. Predestined by policy to end up in poverty and prison. We seem stuck on this track. The truth is much more complicated and liberating.

THE WILLIAMS FAMILY

My mom, Alfreda (Freda), had been working on getting the family out of public housing for a while by the time I came along. I was the youngest of three, the baby of the family, and always treated as such. My sister, Mildred, named after our grandmother, was two years older than me. Granny nicknamed her Trice. Years later, she would visit me in prison and pay me the same honor by naming her son after me, Lil' Cobe. Michael (Boo), my brother, was three years older and never let me forget it. Mom wanted a house near her parents, especially with Dad serving time downstate, so that she could have more room and help to raise us.

My family settled in Chicago in 1963. Grandma Mildred, my mother's mama, grew up with Phillip Williams, Sr., my grandfather, in the relative backwaters of Hamilton, Louisiana, nearly twenty-five miles from Baton Rouge and some one hundred miles outside New Orleans, roughly ten minutes from the banks of the Mississippi River. Go out just past the middle of nowhere, make a hard right—you might find it—or blink and pass it by entirely.

Granny knew that Phil was sweet on her from the beginning, back when they was kids. He was a shy, quiet boy who might never have worked up the nerve to talk to her if it wasn't that she held the conversation enough for the both of them. He was also one of the only kids in town with a bicycle.

And, besides the Main Street and the highway that ran past Hamilton, roads in town were little more than dirt paths or wooded trails, especially back in those days, so bikes were pretty valuable. As Granny always put it, she'd bat her little eyelashes and ask Phil if he could give her a lift into town on the backseat.

Mildred would hop on the seat, wrap her arms around his waist, holding tight as Phil pedaled with all his strength. He'd pedal them to the general store for groceries and back. For years, Mildred played that if she'd had a bike of her own growing up, maybe none of this would have happened. Over time, they got close, literally.

Eventually, she and Phil married. There were no jobs in the South. Granny had one brother, who moved to Chicago after serving in the army. She and Phil came to the Midwest to join him. This was part of the Great Migration that brought Blacks en masse into cities throughout the North looking for work.

The Great Migration was one of the largest movements of people in U.S. history, forever changing the demographics of the country.[5] Approximately 6 million Black people moved from the American South to northern, mid-western, and western states over a span of six decades from the 1910s until the 1970s. It is no surprise my father's family was making their way from Mississippi at that same time to settle in Chicago. During that span, the population shifted from 90 percent of Blacks in the United States concentrated in the South to 47 percent of all Blacks living in the North and West.

This was the promise of a new life, new beginnings. Chicago was the "Promised Land" in that era. Phil found himself a steady job at Allied Steel. They bought the same house I grew up in, located in the Auburn Gresham area, and settled here alongside some five hundred thousand Blacks who made it across the Mason-Dixon Line, more than doubling Chicago's Black population.

Granny had seven children in total. Five of them girls: Hilda, Shirley, Cookie, Freda, and Myrtle. Two boys: Phil Jr. and Ray. They all came up in that same house, which my Granny still owns some sixty years later.

Gramps woke before dawn every day to make the commute to the steel plant outside the city. They made pipes for electrical conduits. It was long hours, often mandatory overtime, working in extreme heat near open flames. Backbreaking labor with heavy machinery. Blast furnaces, smelting ore, embers flying, flashes of molten golden-orange steel pouring like lava, raining down in the factory all day. Descriptions sounded like hell itself, yet this was an enviable job in the community: steady wages, consistent hours, good benefits.

He would cash his check every Thursday and leave the cash sitting in stacks on the counter for Granny to cover the bills. He took care of his family and kept his priorities in check. He was a provider with almost no vice—unless you count being a Cubs fan.

On weekends, he listened to the game on an AM/FM radio. After yard work, he'd set his folding chair out on the front lawn in a tiny patch of shade. The air smelled of freshly mowed grass. He'd nurse a beer into the midafternoon. Inning after inning, he fed squirrels peanuts by hand. He'd dig a shelled nut out from his pocket with a calloused hand holding it out between pointer and thumb. The squirrel would scurry up his pant leg into his lap. It would take the nut, shell and all, eating it right there, or leap back to the lawn, oversized treasure in hand, dragging it to safety beneath a shrub.

Stretched in the shade, he'd doze, eventually. The squirrels would hop up into his lap. They'd nibble through the pockets of his jeans while he slept. Remove the peanuts one at a time and scramble down his leg, nimble as if it were the trunk of a tree until they'd emptied his pockets. This happened often enough that he didn't have a pair of denim with pockets intact.

Mildred was a fun-loving, good-natured, shrewd business owner with an enormous heart. At times, she seemed to take care of the whole community yet still managed to maintain a household, run a company, raise a sprawling extended family, and keep a beautiful flower garden on the front lawn. On weekends, she'd give her daughters a break from being moms, packing the living room wall-to-wall with kids—all my cousins, my brother, my sister, and me—nestled together in a giant slumber party that stretched for days. We all stayed there on the weekends, carving out space for ourselves on the floor, forming camps where, by the dozen, we would nestle side by side by side. We'd create a big old fort in the dining room using the table as a base and spreading sheets wall-to-wall. There would be nowhere to step with all of these kids bundled across the floor space from the dining area to the living room into the foyer. She was a good person who looked out for everyone and was always willing to lend a hand.

She also raised a lot of us grandkids in that home. Boo, Trice, and I stayed under that roof most of our formative years. As did some of my cousins. As far as I am concerned, she raised me. She also raised seventeen foster kids besides those of us who were blood.

Eventually, Mom would move us into a place on 77th, right behind my grandparents, over on Carpenter. It was modest but may have been a palace to us compared to our project apartment. I was still a toddler when we first moved in. It was so close that I could run back and forth between houses whenever I wanted. I took particular pleasure in making my rounds at lunchtime, getting something to snack on at each stop.

I bounced around the whole time I was growing up, but I always felt welcome everywhere I went. I was never at a loss. My first lesson in mindset was that we could choose how we see things—appreciating the good moments in these hardships.

My grandparents always tried to teach me right from wrong—I just didn't listen that well. Phil, through his actions, modeled what it was like to be a responsible man. Mildred, through her interventions and lectures, tried to make me decent.

THE BADDER YOU GET

"You think you so bad," Granny said in a calm, even voice, which hinted at anger without giving over to it. "There is always going to be someone badder."

I sat on the couch and picked at a fresh scab on a busted-up knuckle, trying to avoid eye contact. Granny had a way of shaking her head at you to express disappointment. It was often far more effective than anything she'd say. My guys, Calvin, Sadar, Ty, Ollie, Dog, and Lil' Paris, and I had gone to the park to fight. I was a little banged up, with a bruise on my right cheek and some dirt on my clothes. It wasn't as bad as some of the beatings Boo had doled out under this very roof, but I wasn't about to try to make this point. I had a mind to say something, but Granny showed no sign of letting up yet, and it wouldn't be good to try to cut her off.

"I thought we put this behind us last semester, but here you go, getting up to this nonsense again in no time."

I was always into mischief. Even during the good periods, I was into mischief. We were sneaking into places where we weren't supposed to be and sneaking out of places when we were expected to stay put. The Forty Thieves and I would find our way into garages just rummaging around. We weren't set to steal anything, just to explore. We'd also sneak out of class in elementary school to fight the kids at the school down the street. I had gotten caught up the previous semester, just before summer break, sneaking off on lunch to jump some kids from the next block. The principal had seen us from the window.

"Grandma, we were jumped, seriously," I attempted.

It was clear that wasn't true.

"After you went looking for trouble, Cardy," she countered. "And, the thing is, when you go looking, you are bound to find it."

I nodded. Granny was right. We knew some kids were playing up there. We sought them out to mix it up. That was the truth.

There were also misadventures in shoplifting and vandalism in this era. These would always occur outside the community. We'd embark on some sprawling hike to get out of Auburn Gresham so we could throw rocks through windows or trash a front porch. These activities tested our mettle. They were feats of courage in some warped way. Challenges we'd undertake to see who would rise to the occasion to prove themselves. Dares we'd make to each other.

"When you think you're bad, it is just going to make you a target, Cardy," Granny said. I was looking at her now, watching shamefully as her head ticked solemnly from side to side. "Badder you get, the more people are going to try to test you."

It is the tension between social norms in the community. Granny wasn't wrong. Violence was a testing ground. If you can prove that you're hard, courageous, or, as Granny kept putting it, "bad," it makes you less likely to be targeted. That's the irony. Retaliation as law. Eye for an eye. You always cycle between victim to aggressor and back again. Going hard on offense is your best defense to keep from being a target.

It becomes so that the only way you break that cycle is by being more and more aggressive. That's how you get so that you are not a mark, but, as Granny pointed out, you end up in a similar position, no matter what side of the equation, because you will keep getting tested.

Granny's argument had her swimming upstream against a waterfall. Violence was in the air. Arguing against it was arguing against oxygen itself. There were ways that you could live in the community and not participate, but it still touched your life. Maybe you didn't throw down, but there would be someone in your class, on your block, a teammate, a classmate, a neighbor, or a friend who had their lives touched. In that way, even if you were a "good" kid with straight A's who played baseball and avoided trouble, it was still a part of your reality.

She was more successful with other arguments. After the incident with the rock through the window, she had me thinking about what it would be like if a rock came crashing into our living room.

"How would you feel if that happened here?" she'd ask.

I shrugged.

"A shrug isn't an answer, Cardy. Don't we work too hard—your granddad, your mom, and me—to be fixing a broken window made by some little kid with too much time on his hands?" She challenged, with that stern head shaking.

She was on me in similar ways about ditching class, shoplifting, and vandalism, asking me to consider my actions bigger than myself. "Even the smallest thing could have the biggest effect," she'd say. She was connecting the dots so I could see from the victim's point of view outside of my own.

Violence had it that we were all victims, and trying to identify from that point of view just put you back in that loop. It infected the community. It altered the mind. It had a way of affecting everything. When you followed that loop, full circle to its start, the only conclusion you could reach was that fighting violence with violence was always on the defense.

I scratched the back of my hand until the wounds opened. My knuckles had started to slicken with blood.

I had wanted to say, to explain, all this to Granny. That trouble was my birthright. It was more likely to seek me out even if I didn't go hunting in the park. I wanted to explain that if we weren't bailing on a class to rush the playground down the street, the same kids would just as likely find their way to our backyard. I wanted to tell her that I didn't know any other way to act when it came to this than what I was already doing.

Instead, I nodded: "I know, Granny, I know," clapping my right hand over my blood-wet left palm.

Two violent events defined my childhood. The first took my father from me for the first part of my life when I turned three. His absence defined these early years. The second occurred before I was a teenager, taking my father from me forever.

Each was a murder and shaped every day that followed.

FAMILY DAY AT STATEVILLE

Arthur "Slick Rick" Hoover Jones, my father, dressed sharp. Tailored suits, stylish fedoras, fashionable dress shoes, and jewelry. There weren't no Mississippi about him left. Most of the guys in his era rocked sweats and sneakers. Getting dressed up was something for special occasions— weddings and funerals. "Slick Rick" preferred the polished look of old-school gangsters. He believed there was no point in having your best-dressed day in a casket. A true-to-life *Superfly*, already a living legend, long before I was born. Though he opted for somber colors, letting the look speak for itself. He didn't need bright patterns to grab attention, letting the cut of his threads do that for him.

My father was a shot caller in the Black Disciples, a street hustler and drug dealer who ran his own crew. He sold wiki sticks, PCP-laced joints, known as *Sherm*, which were the hard drug of choice in the pre-crack period of urban America. While he was locked up during my formative years, I got to know him only in hour-long increments every few months stretched across the calendar.

On a given weekend, the family dressed in Sunday's best, like it was picture day at school. I wore a colorful cardigan with a striped turtleneck underneath and dress slacks. We piled into the car and drove out of the city, through the suburbs, into the billiard-flat landscape of southern Illinois. Miles and miles of corn, wheat, and soy. Tiny towns with a single-lane Main Street where Confederate flags still flew from front porches.

We drove for over an hour out of the city until we came to the sprawling monstrosity of Stateville Correctional Center (SCC), a maximum-security men's prison in Crest Hill. A 2,264-acre campus of concrete and steel surrounded by thirty-three-foot walls capped with barbed wire and armed guard towers. These were the conditions under which I first got to know my father.

SCC was one of the country's oldest and most notorious prisons, a Level 7 designation, housing the most violent inmates, including serial killers Richard Speck and John Wayne Gacy. Gangs controlled entire cell blocks. Drugs were openly trafficked and used. Corrupt guards created a free-for-all atmosphere.

I didn't know these details at the time, not with an adult understanding, but they still influenced these early family reunions. We would be filed into a waiting room, where Mom had to present IDs and birth certificates, sign us in on a clipboard, and then gather with other families in a cafeteria-like visiting room where we would finally be briefly reunited with Dad. These memories were my early snapshots: intimacy under armed guard, the bustling volume of a communal hall, and the frenetic energy as time passed too quickly.

Years later, I would learn firsthand that it can be worse for the man in lockup, trying to cram a lifetime of what was happening on the outside into sixty minutes in a loud, crowded visiting room. Your children are getting older—growing into themselves, becoming young men and women—before your eyes. At the same time, you are frozen in amber. One monotonous day passes into the next. In that hour, life floods in from the outside. It is like the blast of water from a fire hydrant on a hot day, moving too quickly to quench your thirst.

The family gathered around an immobile table bolted into the ground, seated on a set of equally immobile benches. Mom shared the news about our grandparents, aunts, uncles, cousins, and family friends. On these early visits, I was seated on her lap and squirmed against this adult talk. A full report of what was happening around the neighborhood bored me senseless, like any kid at the grown-up table when the topic turned to grown-up things.

It took some years to realize how important these conversations were to my dad.

Then it was time for each kid to get a little attention. He pulled us in front of him one by one in order of age to have what passed for personal moments amidst the bustle and chaos of the room. Over the din of sobbing wives and squealing kids, amped on anxious energy, excitement, and vending machine candy. A lifetime of emotions, coming out on visitor's day, trying to make up for lost time. It was bittersweet, pain and pleasure, joy alongside sorrow. Everything wrapped up as love, loss, grief, and a bag of Lay's.

He gave Michael a hard time about being a bruiser, poking at him a bit playfully. He teased Trice about becoming a heartbreaker in her brightly colored blue and coral dress with her hair done up in pigtails.

Then it was my turn.

"How you doing in school?" he asked.

I stood to face him. I looked him in the eyes while he straightened my white and checkerboard patterned sweater.

"Good," I said in response with a shrug.

"What's your favorite subject?"

"Math," I offered, shrugging again.

He nodded approvingly, "That's good. That's good. It's all about making that money. Math."

I beamed under his attention.

One of his friends yelled across the room, "Yo, is that Lil' Ricky? What's up, Lil' Ricky?"

"This is my boy," my father said, standing up behind me and cupping the back of my head in his hand. He steered me forward to meet the other family man doing the shouting.

"Lil' Rick. And, you know Mildred, my daughter, Michael, and that's my wife, over here, Freda."

More introductions were made. Other men came over to meet me, my father's son. The guys patted me on the back, shook hands, or slapped five as my father strutted me around the room, showing me off to his buddies.

I felt so proud. My father's grip never left the back of my head or between my shoulder blades when he ushered me forward to meet some of his guys.

If his grip left its hold, even for a moment, I might have floated away on the joy of that attention.

"Let's see those gates," his homie said, meaning to flash the hand sign for the BDs.

Dad went down on his knee and took my hands in his own. One of his mitts swallowed my own tiny kid-sized hands in a single gesture. He contorted my fingers into flashing a three, then bent both hands together to form a star with the digits. The guys thought it was hilarious. In response, they roared with laughter and a round of applause, throwing signs back and patting me on the head.

We took some Polaroids with Dad, posing like doing a family portrait at Sears studio. It was some side hustle for one of the guards to sell the instant images. Then it was all over. It seemed we were in the parking lot before the images even developed. The whole thing was a whirlwind. I was still floating on the high of that attention, though. I could feel my father's palm print, still warm on the back of my head and a sense of confidence rushing through me.

"Why does he have to stay here?" I asked as we piled back into the car. I wanted my father to come home with us and felt I had never gotten an answer to that question.

Michael slapped me upside my head as if aiming for where my dad had held me moments earlier, sharply bringing me crashing to earth. "Shut up! You're not supposed to ask that, dummy!"

I spun quickly to jack him but caught my mom out of the corner of my eye. The weight of the visit had bent her over the steering wheel. She started to cry. I lowered my fists. I didn't want our fighting to add to Mom's grief like the question already had.

"Are you okay, Mama?" I asked.

"Y'all just get in the buckle your belts now, 'kay?"

I jostled Michael one last time with my shoulder, pulling the seat belt across my lap. I couldn't let the strike slide, but I wasn't going to escalate it. We exited the parking lot in silence. Mom sniffled while we stared out the window. Those miles rolled by in reverse. The trip back was the opposite of the ride out: no music on the radio, our energy muted, everything quietly deflated.

After we'd been on the highway a good minute, I placed my hands in my lap and began practicing those signs—a Roman numeral III, gates, a six-pointed star—flashing them absently. I got another small pick-me-up think-ing about showing my friends what Dad taught me on Monday morning.

IMAGES OF MY FATHER

In the years that followed, I pulled together bits and pieces on my father that built on these infrequent visits and the fuzzy images of Ron O'Neal on the late afternoon Black Power Hour lineup opposite badly dubbed Samu-rai Sunday Marathons. Most of us were latchkey kids, raised by prime-time TV dads who dropped problem-solving wisdom just before commercial breaks. My dad, though, had an air of great power, as Curtis Mayfield put it, tryin' ta get over. At this point, I'd grown old enough to recognize that Youngblood Priest from the *Superfly* series wasn't actually my dad no more. I snuck letters written to my mom out of dresser drawers and read them in secret. Every family party became an opportunity for exploration, asking my family or my dad's friends for details on an event that went down when I was barely three years old.

I recalled cops pounding on the front door of my grandparent's place, back when we lived just across the alley, demanding to know where they could find my father—standing in footie pajamas at the center of a living room awash in blue and red lights. Someone rushed me off into another room. I remember the emotional charge of hearing he'd murdered some-one, learning that term early in life but not completely clear on the mean-ing. In my recollection, the squawk of the walkies from towering uniforms with booming voices squelches into the living room. Then, the door is pulled closed between me and the action.

My grandfather waved them off. We don't know where Dad might be, he was telling them. The gravity in the room feels distorted and heavy.

HOW WE MYTHOLOGIZED

It was Dog's ball, but Solomon was being a goof with it. He hefted it over his head with both hands, elbows locked. Then, putting all his weight into it, he hurled it at the ground. Jumped up while throwing it down. It made a hard *thwap* that would spring it back into the air like a leap ball.

Dog was too chill to care, let alone say something about it. It was a ratty ball, just held together for the hoop, skin slightly peeling. Ollie, however, winced every time it slammed into the ground as if it caused him physical pain to see the ball misused like that.

"You're going to mess up the integrity of the ball," Ollie said.

Solomon laughed as the ball slammed again and whirled upward. He jockeyed beneath it, alongside Lil' Paris and Dog, elbowing to get up under it.

"I don't even know what that means, man," he called back.

"Try and get it up even with the garage roofs," Lil' Paris suggested. "See if you can bounce it that high!"

Solomon caught it against his stomach, clutching it like it was a soccer ball, *whap*. "Integrity of the ball. What's that shit even mean?"

"See if you can get it even with the telephone wires over there," Lil' Paris prodded Sol with the nonsense challenge—the kind these days that would fill YouTube. "Bet you can't."

"It ain't like a kickball, made to bounce like that," Ollie explained. "It's your ball, Dog, but be messed up if it was flat by the time we got to the courts. What are we going to do then?"

Solomon put weight behind it again and pitched hard at the ground. The ball bounced upward. It was not level with the rooftops or the wires. Solomon came racing beneath its shadow like he was playing a game of "Killa Man" and scooped it.

"Under the skin, it's all just threads. I seen it before. A busted basketball. It's just a bunch of strings all tied up together, real tight, like a ball of rubber bands, is how it look," Ollie countered, exasperated. "You keep doing that, and the threads gonna come undone. Then the ball goes flat, and it's useless, like the ones at the rec center."

Solomon tossed it Lil' Paris, playing keep-away, as Ollie vied for it. He snagged it a moment and dribbled a bit before Lil' Paris stole it, putting it back into rotation.

"Sure, know a lot about balls, Ollie," Solomon teased.

Everyone giggled.

"Just saying it's Dog's ball," Ollie pleaded. "Might want to take better care of it. That's all."

"I bet you can't bounce it as high as the branches on that tree," Lil' Paris goaded, trying to get the game back on track.

"Ollie, how you know so much about balls?"

"Ollie spend a lot of time playing with everyone's balls, ain't that right?"

"Dog, you let Ollie play with your ball, man? He seems awfully concerned with your ball's int-eg-rity."

Solomon hurled it again, and everyone, including Ollie, scrambled to grab it out of the air. They played like it was a game of "Killa Man" at recess, but the basketball wasn't built for that.

"See if you can get it high as that bush over there."

"That bush? Shit. No problem."

"What's with you?" Ty asked in a hushed tone. We fell back naturally so that our pace was a few feet behind everyone else and then a few feet more.

Normally, I would be in that mix, horsing around with the other guys. Playing keep-away with the ball. Ty could see that something was weighing on my mind that kept me from clowning. It was an anniversary coming up when my father first went away. If any of the other guys were to ask after me at this moment, I'd have snatched the ball away from Solomon faster than he could blink, really giving Ollie something to get worked up about, pitching granny-style underhanded up onto a garage roof for laughs, ignoring the question. No one would be the wiser, but something about Ty always made me feel I couldn't dodge his questions. In some ways, he knew me better than most anyone in my life, before or since. He was my closest friend, my main man, so we could talk pretty much about anything and everything.

"They had a birthday party at the Lounge last night for Uncle Phil's girl-friend I was at," I began.

Granny hosted parties at the Lounge most of the year round. By age ten or so, I was working events. I did little errands here and there for pocket change. I was sweeping up in the back, breaking down boxes, shoveling snow, keeping things tidy. Eventually, I would graduate to barbacking, swapping out kegs, doing dishes, and the like as I got older, but in those early years, it was just simple tasks, like wiping down the bar and stacking chairs.

"TK, my daddy's friend, was there, and they got to talking about how my daddy went away in the first place. I never heard the whole story, like how I got to hear it last night."

"They know you was listening?" Ty asked.

It was a fair question because the versions I heard until that night were edited for my ears. They came out tamer than most of what was on television. That night, I heard enough details to know it wasn't being watered down. I told Ty as much.

"What I heard was that my mom was doing the club sets with her sister, my auntie Myrtle, up at Tiberia Lounge. This, back then, before she and my daddy were married, she had another dance partner," I said. "My daddy and

TK be up there, too, just drinking and having a good time. This guy comes to the Lounge with four other guys, looking for trouble."

"Looking for your dad?"

"Right. Same thing I just said."

"Right."

"So, they come up to my dad mean mugging, trying to start a fight, and tell him, *'You wait right here,'* and leave out."

"You know what that means," Ty says.

"They going to get a piece."

"Exactly."

"TK knows it, too, he says, but my dad just keeps sipping his drink like he doesn't have a care in the world."

"This is what they were saying last night?"

"I made like I was wiping down tables, but really, I was listening."

I learned early in life that people spoke more than they intended when they drank. In the Lounge, I heard people speak on things they'd have never said otherwise, let alone in the presence of someone my age. All I had to do was sit silently atop my perch in the horseshoe booth in the back corner. Watch. Listen. Learn.

People overshared night after night. They were acting against their intentions. I promised myself all that time ago that I would never drink. I've never gone back on my word with so much as a drop of alcohol in my life.

"So, you know TK, right?"

"Of course, TK an OG."

"Right. He tells my daddy, 'Let's see what's happening over at the Bonanza,' another club, trying to get my daddy up out of there before they come back."

"Your dad don't listen, though," Ty says, anticipating. "Would you?"

"Nah. You know I wouldn't."

"Hell no, he is a gangster!"

"It's like some shit in a cowboy movie," he says, eyes wide like he's seeing it right there in front of him.

"TK is like, 'if your stubborn ass is going to stay here, then you need a piece,' because he doesn't want him unarmed."

"Right! It's like something out of a movie."

"That's what I heard," I continue, with growing enthusiasm at Ty's encouragement.

"TK runs home to get his .38. He don't want to sneak in the house because his parents are asleep. He calls up to his sister to throw it down to him from the second-floor bedroom window. He goes to try and catch it but misses. The piece hits the ground and goes off, firing a bullet into the dirt."

"So much for not waking anybody up," Ty laughs.

"That's the same thing Uncle Phil said last night," I respond. "TK is on a mission, though, so he runs back to Tiberia as the lights are going on in the house."

"TK meets my daddy back at the Lounge and slips him the .38 just before these dudes come back through. TK kept trying to persuade my daddy they should hit up Bonanza, where he got friends meeting him, but my daddy, now strapped, cool as can be, just keeps sipping his drink like nothing. So, TK bounce to meet his friends, leaving my dad at the bar with his piece."

Echoing my enthusiasm, Ty asks, "What happens when they come back?"

"They weren't there to have no conversation."

"They were there fixing to kill him."

"They drew on him as soon as they came back through. That man and his friends up they pistols and start shooting," I say, "But, my daddy gets the drop on them—starts firing back."

"It's right outta a movie," Ty says, jaw dropped.

"People are running from the dance floor, making for the exits. Tables be overturning. People pushing each other out of the way. My father is cold as ice as he moves through that place. He drops to the floor and rolls up under a table. He is firing on them from the floor as he rolls. Just like in a movie. A scene out of the Wild West. Bang-Bang-Bang. He rolls up behind a booth and takes out Dude's friend. Bang-Bang-Bang. Get him first. Old Boy is firing back, but Dad got the upper hand. Bang-Bang-Bang. He's firing. Bang-Bang-Bang. Dude's firing. Bang-Bang-Bang. He drops Dude right there before he could get off another shot. Drops him."

"That's gangster," Ty says.

"That's what I heard how Phil and TK describe it."

We crossed the street between alleyways, my guys leaving the shrub behind. They took our cue, keeping pace with the group as if Ty and I were magnets with reverse poles, pushing them to stay slightly ahead of us.

Dog wrestled his ball back from Solomon to keep it from the bushes. They switched up the game, just dribbling back and forth, like the Harlem Globetrotters, showing off their skills. Dog passed overhand to Ollie, who bounced it a few times, sending it back. They went through the motions, first Solomon in the middle, trying to intercept.

Then, Lil' Paris at the outskirts, with Solomon, Ollie, and Dog playing keep-away. As we moved between blocks, this new game of keep-away seemed to teeter on a round of "Killa Man" breaking out.

"So, TK been gone by the time all of this went down. He went to Bo-nanza like he was saying he would, missing the whole firefight. Next morn-ing, he shows up at my dad's place early to get back his piece, but police were waiting on him."

"TK didn't know what went down yet," Ty says.

"He didn't," I respond. "Police say, 'You know Rick?' TK goes, 'Yeah, I know Rick, that's my brother, man.' Police ask, 'You with him last night?' And TK says, 'Yeah, I was with him.' They throw the cuffs on him before they even tell him what went down. He gets put in the back of the squad, and they say, 'You know he's wanted for homicide, your 'brother.' TK starts walking it back immediately, 'Homicide? Not my "brother," man, I'm just saying, you know, I know him from around the neighborhood. You know how we do, every one a brotha, man.'"

Ty laughs.

"When he got word both guys were dead, my dad went on the run. He hid out a few weeks, but eventually, he turned himself in."

"It was self-defense, though."

"There were so many guns on the scene and bullet holes in the walls, there was no way to see it otherwise."

I recalled that night in Granny's living room. Red and blue lights from the street cast through the window. Fear in my chest. Burning tears streamed down my cheeks. A sickly knowing that something is wrong and things will not be the same. My grandfather told police they hadn't heard from Dad in some time. I don't share these memories as a part of the story.

We were coming up to the park just across the street. The courts in sight. The guys still managed to keep the ball from Ollie. Now, he rushed back and forth, trying to get up under the growing shadow as it fell toward them.

"Yo," Ty called to them. "Yo. Y'all ever hear how Cobe's father, Slick Rick, got the jump on some nasty dudes that was hunting him back in the day?"

"Nah. I don't think so," Ollie shouted back.

"No," Solomon answered. He broke from the game and slowly made his way over. "This what he locked up for?"

Ty nodded.

"I didn't hear it before," Dog shook his head.

"Uh-uh," Lil' Paris responded.

Ty set the stage. He turned to me then as if pulling those memories from me. "Cobe, you go ahead and tell them what happened. Tell them the way we heard it."

PITCHING QUARTERS WITH CORNER BOYS

A lot of the older boys in the neighborhood that my father had looked out for when they were growing up started coming around to repay the favor with me. They were no older than sixteen but seemed like giants. Most of the time, they would take me to the park to shoot hoops, hang out, and maybe buy me ice cream. They'd tell me about my father's preference for Cadillacs, the way he conducted business, and how he was just a chill guy.

Other times, I'd tag along as they ran errands, dropping dope off somewhere or collecting money. My first lessons on the street came from these guys: the corner boys, the runners, the lookouts, and the hustlers. At the time, I was still too young to participate, but I had a front-row seat to all the action. I got to see how the whole operation ran. Being the mouth I am, I would start playing that I wanted my cut.

They wouldn't give me a role in the trade just yet, but they would give me a chance to make some money by gambling. Mostly pitching quarters. A quarter would get thrown up against a wall, bounced off a curb from a distance, or tossed just over a crack in the sidewalk. Then, the players would pitch coins to see what could land the closest to it, with the winner taking the pot. I had a goofy way of throwing sideways, like flicking a tiny frisbee, which made everyone crack up. For me, it was as much about the performance as the game.

I would hear this story hundreds of times over the years, listening to these older boys tell it as a legend, reenacting beat by beat, like action sequences from those Black Power Hour lineups with the Funkadelic 1970s soundtrack and elements of old western shootouts. They'd get the dive under the table and the roll as he dodged for cover behind the booth. It was a performance piece pantomiming this sequence of events.

Always absent from these retellings was the pain around the edges. I never thought of its direct impact on my mother caught in the emotional cross fire. There had to be grief and guilt, no matter the outcome. I never thought about the pressure my father must have felt, walking into that situation and making himself a target, because he would have had to settle it at Tiberia that night or spend weeks after looking over his shoulder. I never thought about my auntie, who went out to have a good time but ended up dodging fire and witnessing a double murder.

In our version of events, we never talked about everyone else in the club that night. The version of events I learned never considered the trauma we collectively experienced that resonates outward from an event. Those pieces, jagged with trauma, pain, and bitter memory, get left on the cutting room floor because they are just too much to carry.

Shock waves passed through my family. They traveled down the block. They moved through the community into the homes of everyone there that night and many who weren't for years to come. That event occurred when I was three and impacted every day that was to follow, but this is how we cope.

We numbed to it.

We celebrated it.

We mythologized it.

This was survival.

3

NAVIGATING BORDERLANDS

Auburn Gresham, Chicago, July 2015

South on Racine. Deep into Auburn Gresham. I search for the Caprice that opened fire at Big Folks and his crew this morning. Racine is a dividing line. North and South separate Vice Lords from BD; East and West divide BD from GD.

These borderlines are not as clean as the Chicago grid. It is all mixed up in every direction. Rogue pockets are camped out in different areas, block by block, but for the most part, these boundaries are anchored to main streets, like Racine, carving through the neighborhood. I would have avoided much of this stretch in my youth unless I was fixing for a fight. Now, I plunge in, scanning streets and alleyways. I roll forward. Most everyone these days knows what I am on these days.

My first call is Big Fella, who runs the E-wood office. Violence interruption is a team effort. Big Fella is our captain. He is responsible for coordinating all these moving pieces. Maintaining the twenty-thousand-foot view. Deploying resources. Making sure we all stay on the same page.

I run through the morning events with him. The Caprice. The shooting. My read on everything. D-Boy. Big Folks.

"I got through to most of the guys for the time being," I relay. "We got their word. They holding back, but Big Folks wasn't feeling it, you know? He gave me his word. I am not sure it is going to be enough. Everyone follows his lead. We should try to get him one-on-one."

Big Fella used to oversee a whole empire. This was a generation before my own. Now, he runs CeaseFire Englewood out of a storefront office. If you trust the police or the press, which I wouldn't recommend, Big Fella started as an enforcer who rose to be the number one dealer on the South Side for a time. Police and the press needed a bogeyman, and Big Fella filled the role for a time. A different era, though.

Nowadays, he spends his time coordinating shooting responses, candle-light vigils, outreach efforts, and violence interruptions from our office—the activities of peacekeeping. Big Fella is trying to give back to a community he took so much from—he was part of the problem and now works to be part of the solution. A sign in the window puts the number of days since a shooting at zero. We're on it.

Signs like this work to reverse social norms. They aim to get the community to celebrate the absence of violence. Declaring victory when a conflict isn't resolved with violence.

Big Fella listens closely.

Then responds in a voice that sounds like gravel in a concrete tumbler: "So, who you think steps in with Big Folks to sit on the situation while you out?"

An inverted colonel with orders to dismantle a war.

"Hot Rod can check in on the situation," I tell him. "He doesn't know those guys, but he can at least monitor while I'm not around."

Rod is my right hand in the Englewood office. I know him from way back. We didn't do time together, but I met him when I was in County. I was locked up. He was there visiting a friend. This is before CeaseFire, Cure Violence, or any of my violence prevention work. Some guys in there were trying to mess with his friend, who was locked up with me. Hot Rod asked me to look out for him while we were both in there. I wouldn't let no one mess with his guy, and Hot Rod never forgot what I did for his friend, so we've been jam ever since.

He don't know D-Boy, but Rod has influence and access to the guys. He can monitor the situation. Pop in if necessary. Keep heads cool and hold everyone to their word.

This is important. Everything is word until it isn't. Guys get to drinking or smoking. Someone gets in their ear, whispering, "You got to do something. How it going to look? Y'all giving permission for them to come through any time they want." And so on.

Then, it is easy to go back on an agreement. They get to rationalizing, ain't no other way to handle this situation. By staying in tune with them, Rod makes that more difficult for them to act out.

"Bet," Big Fella confirms, then after a beat adds, "Let's put Joe on it to come at this from the other direction."

His tone is measured and thoughtful, referring to John "China Joe" Lofton, a one-time national leader of the Imperial Insane Vice Lords, many years older than me, from another generation, out of the West Side.

I drive into Vice Lords territory, literally, "the other direction." Tattered homes alongside boarded-up houses. Empty lots. Abandoned buildings. Vacant apartment complexes. Overgrown playgrounds. They drift by outside my window. Fire scarred and shuttered businesses. Storefront churches and liquor stores, each preaching their own brand of hope, nestled side by side. We all lost out here, trying to find our way. I am less than five minutes away from where everything went down beneath a train viaduct and into another land entirely.

"China Joe" is a sinewy dude with a mellow vibe and sleepy eyes. Far as I know, he is not actually Asian, but some of the features that earn him the nickname may come from Cherokee blood on his mom's side. Lofton was a talented boxer with lightning-fast footwork who, rumor has it, could've gone pro. He took over the faction instead of pursuing a career as a prizefighter.

At the CeaseFire-Englewood storefront, former GD, BD, Vice Lords, and Stones of high rank and legendary status share office space. Desks are pushed together beneath a map that carves up our corner of the city. We mark it with recent shootings and killings, divided by cop beat for statistical purposes and organized by a hidden history of invisible kingdoms.

Interruption work focuses on making inroads into these groups. On one level, it is about information gathering. *Who knows who? Who knows what? What's going on? How can we find out? What is going down and why?* It's about collecting intel to get at the bigger picture.

Referring to street organizations as Group A and B, opposing sides, or rivals keeps the actual names and history to a minimum. We do so for a few reasons. First, practically, it is just good sense. You never know who is listening.

As a rule, we don't share information with the police. Our work depends completely on trust. A relationship with the community. A relationship with active members of street organizations. If information falls into the wrong hands, that can be dangerous for everyone involved.

Big Fella is also always quick to point out that his own empire came apart when he was brought up on Racketeer Influenced and Corruption

Organization (RICO) charges back in the 1980s. The prosecutorial tool allowed law enforcement to go after entire criminal organizations for the actions of individuals.[1] Initially, it was used in New York to convict the heads of the Mafia's Five Families, but it didn't take long before prosecutors all over the country started using guilt-by-association conspiracy charges to go after any manner of street organization. Eventually, Chicago gangs, including the organization Big Fella helmed, would be swept up in its wake.

In his justified paranoia, Big Fella is concerned that law enforcement would try to find a way to target community violence initiatives. Since our workers are often aware of a crime or the intent to commit a crime before it happens, Big Fella has always been concerned that some savvy anti-violence prevention prosecutor would try to bring charges against activists for the very crime they are trying to prevent. That hasn't happened yet, but our guys always get extra scrutiny from the law, which has a bitter irony to it.

So, it's Group A and Group B, just to be on the safe side.

Second, it is symbolic. We've moved past our past. That history is history. We need to distance ourselves from the identity we once owned. It is often one of the hardest things I've seen workers endure. Across the country, so many of us have relapsed because we are unable to turn that corner. You start behaving in your old ways. I was born and raised a Black Disciple, but if you are going to be on something else, you have to transition away from it. CeaseFire is my ride now.

Third, it helps prevent triggers among the team. Whether you were born in the way Joe and I were or you jumped in, meaning recruited to be a gang member, you inherit a war with casualties. You got kids that come into this life expected to kill for a beef; that started two generations before they were born without any knowledge of how it originated. When there is unresolved trauma and a body count on both sides, letting go of that baggage makes office politics less volatile. You don't want coworkers cracking skulls because someone forgot to refill the copier.

Keeping it Group A and Group B keeps the peace.

If this is Vice Lords who is responsible, "China Joe" can try to get a read on who is involved and why. When you got two groups into it, you need to understand the motivation of both parties. You can't come to half an agreement. If you resolve only half a conflict, you haven't resolved anything, really.

Most everyone ranking on our team is Hood Famous. Fact. There are some legendary figures out of the CeaseFire Englewood office. Street royalty. Big time on the block. That's the other part of interruption work. It is about influence. Being in the know is important. Being able to persuade, more so. Having a reputation that lets these guys stand down and still save face.

"China Joe" has the rare distinction of being one of the first among us to become legendary as an interrupter.[2] Years ago, Joe was in the middle of negotiating a turf war between rival drug dealers. Trying to get these guys to split up the territory in a way that don't end in bloodshed. "Woo. Woo. Woo. You go over there. And, you. You go up over there." He's mediating both sides to find an agreement.

So, just as he is wrapping up, he gets a call. A set of hotheaded, young Vice Lords are trying to force their way into a woman's home across town. She calls Joe. "They are gathered on the front porch, threatening to shoot up their way in," she's telling him. "There are kids inside." She is terrified for her own safety and for the safety of her children.

Joe goes, "I'm on my way," but before he can jump in his ride and head over there, the guys from both sides of the beef he just squashed tell him they're coming too. The whole crew, both sides of the conflict, ride along with Joe to settle up. It was like he deputized everyone on the scene as peacekeepers, and they helped resolve the second conflict.

Now that is some other level mediation work. When your long-term strategy is to change the social norms of a community around violence, these are the kind of legends we need to be sharing.

"We put 'Head' on it, too," I tell Big Fella, suggesting our guy in the office work with the remaining groups in the equation. If there are any loose ends or if our read that it is coming from Vice Lords is wrong, Head will get on it. "Since we don't know for sure where this is coming from, it'd be good if he can ask around some." He is plugged in with the Gangster Disciples and can keep an ear out if anything is happening there that may be related.

Big Fella grunts in affirmation. I imagine him standing in front of the map in the main conference room. His pointer finger traces Racine, the same route I'm driving as if he is following my path.

GD, BD, Vice Lords, and Stones under one roof, working together, that means something—symbolically. It represents some kind of hope out there. We've more common ground than anything that ever set us apart. Our entire destinies become bound up by zip codes and intersections. We see it now. Our identities are altered by which side of a cross street we come up on. Lives forged by geography. False divisions.

On our maps, small red squares look like chalk outlines, marking homicides. In tight grids, one over the other, they represent lives lost. Shootings appear as black dots, freckled in clusters. There is so much overlap that we have to print additional maps so details don't get washed out. That stretch from 35th to 138th looks like pools of spilled ink smeared across the grid.

Nationwide, cities experience the highest rates of gun homicides and assaults.[3] Communities of color are disproportionately impacted. Seeing it on the map like this is more striking than an open-palm slap. Young Black men and teens are killed by guns twenty times more than their white counterparts.[4]

On the Chicago map, a mass of polka dots and red squares could easily show structural inequities. Dots could indicate redlined communities, economic disinvestment, unemployment, job loss, and poverty. They layer over these same stretches street after street like a topography of systemic racist policies.

"Right. Right. Right." Big Fella responds. "I got you. I know. They into it with them, you think? Or this just random?"

I see where Big Fella is going with this line of questioning. Random makes it a little more manageable. Something popped off. We find both parties and put it to rest. It's an incident, some friction, personal. You address it and move on.

Most of what passes for gang-related events can be chalked up to interpersonal issues in fact.[5] Domestic issues. "Are you looking at my girl?"–type conflicts. A "so and so said such and such about this and that with you" kind of thing. Violence of the "he say/she say" variety. "Gang-related," though, is a convenient narrative that ends up on the evening news and earns political clout. It gets tossed around because it increases police budgets, secures reelection, and sells the news. The numbers don't actually add up to what the narrative has been saying for years.

In the country as a whole, gang violence accounts for only 20 percent of homicides overall.[6] That doesn't stop the label being slapped on just about every kind of urban crime there is over the past several decades.

All of these events get put in the "gang-related" category. Remember what I said about the press and police wanting a bogeyman? It makes the world seem less uncertain and easier to control by saying, "Gangs are the problem." It isn't that topography, dense layers of racist social policy reinforcing poverty, burying those red square chalk outlines and black dots. Nah. If it is gangs, increasing police presence and power, militarizing law enforcement, and creating harsher punishments with longer prison sentences, start sounding reasonable.

If it is social conditions, addressing them with other layers on the map starts making more sense. Social service programs. Jobs. Opportunities. Start making more sense. Creating channels to build Black wealth, investment, and home and business ownership start making more sense. "Gang-related" like "Black on Black crime" is a dog whistle. It keeps people in fear and rationalizes whatever the police do to stop that crime. "Gang-related" becomes a scapegoat for those racist policies detailed on that map.

If they are into it, the situation is more complicated. More moving pieces and more people are involved. Those rare events that are actually "gang-related" mean that we got to go deeper into an issue to find out all the players involved. It could be a lot of issues tied up in these situations. Losses on both sides keep people into it. Rationalize their own behavior. Justify their actions. Those situations can be harder to untangle.

"Couldn't say yet," I reply. "Trying to figure it out myself. Big Folks seems legit surprised. It wasn't something he saw coming. That tells me it's rogue. Who knows, right? Could be they just trying to make a name for themselves. Could be something bigger going on. A power move? Maybe? I don't know yet. Maybe they are making a move we don't know about."

"Kids today," Big Fella offers wryly.

He is in his sixties now. Plays at sounding every bit his age. His humor always runs dry as he puts on his best "back in my day."

"It's anybody's guess what they up to here. Could just be 'bout sneakers, or could be no move at all."

I hear the scraping sound of his hand running over the stubble atop his head.

I turn down a side street and move through the neighborhood, looking for a few corners to hit up. I want to see who knows what. On my left, the shell of a former trap house in an old bungalow comes into view. Front porch to attic window, charred. Furniture scattered across the lawn as if the house threw up its contents: sofa, loveseat, kitchen chairs. Front yard is the new living room. On the street, at the curb on the corner, a fire-wrecked four-door sedan. As if the two, house and car, come as a matching Chiraq playset. Order now and receive a homeboy hustler with a dope-slinging action grip! Windows smashed. Interior torched. Wire mesh beneath gobs of melted upholstery. Asphalt singed beneath the vehicle, shimmering with broken glass.

These relics of urban decay get Chicago rebranded Chiraq. Fallujah west of Racine. The street dead-ends opposite the burnt car. Corner boys could hold this spot and control the traffic. A single entry and an exit for the block, like a drive-through at a fast-food joint for coke, crack, fentanyl, and H. Control the choke points. Position lookouts. Staggered in gangways up and down the block, eyes are everywhere. Put runners in alleys between streets and behind houses.

Every generation will always say the one coming up behind is wilder. They more out of control than we ever were, the saying goes. It is a time-honored truism. One generation scratches its head about the one coming up behind, as applicable to music and fashion as it is gangbanging and drugs.

Except, in this case, it's true.

I came up in the last age of kingdoms. Gangs of the 1960s, 1970s, and 1980s—what my father, Big Fella, Head, China Joe, Little Fred, and all these guys came up under—began to fade by the time guys like me came of age. We were the last generation to grow armies citywide with national networks.

There is a reason RICO has been known as the "atomic bomb" of prosecutorial tactics. When they went after the Mafia's Five Families in New York in the 1980s, it was explosive—all scorched Earth and nuclear winter. They got convictions on three of the five bosses with a century of sentencing. A fourth was gunned down in the streets. Everything exploded. This was considered a success to the law.

In Chicago, RICO tactics targeted Black gangs. A similar strategy. Everyone gets charged—guilt by association. RICO allowed them to pin crimes committed by an affiliate on other gang members. Shot callers held accountable for foot soldiers. Leadership charged with the events that occurred at the street level. Another reason "gang-related" is such a loaded term. You sweep up all the guys on the corner near a shooting rather than just going for the shooter themselves. Overnight, power vacuums were created.

My generation saw the fracturing of kingdoms. Our leaders summarily rounded up with our rank and file. Civil wars kicked off as guys started vying for power. This was our warring states period as empires disintegrated. Our story is one where scattered factions squabble over whatever scraps were left in the margins. A lot of bodies behind that.

Throughout the 1980s, they cut the heads off the beast, taking down the hierarchical street organizations that were running like corporations. They made a big to-do of putting all these gangsters behind bars in the Fed. Dragnets aim at entire memberships. Police, prosecutors, press declare victory for the good guys. Photo ops with bricks of cocaine on the evening news. Saran-wrapped bundles of cash on front-page headlines. Political careers are made over these events.

The result: some kind of wicked problems created.

Policymakers refer to wicked problems as difficult-to-solve social issues that emerge from addressing another issue entirely. The complex interconnections of various social issues create a situation where fixing one piece of a puzzle kicks off all kinds of complications in another area.

RICO was an immediate solution for law enforcement to get guys off the street. That act, though, created a cascade of other interrelated issues. In Big Fella's day and my own after it, we had a chain of command, laws, by-laws, systems in place, and discipline. There was an order to things. In the simplest terms, there was motivation to keep the heat down. Bodies meant cops. You had to limit your exposure. The collapse of the power structure created a vacuum, kicked off a civil war, ignited new levels of violence, the issues became amplified and dispersed.

This generation is suffering the fallout from these explosions. Now, gangs devolved into sets and cliques—smaller and smaller units. Big Folks and crew operate independently. The rogue Vice Lord crew that most likely road down on them operates independently. Other fractions and factions operate independently. No one up under any shared banner. In a couple of blocks, you could have a handful of cliques vying for power. It's all Wild West. The city is home to 625 factions that carve up territory.[7] No structure. No command. When researchers start asking how Chicago became the most violent city in the country—this splintering always tops their list of reasons.

This happens to be Chicago, but it is true of every city everywhere USA. In Milwaukee, my brothers and sisters in the movement are even more on point. They call them "Pain Cliques." Groups form spontaneously after a loss: "Evan Daniels Boys," "D'Angelo Jackson Crew," and so on. Their only bond is through the grief, loss, pain, and revenge they seek. These, too, number in the hundreds.

This is not to say that we need to be going back to the old hierarchical structure of street organizations. Still, it does explain where we need to focus our efforts on changing the underlying social norms that reinforce violence. There are also ways, which I will explain later, that we can recreate these decision-making structures without replicating their violent roots by empowering groups toward self-governance.

A woman pushing a stroller follows me with a wary gaze, not knowing what I am up to here. The street is relatively empty otherwise. I keep on. We could be in the burbs down the block, just a little from the Chiraq scene.

Parked cars gleaming. Green front lawns. Sprinklers running. Kids on front porches.

The controversial name, Chiraq, speaks to stats comparing violence in the city with those coming out of war zones. Englewood has a homicide rate one-third higher than the most violent countries in the world. So, politicians across the aisle can agree, at least in passing, on that one thing: Chicago as a national symbol for urban violence.

It is no coincidence that a spotlight is suddenly beamed on Chi-Town when Ferguson, Baltimore, or Minneapolis start getting prime-time attention. When the national conversation turns to systemic racism, and we start making a closer study of that map, I get calls from CNN to talk about my work. Suddenly, everyone wants to talk about "Black on Black" crime as if it invalidates "Black Lives Matter" arguments.

From time to time, when CNN calls a Top Cop in a given city—Chicago, New York, Baltimore, Minneapolis, St. Louis—gets up on the mic to mix apples with oranges. They will ask how we are going to worry about police killing Black men when the percentage of violence by police against citizens is so much smaller than the percentage of Black men killing Black men.

As if, somehow, these skewed figures make police brutality a minor problem in a larger context. "Black-on-Black crime" is put under the microscope so it can be used to create more aggressive policing policies and higher rates of incarceration of Black people.

What they are trying to say when they say this is that Black people can't look out for themselves. The code that is being broadcast to the world is that police need to occupy these communities because if we are left to our own devices, these neighborhoods will burn. So, when we talk about how things used to be, this isn't a nostalgia trip for a simpler gangland, so much as recognizing autonomy and self-governance long before formal community violence interventions.

"Okay, Old Man," I play, maneuvering back off the side streets onto Racine. Big Fella is on speaker, but I'm already on to the next task. My car is idle at the curb before pulling into traffic as I text Hot Rod an update.

"That's Boss Man to you."

"Fair enough. I'm still staying off your lawn."

"Keep me posted if anything changes."

"Will do. Same."

I end the call and push send on the text in quick succession. Phone chirps. Then I pull out, heading toward a gas station that is recognized in federal statistics as one of the most dangerous in the country.

4

AIN'T TOO DUMB

Englewood/Auburn Gresham, Chicago, 1980

Uncle Phil was flirting with the substitute nurse at Oglesby Elementary when he came to scoop me up just before lunchtime. Phil was smooth. He wore his hair long, flattened, and tied back in a ponytail. He dressed sharp. The nurse swatted his chest playfully, giggling, as I sat cross-legged on the front bench of his boat-sized Oldsmobile parked a few feet away.

He was the eldest of Granny's sons on my mom's side. Phil was a father figure the whole time my daddy was in prison and most of my life after. He was a player and prankster with a big personality, a bigger heart, and a rapid-fire sense of humor. Phil worked as a bartender at the Lounge. For a time, he followed in his father's footsteps, working at the steel mill, but it wasn't for him.

He stayed in an apartment downstairs from Granny. It was an in-house bachelor pad with silk sheets on an oversized waterbed, mood lighting, and a remote-controlled custom sound system.

More importantly, since he worked all night, Phil was home after the first period, when, at least once a week, I would make my way to the nurse's office, feigning illness. My illnesses were usually exaggerated versions of actual symptoms blown out of proportion: an upset stomach, headache, sore throat. That prompted any number of weekly stomach bugs, headaches, colds, and flu. Phil would pick me up from school. I'd have done it every day if I could have gotten away with it, but then I wouldn't have gotten to see my friends.

Phil asked the nurse to swing by the Lounge that weekend, promising to make her a signature cocktail. Nothing too sweet now, she pleaded playfully, writing down her number. He made his way around the driver's side. I took that as a cue to hang my head and hug my knees against my stomach, letting out a pained groan.

"You alright over there?"

I nodded.

"You hungry?"

I nodded.

"Trick question. You always hungry."

I nodded.

"Burnt ends?

I nodded.

"You want them extra crispy?"

I nodded.

He'd cranked the ignition, turning the engine over. Waved good-bye to the nurse one more time.

"You want them extra hot?"

I did.

"Lemonade?"

Yes.

"That jumbo-sized with easy ice. You want sugar cookies?"

I nodded.

"You know what, though, Cobe? I don't know what I'm thinking. You can't eat all that with an upset stomach." He put the car in gear and circled the lot slowly. "That was inconsiderate of me. How about I just get you a piece of bread and a cup of chipped ice? You think you can handle that?"

I didn't say nothing, but I stopped the moaning.

"You know, I was born at night, but not last night. I was really young at the time but grew older with age."

I couldn't help but laugh.

"How you going to eat all that while your stomach is hurting? Thoughtless. Thoughtless of me."

I couldn't stop now.

"And, laughing like that! In your condition! Hazardous! You'll rupture a spleen! You'll bust a gut! You're going to bust a gut."

I kept laughing.

"I may be one dumb, Cobe, but I am not—what?"

"—too dumb," I said in response.

"That's right," he replied, "and not nearly as dumb as you look."

We ate lunch together from Styrofoam containers on the front porch at home. Extra crispy, extra hot, burnt ends slathered in BBQ sauce situated on a bed of fries. Two slices of white bread wrapped in wax paper on top. A large lemonade with easy ice, as ordered.

"Math still your favorite subject, Cobe?" he asked.

I nodded.

"What do you like about that?"

"It makes me think of money."

"Especially subtraction, huh? Watching all that money go."

"Nah. Multiplication. Watching that money grow."

He laughed.

"What do you know about multiplication? You don't know anything about that."

"I do!" I protested.

"I'll quiz you. What about two times two? What do you know about that?"

"Four."

"Oh. Okay. Two times four."

"Six. No. Eight."

"Okay. Okay."

"Five times five."

I got to use my fingers to count up by five, but I'm quick with the right answer.

"Twenty-five."

"Nine times nine."

I shrug. "I'm not sure," I say after thinking on it.

"Okay. Okay. Finish up. We got to get you back to school. We got to get you back immediately, you don't know nine times nine."

I laughed. "Ninety-nine. No. No. Eighteen. Wait."

"We got to hurry. You are getting dumber by the moment. Come on. Wash up."

We washed up, consolidated the leftovers for the fridge, and threw out our garbage. He packed me into the car to head back to school.

"Cobe," he said, sliding behind the wheel. "I want you to know something. Next week or the week after or next year even, I'm going to come get you, any time it is that you need to be picked up, okay?"

I nodded in response.

"Just so long as you always with a nurse as fly as Ms. Henderson."

HOW TRAUMA FEEDS THE SCHOOL-TO-PRISON PIPELINE

Knowing what I know now, I see how trauma played a big part in my education. I recognize myself in the kids I mentor. Growing up where we grew up, I don't know how anyone can concentrate on learning anything. Gunshots ring out, breaking your focus. Seems impossible to stay in your seat. Fight. Flight. Eyes front. Stayed focused. Pay attention. Sit still. Stop fidgeting. You want to duck, run, hide, swing, or just about anything that puts you in motion. Thoughts race too fast to focus on your studies. Can't attend to the open book on your desk when you got to scan the room once more to make sure nothing is coming at you.

This repeats all day, every day.

Even the physical symptoms I experienced—stomach pains, sickness, headaches, body aches, tremors, tension, fatigue—that amplified into faking illnesses from first grade through eighth are signs of chronic trauma. Exposure to violence can be extremely traumatic, leading to physical, emotional, or psychological problems.[1] It is funny because if you had asked me, I never felt I was really sick, but thinking back, knowing what I know, I got to wonder how much of my put-on might have really been at some level legit. Real symptoms of an unspecified, unrecognized illness—trauma—are suffered by a whole community.

When you are traumatized, you are always thinking about what might be waiting for you after school on the block. I have homies that can't hear fireworks without hitting the floor, thinking it is gunfire. Friends walk out of their way, going back and forth from the grocery store to avoid the street where they saw their cousin gunned down years before. Guys who can't sit with their back to a door throughout an entire meal. It gets so you won't be at ease even in your own living room. You can't sleep through the night without having to check every lock in the house at 2 a.m. (sometimes checking every lock more than once to be on the safe side).

If you are always looking over your shoulder, it is hard to see what is written on the chalkboard. It seems impossible to focus on what is happening in school. So, you are fidgeting, unfocused, jumping out of your seat, can't stay still, and the teacher is thinking you're misbehaving. You get labeled ADHD, anxiety, or, worse yet, a bad kid. Those labels stay with you for years to come, put in your file, passed grade to grade, teacher to teacher, who get weary of you before day one in their class because they know your type. Those labels are hard to shake. They follow you year after year until you are eventually pushed out of school.

Discipline case, someone got to be sent to the assistant principal's office, in our case, Mr. Cox, who set kids straight with a wooden paddle, thickened by layers of black electrical tape. Cox lived in the neighborhood, only a couple of blocks from school. He knew our comings and goings in the halls and in the hood. Getting sent to his office was a big deal. He handled any discipline issue with an old-fashioned whupping.

These labels have long-term consequences in our neighborhoods. Discipline case, sent to the assistant principal's office enough times, catches the attention of school security. That file grows thicker than the electric tape around Cox's paddle. Offenses, allegations, detentions, suspensions, in school and otherwise, add density. Just like the police, school security—often an officer moonlighting as a guard—knows the trouble kids. Problem children, repeat offenders get a rap. They are rounded up whenever some school supply goes missing, or something is scribbled in a bathroom stall. They are rounded up, usual suspects, paraded down the hall, and made an example of at every infraction.

The school-to-prison pipeline conveyor belt feeds these kids from the classroom to the detention center.[2] Discipline case gets flagged enough times that the kid is bound for the justice system. Those of us acting up in the back of the class are often the first shipped off to juvenile detention centers.

The problem kid is removed from learning opportunities, pushed further and further out of school—expelled, arrested—increasingly for lesser and lesser offenses. Smoking a cigarette, violating the dress code, or using a cell phone in a zero-tolerance environment can get a kid booted.

C-MAN

Calvin's mom didn't want him to go to Oglesby. C-Man was the nephew of King Shorty Freeman, the founder of the Black Disciples. Ty and G-Free, C-Man's cousins, both were a bit older and attended Oglesby. Ty was my main man, and G-Free, his brother, eventually became our leader. King Shorty would meet with his top lieutenants in C-Man's mama's house over on 82nd and Woodlawn after his parents split.

C-Man, at age ten, was enrolled in a school close to home, and his mom wouldn't budge on that point. Now, a lot is made in the media about shorties in grade school being recruited into the drug trade or caught up in violence. No question that does happen. Children catch a stray bullet often meant for someone else. I was certainly a D-boy, selling drugs before I learned to ride a bike. Youngsters get put to work as lookouts or runners for corner boys, but that is more the exception than the rule.

For the most part, the unspoken law is kids are off-limits. That is just understood. We get into mischief, throwing up signs in the park to represent. Throwing down signs at passing cars on busy main streets to disrespect. Vice Lords would sometimes chase you through the neighborhood, but at that age, it was sport. We took ourselves seriously—that much is a fact—but in the big picture, we were mostly playacting. Even those who were born in still weren't expected to be soldiers yet. You are mostly going through the motions.

Drawing signs on just about any surface we could find. Brown paper bags folded into DIY textbook covers, two-pocket folders in BD colors, trapper keepers with Velcro latches, and even our Adidas kicks, before Nike embraced Jordan, were just a blank canvas to be filled. This identifies the at-risk kids from the high risk, but it is still a game at that age.

Even the dustups we'd launch against the opposition at Stagg were more training ground than main event. They might leave us scuffed and tattered, sneaking back into school bruised, bloody, and disheveled, but the consequences were lower. They were not life or death.

In those early elementary school grades, you might even count a Stone, GD, or Vice Lord "in training" as a friend. Many of my guys in grade school would end up on opposition. Divisions were not rigidly maintained at that age. We still horsed around together at the back of the class, even years after those early affiliations were made.

We'd mess around on the playground, hosting gymnastics tournaments. The silliest booty flop stunt got the highest score. We'd use the monkey bars and rings for feats of daring, race one another, giving points for goofiness.

After school, we'd play arcade games in the back at Turner's BBQ, where the controls on *Space Invaders* were half coated in grease. Players propped quarters on the lip of the plastic casing that housed the video screen to place dibs on who took on the winner.

Years later, when we were at odds in high school, some of those same grade school friends and I actively avoided each other even while our crews clashed. We would all be mixing it up in a game room, squared off with our respective crews into it with each other right there on the floor, but we would keep our distance from one another out of mutual respect. We never traded blows.

Eventually, many of those guys, decades later in adulthood, would work alongside me as trainers for Cure Violence Global. In those days, everyone would be squared against everyone else regardless of affiliation. You were constantly testing or being tested. Win, lose, or draw, you had to fight. You might be pit against another BD just to try them on. It wasn't for keeps, but it defined hierarchy.

We organized ourselves through these battles. On the playground, in the hall, at the back of the room, during a lecture when teacher wasn't looking, after class, in the park, in the street, or anywhere else you could go heads up, toe-to-toe.

If you tried to avoid it, outright refused, hid from conflict, or ran away, you'd be branded a "high-powered coward." A label that marked you as a target to be bullied, booked in the halls, made fun of and mocked, pelted with spitballs, and chased after school. It was a fate worse than Cox's office and another disciplinary write-up in your folder.

The year C-Man eventually wore his mom down, getting him transferred to Oglesby, was fifth grade. It was the year he officially became a part of our crew. That was the year everything changed.

I was ten years old.

DAD RETURNS HOME

When my father was released from Stateville, we all piled into the car for one last drive downstate to fetch him. Grandpa Phil drove. Granny sat in the passenger seat. The three of us kids—Boo, Trice, and myself—squeezed into the backseat with Mom.

Any of the usual griping we kids might put up on a road trip was set aside. We took turns sitting crammed in the middle on the bench, between our sibs, without complaint. Rotating who was saddled with the undesired seat. There were no elbows to the ribs or smacking upside the head that usually accompanied a round-trip journey. No backseat brawls. We were uncharacteristically patient and cooperative. Any drama set aside. We drove in excited silence, eager to be reunited as a family.

We picked Dad up out front. Exchanging warm affection. Handshakes and hugs. Inside, guards policed against physical contact. Hugs, broken up. Touching hands could result in thunderous crashes down on metal table-tops. The clash of cymbals being pounded on with fury, startling to make the point: "No touching."

Any intimacy inside is punishable.

Outside, I could wholly lean into my father put my arms around his waist. I could hold him in a proper embrace alongside my brother, sister, and mom.

That evening, we celebrated at Mildred's. The Lounge was filled with family and friends. As customary, a pitcher was passed throughout the night, stuffed full of cash for the newly freed to have a fresh start. Envelopes filled with bills. Wads of money to get life going on the outside. Drinks flowed. Uncle Phil tended bar. Dusties played on the jukebox. My parents danced as if it were their wedding night.

Dad was interested in making up for lost time from the jump. He needed to make up time on the streets and time with his family. He put his crew back together. He was a savvy leader and skilled businessman who kept things tight. He scored some product, liquid PCP, which he dipped individual cigarettes in to get started. It had a chemical smell like the toner cartridge in a copy machine. They were relatively easy to manufacture and sell on the cheap. He set up an assembly line to open packs of smokes, dip individual loosies into the liquid, lay them on a paper towel to dry them out, place them ready-to-go in plastic baggies. In a few weeks, he was back at the level he was at before going away.

This time, though, more people wanted in on the action. Dad had made some connections behind bars who wanted part of his operation. That meant building up bigger than before. He had always kept a tight crew that ran under the radar and wasn't afraid to shut down for a few months to let heat blow over if necessary. Under this new system, that wasn't an option anymore.

At the same time, we moved into a two-flat around the corner from Granny's house, only a couple of blocks away, taking over a second-floor unit on 76th and Peoria. It was nice digs with a fenced-in front yard. For the first time, we had plenty of room. We each got our own bedrooms, and there was enough space to move around that we weren't on top of each other all the time.

Life was good.

MY APPRENTICESHIP

"Whoa!" Doc yelled as we headed out the schoolyard exit, cued by the end-of-day bell. It was one of those rare occasions where we made it through a whole day without skipping class. "Check it out!"

We ran in the daily stampede out of the building. Past Mr. Redman, the phys ed teacher, blowing on his whistle at us escapees: "Slow it down! Slow it down!" Past the door holders propping open the exit. Past the stairs, which we took in a leap. Along the metal fence that ran the length of the schoolyard out onto the sidewalk.

My father's Cadillac sat out front. Dad propped against the hood, waiting. He wore a fedora that matched his custom-tailored suit. There was a chill in the fall air. He braced against it in his full-length fur trench coat.

Doc saw him first and stuck me in the ribs with an elbow.

"That's my dad," I told him.

I was unclear why he was there. It had me a little jangled for a moment.

"Who is this, then?" Dad asked.

"This is Doc, and this, Solomon."

"How you do, Doc?" My dad asked. "Solomon?" Shaking their hands like they're men. Fishing out a thick billfold, he peeled off a couple of fives, big money in grade school dollars.

"Can you guys give me a bit of time with my son? Go buy yourselves some candy."

"Thank you, sir," Solomon responded. They give wide-eyed disbelief, snatching that money.

"Did I do something wrong?" I asked when my boys were out of earshot.

"I don't know, did you?"

I shake my head.

"Good. Get in. I need your help. How you want to earn some money?"

"Yessir."

That day started my apprenticeship.

I climbed in on the passenger side. We drove all around the city until it was dark out. He collected cash from his corner boys and introduced me around. He'd pass money to me to count. It was more than I had ever seen at that point. He'd hand over billfolds thick with cash. I'd stuff it into an envelope.

My mind would reel as the counts climbed into double digits: Twenty-five. Fifty. Sixty. Seventy-five. Eighty.

Onward into triple-digits: One hundred. One fifty. Two hundred.

Up. Up. Up.

He'd often close out our "shift" by telling me the total take that day, which my mind struggled to comprehend. He broke down how much had been collected overall, what percent was our take, and what got kicked upstairs. He'd give me an idea of wholesale costs on the smokes and the dust with the markup street value of sticks.

"What is your profit then?" he'd ask.

During this period, we never wanted for anything in my house. When he was locked up, we sometimes struggled to put food on the table, but Dad often ended our errands with a stop at the mall. He'd buy me new clothes, fresh kicks, an Eddie Bauer backpack, a Member's Only jacket, designer shirts, and Guess jeans.

Overnight, I had school supplies, a brand-new Walkman, cassette tapes, and movies. Dad took care of all of us kids. It was Christmas around the clock. That summer, as an early birthday present, he came home with a bike for me. My brother and I had new sports equipment for the first time in our lives: baseball mitts, hitter's gloves, bats, balls, a pigskin, and a basketball. We wanted for nothing.

We'd replenish supplies at trap houses throughout projects all over the city. He showed me the logistics of our trade. The way distribution worked. Ziplock baggies packed full of wet smoke. Angel dust. Wicky sticks. The design that went into keeping the enterprise going. Dealers corralled traffic on one-way side streets to ensure that we kept control of the block. In high-rise towers in Henry Horner, Cabrini, or other projects around the city, we controlled floors to the same aim. Stairwells barricaded. Limited elevators in use to manage traffic.

Occasionally, I would be lookout. Dad would point out an unmarked cop car. He'd tell me to lay on the horn if anyone made a move for the building while he went inside. As we slowly passed a squad car, idle in the parking lot of a housing complex, he handed over a Saran Wrap bundle of Sherm.

"Son, stuff these in your socks," he'd tell me. "You got the right kind for it, you know, with the elastic band."

I never seen a pair of socks that didn't come with an elastic band, though I did as I was told. I yanked the cuff away from my leg and jammed the smokes down into the gusset, the V-shaped stretch of fabric between the heel flap and the instep. Angel dust needed to be handled carefully so my sweaty ankles didn't activate those chemicals. I'd fidget with my pants leg and adjust my shoe until it would sit right, concealing the package.

My dad banked on the police not patting down a minor.

For months, I explored the city with my dad, absorbing everything I could about the man and his work.

One morning, I woke up thinking I could pinch a few marijuana ciga-rettes from my dad's supply and sell them to some older kids on the way to school. It just popped into my head as something I wanted to try.

Fact is, I didn't need the money. I'm not sure what I'd have done with all that cash at that time anyway. Dad was spoiling us. There wasn't much of anything I could imagine having that wasn't already being provided. Most of the time, he was kicking me down a little spending cash on the side for running errands with him anyway. A kid can eat only so many Fun Dips, Wax Lips, Pixie Sticks, Bottle Caps, and penny candies.

So, it wasn't about the money that day.

The only thing I can figure in retrospect is that it was going to make me look cool. A ten-year-old isn't usually worrying about their rep. I am sure the opportunity to be a bona fide D-Boy before all my friends might have been too much for me to resist.

I pinched a few joints that I didn't think he'd notice.

Sadar's grandmother owned a candy store with a game room next door that was on the way to school. We'd usually group up there to make the rest of the trek to school, coming from different directions in the neighborhood. Then our whole crew, loaded up on our treats, would mob up the rest of the bands of kids that flowed into school in the morning.

That day, I sought out some of the older kids from school that we passed on the way. Even now, everybody says how I used to be able to talk to just about anyone anywhere. I started talking to them. I don't know if it was having spent all the time in the Lounge or what, but it was never really a problem for me.

"Y'all want to buy some weed," I said, walking up all cocky and confident.

They fell out laughing at first. The whole thing must've been a bit of a cartoon. Here, this pint-sized D-boy, slinging like he thinks he is a pro. My guys fell back laughing, too. They couldn't believe it.

I showed them the baggies. They knew enough of who my dad was that they didn't roll me right there. Instead, they made good with the money. My first drug deal was on a Tuesday morning before the 9 a.m. bell, only a few blocks from school in fifth grade. They bought all the smokes off of me in a single exchange.

Of course, it got back to my dad. I don't know how I thought it wouldn't. Even if some of the older boys didn't narc me out, which they did, my dad kept a tight watch on his inventory. I came home, and he was in the living room waiting for me. It was just after school when I got home, too early for him to be there, so I knew something was up. He was calm, not pacing the living room, wearing a path in the carpet, the way my mom would at times. He wasn't seated either, just standing in view as the door came open. I knew what was up immediately.

I'd gotten whuppings before for far less. This was just how we were disciplined. Horsing around one time, I'd caught a stunning blow so hard upside the head that I saw stars. Another time, I got a beating for mouthing off in class. I'd seen Boo take one for acting out that left him looking like a prizefighter gone a few rounds. My brother often clashed with my dad. Even my mom had occasionally been on the wrong side of my father's temper a few times. Late at night, when they both were drinking, a ruckus pulled me out of bed into this same living room when I should have been sleeping. I watched them get into it.

Dad had a cold rage. It wasn't the kind of anger that comes over some dudes when everything goes tense—balling their fists, a vein in their forehead pulsing. They run hot. Seething. Nah. Dad was always cool. There was no tell. He'd be stoic and stone, then—Bam!—pop you so quick, it was like blink.

I braced myself for impact.

Those "offenses" I had committed before were nothing on the level of what I had just done. I was sure going to get it.

"Are you selling drugs?" Dad asked.

His voice was cold and measured.

I shook my head no and started to play like I was crying. It was my only defense, I thought. Even before he moved, I started whimpering a bit. Figuring the act might get him to go lighter on me.

Meanwhile, I tensed up. I steeled myself to catch a blow.

"Well, don't cry, son," Dad said gently.

He was laughing a bit. That mischievous smile, which everyone tells me I inherited, on his lips.

"Don't cry now."

He placed a hand on my shoulder.

There weren't any tears yet to wipe away. I was just making the sounds, but I ran the back of my hand across my face anyway and looked up at him.

"Don't cry, son. Get your money. Just don't lie about it."

WHEN C-MAN GOES TO OGLESBY

When Calvin transferred to Oglesby, he had already heard about me from his cousin Ty. C-Man couldn't believe there was a D-boy our age. That was fascinating to him. Even before we met, he had heard about me dealing dope to the older boys. The idea of a D-boy at ten was unimaginable at that time and place.

C-Man became a part of the crew overnight. We hit it off instantly. The whole group of us was inseparable. It helped that he was related to Ty and G-Free, but we'd have bonded regardless. We had the same sense of humor, and he encouraged my bombastic, outgoing personality. I'd have him rolling by starting random conversations with strangers at McD's or enthusiastically greeting people I never met in a parking lot as if we were lifelong friends.

Even though C-Man was related to the Big Man, King Shorty, he still wanted to hear all my stories all the time. I could hold court at lunch in the cafeteria. I would describe in detail where Dad and I had been this week or that.

In exchange, he would detail the meetings his mom hosted with Shorty's lieutenants. We didn't always understand everything we were exposed to but knew enough to put pieces together. We knew when someone was moving in on BD territory, when they were into it with somebody, or when things were escalating to full-scale war. We exchanged this gossip as if it were our own, even when we didn't know everything being said.

Midway through the school year, Calvin acquired a bully. To us, he was a giant—older, bigger, meaner. He was in eighth grade. Already a teenager. He could toss us around like rag dolls and not think twice, but Calvin was his favorite toy.

In the hallway between classes, he'd come up behind Calvin and give him a shove. He'd knock books out of his hand or hip-check him into the lockers. He also watched way too much wrestling. His favorite move was the full nelson. The wrestling hold where his arms would twist up behind C-Man's neck, pushing his head forward by pressing his hands into it from the back.

It was easier to execute in passing than a suplex, though if he could've gotten away with it in the halls, I am sure that would have been his go-to move. This was typical bully behavior. It didn't have anything to do with gangs, and, come to think of it, it might not have had anything to do with bullying. He didn't really realize his strength. In his mind, he probably thought we were all messing around. I don't even know for sure if he was aware of who Calvin was at the time. For the most part, that fact went unnoticed even in our own circle.

In fact, it might be said that Calvin didn't even recognize the full scope of who he himself was yet.

"I told you quit!" Calvin was yelling.

"Ima mess you up!" the bully growled.

On the playground, he was pushing Calvin around. He came up behind him, the same as he did a dozen times before, grabbing him up. He was much taller than us, so he could get Calvin's feet off the ground while squeezing his arms backward.

"I ain't playin'!"

"Roooooooaaaaarr! Ima tear you in half!" He bellowed with laughter.

Then, as fast as the whole thing happened, he dropped Calvin flat on his ass and stalked away.

This happened all the time. Calvin was a tough guy. He could scrap. Over the years, I'd come to rely on his skills. He'd saved my ass on more occasions than I could count. The bully was three years older, three times bigger, and just too much for us at the time.

One of Shorty Freeman's top lieutenants, Dirty Mike, took a liking to Calvin. Whenever C-Man's mom would host meetings, Dirty Mike would give him a few bucks. He always showed kindness to C-Man. He'd talk to him like an adult. Ask if he caught the game last night. Ask who he was rooting for that season. Talk to him about school, about sports, favorite foods, favorite music.

"C-Man, if you ever need anything, I got you!"

Now, a fifth grader doesn't need much, but Calvin took him up on it the next time Dirty Mike offered. He explained the situation he was having with the bully at school.

Dirty Mike held up his hand, like, "Say no more."

"I got you." He told Calvin. "I got you."

The next day, Dirty Mike drove through the Henry Horner Housing Project, rounding up his soldiers. He got no fewer than thirty D-boys to come off the block and ride down on Oglesby. They surrounded the grade school.

As the students came out, the D-boys went up to them asking for the bully by name.

They asked one by one.

When Calvin came out, Dirty Mike called him over.

"C-Man, I want you to point out the bully for me."

It was an intense show of force. The bully was nowhere to be found. He'd gotten a heads-up that a mob was up at school looking for him and managed to hide at a friend's house across the street. He watched the whole thing from the front-room window. It didn't matter, though. Word got out. C-Man wasn't someone to fuck with anymore. Not just for the bully but for everyone in the neighborhood. He had juice.

Dirty Mike never intended it as a recruitment effort for BD—he was doing Calvin a solid helping him stand up to his bully—but that is exactly how it worked out. Sadar, who already hung with us every day, speaks about that incident as the moment he officially wanted to join.

He wasn't alone either. Things changed that day for a lot of our classmates. In our generation, in the 1980s, nobody ever saw guys mob up like that in unified coordination. It commanded respect.

5

THE MOST DANGEROUS GAS STATION IN AMERICA

Englewood/Auburn Gresham, Chicago, July 2015

In Englewood, at the intersection of 67th and Halsted, sits a gas station dubbed the most dangerous in America. Press, police, and politicians do love their hyperbole, especially when it serves to reinforce power.

I've known a gas station that bears this name at one time or another in Detroit, Cleveland, Camden, Los Angeles, New York, and New Orleans. I've probably filled my tank at each of them. As with similar designations like "Most Dangerous City," these labels grab attention. The FBI keeps score. Media report. Politicians scramble in response to announce policies. This is how the machine works.

There is perennial hand-wringing. Gut-wrenching discourse and debate follow. Reporting on violence in this way is sensationalized. It is not that this label is inaccurate, but the way it is exercised as a spectacle is calculated to create fear and fuel election cycles.

Violence doesn't behave in tidy cycles over quarter-length spans to fit political terms. Violence doesn't happen according to citywide budgets or make tidy line items on Excel spreadsheets. It isn't driven by seasonal changes or shifts in the weather. In the randomness of violent attacks, waves of crime, and shooting spikes, there is a tendency to promote patterns that offer some illusion of control.

Sunny weather in spring and summer do bring increases in shootings and killings. Predictably. Bullets go astray at backyard BBQs. They ricochet off the wall of a park fieldhouse, shattering the femur of a high school basketball champ bound for the pros. A child riding Big Wheels down a paved park path is caught in a crossfire. These tragedies catch headlines. In a desperate search for answers, things like seasonal shifts in weather start to make sense.

In reality, the context behind these summer spikes really means more people out and about. More people on the street increase the likelihood you will have a run-in with someone carrying a beef against you. It has nothing to do with the heat or weather, only the increase in visibility. More people on the street mean more people crashing into one another.

These efforts to identify simple reasons are as contrived as the efforts to propose simple solutions. Gas stations offer a metaphor on how this whole game is rigged. A convenience store gets attention for a high body count. It catches attention for robberies, fights in the parking lot, shootouts, and drug dealing. It earns a reputation. City inspectors are sent to issue code violations. They ticket on fire codes, health codes, building codes, any department they can mobilize makes it out. The owner is slapped with all kinds of fines and shuttered for a time because the hot dog carousel is too close to the nacho cheese spread and the orange heat lamp doesn't burn hot enough. The gas station gets shut down a spell. Violence in that hot spot is quelled, and the city declares victory, but really they've just moved it somewhere on down the road.

If violence were measured as an infectious disease, transmitted person to person, retaliations amplifying spread, it would look more like epidemic waves—graphs with spikes and drops over longer transmission cycles outside the realm of politics. Measures would focus on "hot spots," areas of concentrated violence, the way they map any outbreak. Red bursts of high-risk splotch over blocks.

Dots of orange and pink speckle streets in a widening circle until they cool pale blue.

Gas stations often make the top ten fed lists for most violent crimes. They are the big red dot in the center of that splotch. Convenience stores (more so if they sell liquor), restaurants, and parks also rank. Violence isn't as random an act as we like to imagine. Statistics are broken down annually by reported violent crimes: homicide, rape, aggravated assault, burglary, larceny, theft, and arson.

In our office, as well as in community violence intervention offices around the country, we keep large maps labeled with hot-spot locations. It is one of the first things we do in a community. We pull police department data, crime statistics, public databases, and FBI figures. When setting up a new site, we look at the last three to five years of data in a given area. This

gives us the target area within the city. We want to narrow this down to a fo-
cal point first—areas with high rates of violent episodes compared to other
parts of the city—which we look at as police "beats" or "zones."

We print off these wall-size poster maps at the local FedEx and splay
them over a table in the center of the community-based office. E-wood,
where we've been established for some time, these posters cover the walls
throughout the office. After more broadly identifying the target area, we
get specific, mapping hot spots. These are the places where there is a high
potential for violence. Spots where groups gather, drugs are dealt, cars are
jacked, and other assorted mayhem transpires.

At the end of this stretch, at an intersection between three gang territories,
I pull into the gas station. It hums with activity. Cars cue at pumps. Hypes
mill, asking for change. A few cars sit parked or abandoned on one side of
the lot. On the other end is a couple storefronts in a brick building. Half
empty of shops, an abandoned lot next door, it abuts the station. The two
are connected by cracked and faded gray asphalt. Buckled concrete on an
uneven sidewalk between them. There are few lights in the awning overhead and few windows in the station itself. Only a single, bulletproof slab of
translucent acrylic, yellowed by cigarette smoke, separates the cashier from
the outside. The window has put in work. There are visible dings where the
"glass has stopped bullets." An alleyway, separated from the lot by a wooden
fence, runs the length of the back end of the station.

An older man in a dirty coat, too heavy for a summer heat wave, makes
his way past busted handles of idle pumps down a row of cars. He holds an
unmarked spray bottle in one hand and a window squeegee in the other.
Filthy rags tucked in the belt of a pair of sagging slacks. Most drivers shoo
him off or give him a couple of bucks to leave their windshield alone.

The air smells of gasoline vapor and skunk weed.

Since the station is at a busy intersection, it operates like an open-air
market. Guys peddle bottled water to cars at the light. Loose cigarettes are
sold from the pack on the sidewalk out front. Makeshift vendors set up stations on public sidewalks spread over blankets selling clothes, electronics,
hair products, and any number of odds and ends.

Other goods are sold in the alleyway, round back.

When a community violence intervention office is launched, strategy
guides everything. We look at city data to find the most violent areas in the
past three to five years. We gather the backstory to give those data context.
In this instance, BD, GD, and Vice Lord have territory leading to this spot.
We try to spot trends, map hot spots, assess all the components of that target area—who are the highest risk, who are the major players, what groups

operate there, what kind of inroads our guys have—plotting everything, including stations like this one, on the map.

Violence interruption is as much a science as it is an art. When I first started, we didn't use data. We weren't structured; we didn't have a strategy. Back then, it was mostly guys who turned a corner and knew they wanted to make their communities better but weren't completely clear on how they were going to go about doing it. It was far more art than science back then.

We plot stations like this one on the map as part of the target area strategy. Liquor stores, lounges, convenience stores, bars, and clubs, anywhere that the highest risk might hang. Places that have a reputation for violence. Even before the data are pulled, our guys will usually know the ones. These locales got a reputation, hard earned.

We plot conflicts on the map best we can, too. Groups and individuals into it with one another. Alongside major reasons for those conflicts. Interpersonal, debt, territory, gambling, abuse, or some historical beef.

I come through. Drive streetside. Circle the pumps. Five guys stand at the back bumper of a couple of cars parked side by side in the lot. A third car, abandoned by the dumpsters, looks like it was towed in and left. I maneuver my car this way to avoid getting pinned down. I make a show of swinging the car around so no one thinks I am creeping.

One dude sits propped on the trunk of a car, hugging his knees, hitting a joint, and holding court. Other guys are positioned around him in a semicircle, fanned at the bumper and tucked between the two cars. The joint passed between them.

Dude on the trunk of the car I recognize as JB, a Vice Lord. He is a wiry guy, tall and lanky, with a nervous tick. JB has an animated way of speaking, punctuated by exaggerated hand gestures. I ease my car up to the group and pull a healthy distance away, close enough now to make eye contact yet with enough distance to pull away if necessary.

The car is a Caprice.

The Caprice.

I jerk the gearshift into park.

Zo, another Vice Lord, stands to the right of JB, propped on an elbow against the car. He spots me first, pushes off the car upright, and jabs an elbow at JBs thigh to grab his attention. Nods in my direction.

The guys angle out now, opening the semicircle up, five total, though I recognize three. It feels a bit like crashing a party, not unwelcome but not exactly greeted with open arms.

Pulling up is like being left out of an inside joke.

"Sup, CeaseFire?" JB grins through a mouthful of dense smoke. He raises his hand in greeting.

The guys laugh. I wave through the window and climb out of the car. A cloud of weed floats skyward.

An energy runs through the members of a group who have just been in some shit. I've felt it myself more times than I can recall. I imagine that it is the same among any soldiers fresh from a battle. The shared experience of violence, an adrenal charge, crackling like electricity, bonding the group. Everything pulses. Senses ratchet up to twelve. Heightened. Colors are more vibrant. Everything has an energy to it.

I enter at the tail end of a comedown. Neurochemicals still coursing through collective systems, being blunted by weed, which softens the edges.

"Sup, JB? Zo? What's going on?"

I make the rounds. Shake hands. Introductions.

"You all know, Cobe? He with CeaseFire."

"That the gun group?" Someone asks.

"CeaseFire just trying to stop these shootings and killings. Period. That's it," I tell them. "I'm a violence interrupter. Keep things calm. Provide options. That's what I do."

"As seen on TV," JB says, laughing. "You never seen those candlelight vigils? They always be out there."

CeaseFire in Chicago has been around long enough that it is easy to offer a shorthand. We have media coverage on all the networks. Bumper stickers, swag, window signs, and pub ed get plastered all over the place, which builds a lot of name recognition. I don't have to work so hard to explain myself.

It helps that I know JB, Zo, and Brian. That makes this first encounter a bit smoother. Having these guys to vouch for me.

When I am coaching set up on a new site, these encounters require a bit more backstory. I might have a new worker explain the mission of an organization, provide some history, explain who they are and why they are out there in the first place. The swag that is ubiquitous in Chicago because of our years in operation is going to look different at a brand-new site in Brooklyn. People will give you a side eye when you are starting out. Suspicious that you might be a cop. I always tell my guys to have something on hand: a bumper sticker, a flyer, a magnet, a key chain. Offer up something as a gift to break the ice before you launch into your whole presentation.

Mentioning jobs is often a good hook. It gets people to lean in and listen. Even if they are not looking for a job themselves, everybody got somebody out of work, somewhere. Options and opportunities are bridge builders.

I also encourage my teams, especially when they are just starting out, to get out there even when nothing is going on. The best time to make connections is when you don't need them for anything. Build relationships when the stakes are low and there is nothing to mediate.

"Just coming off Aberdeen," I add.

I got enough of a relationship that I can throw that out there. I am testing the waters to see how they respond when I drop the mention.

I read the body language, following a shudder that passes through the group. It moves between them more subtly than the joint—and ten times faster.

Zo pulls a hit and passes. Plays cool. His hands in his pockets. All coy and casual. Shrugs.

JB, the trickster sporting a broad, glassy-eyed smile, drops the grin instantly; it vanishes like exhaled smoke. A moment later, the smile returns, twice as wide, a little forced, with more visible teeth.

The dude on Zo's left, partially between the cars, rocks on his heels. Nervous energy. He fidgets with his belt and looks down at his shoes. The guy who asked me if CeaseFire was the gun group seems to catch it next. I sense the movement counterclockwise. Shoulder to shoulder, until it comes back around, back to Zo, shaking his head.

Over the years, one of the things this work has taught me is to read the invisible. Nonverbal gestures. Emotions weighing in the air. An action before it is taken or the residue of an action after being made. Truth hidden in the gossip. Motivation behind a behavior. Many of these skills are introduced at an early age. A micro-expression at the corner of someone's mouth, an instant before they speak, can be a tell to the veracity of its content. An extrasensory perception to assess a shift in emotional energy likely first developed in a volatile home on a violent corner in a chaotic community.

As violence interrupters, we are trained in tumultuous environments. We take the temperature before walking through the front door. If we grew up with unpredictable, erratic, violent behavior, then survival often depends on how early we can detect the mood of a space as we set foot in it. We are also constantly updating that information for status changes. If you miscalculate, the same funny quip can play for laughs one evening and get your head put through the wall the next.

You are looking for signs as you come up the block around the corner to the kitchen. Taking samples of the air. Measure its content. When you grow up like this, you become an alleyway psychologist, a street social worker, and a back-channel behavior change expert because your life depends on it.

"We didn't do nothing wasn't asked for in the first place," Brian says flatly. "We ain't in the wrong here."

He steps forward. JB shoots a look, surprise. Zo shakes his head again. The shoegazer drops his head to stare at the lines in the parking lot.

"I got you. I'm not saying you did anything wrong." I look Brian in the eyes to show I'm sincere. "I'm just trying to know why you would come through like that in the first place."

"Got to stay informed," JB quips.

"Got to stay informed," I repeat.

"If we came through, we'd have a reason," Zo says.

"A good one at that," Brian adds.

When you grow up in a violent home on a violent block in a violent neighborhood, these skills are programmed into you naturally. You learn them in the hood, reinforce them at school, and they become second nature—a part of life. You learn to hone this skill when you get into violence prevention work. This is the science behind the art. You learn to read the cues people give when holding back because they don't want to out someone and the cues they hold back because they are afraid. There are signs and signals in posture and stance. A head cocked to one side or a squint that lasts a second too long.

"Gimme a good reason why y'all might roll through like that, huh? I know y'all too smart to stunt like that just to flex."

Brian looks up and over to JB.

I continue, "Let's say hypothetical, like, what might cause someone to come through like that?"

JB offers a broad, glassy-eyed grin, "High-Po-Thet-Ick-Al," encircling syllables in smoke rings like the Caterpillar from *Alice in Wonderland*.

Zo leans forward. "If we did this thing, then it must've been in response to something."

At this, Brian looks up and scans the semicircle. His eyes come to rest on me. "Yo, man, the question is, what are you going to do with this information once you have it?"

"That depends," I answer honestly, "but my goal is to stop the shooting and killing. Anything that can be done to keep this thing, whatever it is that went down, from escalating further."

"What about them?" Zo asks.

"We're going to take it one step at a time."

Neither JB nor Zo makes a statement. Brian steps forward. "They robbed one of our shorties," he says.

"They rob you?" I ask.

I hadn't heard this bit of the story. The information hits funny. As if someone slipped the wrong piece in a puzzle box. A misshapen fact with rough edges. If the shorty who did the stickup was one of Big Folks' guys, it was not sanctioned, which could cause bigger problems.

"What we supposed to do?" Brian asks.

"Can't let that shit slide," someone snaps.

"That kid didn't do nothing in the first place," someone else says.

"We let that shit go, might as well just give everything over to them," Brian says.

"Little Homie was minding his own business," Zo affirms. "He lives over there."

Maybe someone was stepping out of rank on Big Folks. It could be a power move internally and something to just stir up trouble. Or it could have just been a routine robbery, somebody on Big Folks' crew moonlighting as a stickup guy. They needed quick cash and decided to shake down opposition without getting permission.

No one here is thinking bigger picture. No one is considering potential consequences.

"You know it was one of Big Folks' guys over there?" I ask for clarity.

"We know where it went down is enough," Zo answers.

"They were trying to send a message. That much is fact," Brian answers.

It isn't a fact, of course. That the stickup came from Big Folks' crew isn't a fact. That it was under his direction isn't a fact, either. Nor is it a fact that it was intended as a message. I roll this over in my mind.

"You figure just cause it went down in their hood, they responsible?" I say out loud. "You don't know that for sure, though. How he look? Describe him for me."

"Shorter light-skinned dude," Zo answers.

"He alone?"

"Weren't no one else around."

"But you didn't know the dude?" I ask.

"Only by description."

"You just assumed it was those guys over there?"

"That's right. Safe bet."

"Safe bet, but to be clear, you didn't know him."

"That's right. We knew him we'd know who we riding down on, yeah?"

"Yeah," I affirm. Collective punishment. They were sending a message of their own. If Big Folks and his crew weren't actually involved, though, that message was falling on deaf ears.

"What he wearing?"

"Tan Timberlands. Beige skully."

"How much they take?" I ask Brian directly.

"Fifty dollars."

I sit with this for a moment. Fifty dollars. The ethical economics of a human life doesn't enter into the equation just yet—a life on the line less than the cost of a designer tee—but instead a kind of conflict calculus.

In my wallet: a few twenties, a couple of tens, a five, some singles. That life, more than twice over. Could I afford to buy peace at cost? We will leverage whatever we can to keep down the shootings and killings in a mediation like this one. We've had guys resolve their differences head up with fists in the ring at a local gym to keep someone alive. We've negotiated settlements to make things square between both parties. We've redrawn boundaries to resolve tensions over contested territory.

"I don't normally do this," I tell them, fishing out the cash from my wallet. I fish out two twenties and a ten. I hold up the bills fanned out and folded in half. What is in my hand might end this right now. "But, y'all take this now to consider the matter settled?"

I am looking at Brian. Scan between JB and Zo. Rotate my gaze through the guys and back. Silence. Brian nods.

"That goes for all y'all."

"Bet," JB responds.

"Understood," Zo says.

"Understood," Brian repeats, reaching over to snag the fold.

I pinch the bills between my fingers.

"That means y'all let this thing drop, drop. For real. I don't want to hear any of you or any of your guys coming through there again, okay? No more coming through there for anything. Just let it drop. You got to go through those parts for whatever reason. You take the long way round if you have to. Avoid that street. Avoid that neighborhood. Okay? Can we let this thing go?"

"I got you," Brian says. "I got you. That works."

"That works," Zo repeats.

I survey the scene. The guys in between the car are nodding.

"Cool," JB says.

"Cool," I echo.

I let go of the money. Brian crumbles it in his fist. He shoves it in his pocket.

Another round of handshakes. I head back to the car, climb behind the wheel, turn the ignition, and crank the engine. My mind goes over everything I know about the robbery. A light-skinned guy in a beige skully and tan Timberlands rolled a Vice Lord for drug money near the spot on Aberdeen.

Shorty reported that up the chain of command to Brian. They took the act as a gesture. It was not a cash grab but a message. This declared open season. Brian tells Shorty he'll handle it and gets his boys JB, Zo, and the crew to mobilize against Big Folks, who they know operates over there.

Big Folks and his guys don't know nothing about a stickup or a stickup guy. At least, they don't know nothing in any way that could connect to the shooting. Most likely, the stickup itself happened under the radar. No one had permission.

I call Big Fella and Hot Rod in that order to give them an update. I tell them each I found the car. I offer a rundown on what I've learned—who did the shooting and why—explaining what went down. We strategize on what has to happen next. Even with the commitment from Brian, JB, and Zo, there are loose ends on the Vice Lord side of the equation. China Joe or Head or someone with the right connections needs to get on that.

"We want someone checking in with all of them," I tell Big Fella. "Should follow up later today, even just to make sure everything is good. I think they'll respect the decision. So long as Big Folks and crew maintain their end of the bargain. But, can never be too sure."

Internally, we refer to this as "babysitting." The technical term, though, is "constructive shadowing." We pair up our guys with those involved in the conflict. Even when we have their word, as in this case, we want our guys to check in with them. Make sure they keep it. Provide support. Talk through anything that might come up. Keep them from flip-flopping on their convictions.

"Specially when they get to doing drugs or drinking," Big Fella observes. "I never known weed to make a cold-blooded killer out of anyone, but sure do cloud judgment."

We share a laugh.

The tensest moments in negotiating a conflict are in the immediate aftermath. You can't just accept anybody at their word. People get in their ear. Drugs or alcohol get in the mix. It is easy to upend any progress. Thoughts get twisted. No matter how seemingly airtight, any agreement can go sideways with enough outside pressure.

"We should probably find out who Shorty was got robbed in the first place," Big Fella suggests.

"Agreed. Gotta get somebody on that for sure. We don't want all this ironed out with Brian and the crew only to have some kid decide he got to take matters into his own hands."

"At the very least, we should recognize he did right to bring it up the chain of command."

In Chicago's Austin community, over on the West Side, CeaseFire workers had built a leadership council representing the three biggest gangs in the area. Austin interrupters and outreach workers recruited the heads of the most influential cliques in the area. Operating independently, each of these groups would hold its members accountable. Rather than allowing them to act on their own at a slight, no matter the size of the grievance, members would now have to bring the incident to leadership to make a decision. They would give permission to act or stand down, effectively reintroducing the hierarchy wiped away in those RICO sweeps in the 1980s and 1990s. More importantly, they introduced peace councils, creating a mechanism for the gangs to police themselves.

They called their own soldiers to do as shorty had done with Brian: something goes down like a robbery, or your guys into it over a girl, or someone is making a move, you bring that to your representative on the council. Leadership makes the call on whether this is something worth acting on or if it should be let go. They were getting active members to serve as mediators for themselves. If a situation escalated beyond the gang's immediate influence, the representative brought that to the other members of the council—even if they were all opposition.

As a council, all three leaders and representatives met biweekly to discuss conflicts brewing between their rank and file. No matter what was happening on the street, who was into it, with whom, why, whatever tensions were rumbling, this council met and discussed. Self-governance at its best. They became the de facto interrupters, arbitrators, and leaders in their community, even if they were into it with one another.

It was impressive the kind of system they created over there.

Finding the shorty and acknowledging that bringing the robbery to Brian was the right move could be the first step in replicating it on the South Side. It was still a way off from being structured with the same sophistication, but being able to repeat it would be a huge win for the community.

"Agreed," I respond. "You know anyone got a relationship with Brian specifically?"

"We'll find one," Big Fella answers and waits for a beat before adding, "You think it was a message?"

I've been thinking on this one.

"Not sure," I concede. "I don't know yet."

We sit in silence a moment.

"Find out," he says.

"Bet."

A few moments later, I circle back with Rod. The phone, set on speaker, rings.

I pull into another gas station to fill the tank.

"You get up with Big Folks again?"

"Not yet," I tell him. "I am heading that way now. My next call."

"Okay. Lil' B been looking for you. Call him first. Seemed urgent. Get them up to speed."

"Bet."

The ticker on the pump rolls through digits. Twenty. Twenty-five. Thirty. Thirty-five.

"I'll see what I can find out about dude in the beige skully," Rod offers. "Just ask around."

"That'd be good."

Forty. Forty-five.

"You think Big Folks was in on the stickup?"

I sit with that. Been rolling it around in my mind.

"Not sure," I respond.

Fifty. Fifty-five. Sixty. Sixty-five.

The value of human life is mostly the domain of faith leaders and philosophers. It is above my pay grade. Here, the anger and desire that motivated the shooting were not just about the $50. I get that. It's the principle of the matter, not the money. Culture underlies everything. Still, it is hard not to recognize that a human life, perhaps several, was on the line for less than it cost to fill my tank.

"It makes a difference how we approach that," Rod says.

"I'll see what I can get out of Lil' B when I call him."

Agencies of the U.S. government use a formula to determine the value of human life. Being in public health, I've attended conferences with health economists tasked with the morbid calculation of whether a public health intervention is worth the cost of implementation. They crunch the numbers on safety measures for motor vehicles, health regulations, and environmental impact figures to determine the cost of human life.

Hint: it is more than fifty bucks.

"Okay. I'll see what I can find out on this end, too," Rod replies.

Ten million dollars. That is the figure that is usually calculated. The value of a human life on average to the U.S. government. Ten million dollars.

I replace the nozzle at the pump. Fasten the fuel cap. Close the hatch to my gas tank. Scrolling through contacts looking for Lil' B.

A couple of years ago, Brent Decker, director of Cure Violence's international programs at the time, and I went down to Ciudad Juárez along the Rio Grande just across the border south of El Paso, Texas. The public health department wanted to see if our Cure Violence model could be applied to the escalating cartel war. We drove through sleepy desert towns that looked like something out of an old western in a black SUV.

"Progress," said an activist priest sitting in the truck's backseat, "would be if the cartel stopped killing ordinary civilians and just focused on each other."

Brent and I exchanged a look, like "Whoa."

"You can put a contract on someone for around twenty bucks, U.S.," the priest said, "so a hit squad will come in and shoot up an entire discotheque on a Saturday night to get their man, killing anybody who happens to be in the way of their bullets."

"Damn."

"If you could create a campaign that just says, 'don't kill bystanders,' we'd make a lot of progress."

I get back behind the wheel, ringing up Lil' B. Clock is ticking for Big Folks and his crew. They are running out of patience. I pull out on the street, heading in their direction.

6

A CHICAGO WINTER

The "Low Ends"/Auburn Gresham/Englewood,
Chicago, December 1983

Snow fell the day my father was beaten to death in the stairwell of a tenement building in the "Low Ends" over on South Federal in the Dearborn
Homes housing projects. It was December 29, four days after Christmas, so
the holiday season was still on display. Windows frosted with condensation
glowed Christmas red and green. String lights framed porches. Evergreens
in windows. Wreaths on doors. Candy cane–lined walkways. Snowmen in
front yards.

Snowfall slashed at an angle in the glow of streetlamps. It stuck to the
sidewalk. Piled up on the ground. Blizzard conditions. Harsh even for a
Chicago winter. That year is documented as the coldest on record. Fact. It
was known as the "Great Freeze of '83" as temperatures plummeted to an
all-time, record-setting low of twenty-five below earlier that week.[1]

I don't remember the cold. The holiday that year was dubbed the city's
"Frozen Christmas." I don't recollect it.

I watched Dad climb into a Caddy packed full of *his* guys. Five of his
men. It fishtailed down the block in rear-wheel drive. Sliding along the
slush-slick street into a blizzard-glazed night. Taillights, Christmas red,
winked from view.

That night was the last time I saw my father alive.

We were still over at the two-flat on 76th and Peoria on the second floor.
Auntie Hilda lived a floor below with her only child, Martise, my cousin,
who at that time was raised like he was a bonus sibling. Hilda was easygoing,

warmhearted; she liked to have fun. She left her door (and she would say her fridge) open for us. We always had a place to stay.

In those days, I could pop by Granny's for lunch, head to Hilda's for a snack, and come home for a second sandwich at my own kitchen table. I felt loved and looked after during those years.

I don't remember the tree that year—though I've tried.

I am sure it was decked out: string lights, garland, ornaments, and an angel on top. Beneath the tree in the living room, I imagine it was piled high with presents. My parents were doing well. They were both trying to spoil us. My mother has always been that way. My father gave everything to make up for all the Christmases behind bars. They would have gotten every toy in our letters to Santa that year, but I don't remember any of my gifts.

LYING AT THE LOW ENDS

Anthony Bogan, a BD just like my father, told the court that he spotted Dad from behind the wheel of a stolen car in the parking lot near 2901 South Federal Street.[2] Bogan had fallen on hard times. He was sleeping in elevators and hallways in tenement buildings. To keep warm, he would ride buses to the end of the line or steal a car. It was a brutal winter to be without a home.

Dad, wrapped in a full-length fur coat, cinched against the bitter cold, strode across the courtyard of the Dearborn Homes, heading for the vestibule. Bogan had spent the day robbing people. He thought Dad looked like money, so he followed him into the building, he claims.

I'd been over there a lot with Dad on his rounds. The public housing complex on the South Side in Bronzeville. It was sixteen acres of midrise, six-story, and nine-story buildings along a stretch known as the State Street Corridor. That stretch encompassed six housing projects at the time, a nearly continuous stretch from 20th Street in the South Loop to 54th Street in Washington Park, including Robert Taylor Homes, Stateway Gardens, Harold Ickes Homes, and Hilliard Homes flanked by the I-90 expressway. Collectively, they were dubbed the "Low Ends."

Dad ran them all for a time.

Over the years that followed, I heard multiple versions of what happened next. Bogan claimed to have acted alone. He sent a bat across the back of my dad's skull for pocket change. Bogan said he came up behind him and started beating him without hesitation right there in the foyer of the building.

He took barely enough to cover lunch, he explained to the court. He also took Dad's watch, wallet, hat, and jewelry. He would have taken his fur, too, but it was covered in blood.

Bogan said he didn't mean to kill him.

I don't believe him or the court documents.

AIN'T NO LOVE IN THE HEART OF THE CITY

Other things I remember from that winter break. Auntie Hilda worked as a DJ at the Lounge, occasionally filling in as a bartender when a shift needed to be covered. She was constantly revising a set list for the New Year's Eve party that year. Bobby "Blues" Bland crooned "Ain't No Love in the Heart of the City" into the hallway from speakers as tall as me on a state-of-the-art stereo system. It echoed into the stairwell with the crackle and hiss of a needle on vinyl.

I am sure that there were also Christmas carols played that year from those same speakers. Other dusties—Smokey Robinson, Quiet Storm, Lou Rawls—destined for the set list to usher in 1984 must have been piped into the hall as well. "Say Say Say" by Michael Jackson and Paul McCartney topped the charts that month, playing on the radio everywhere, endlessly.

Still, I only remember Bobby Bland's haunting baritone.

THE GREAT FREEZE

One day, Martise, our cousins Tony and Leon (Auntie Cookie's kids), and my brother Boo got into serious mischief. We spent a whole morning packing dozens of tight snowballs, one after another, piling them into a neat little stack in our sled. We dragged that arsenal down to an intersection just off Racine, a little way from Granny's house. We hid behind garbage cans at the mouth of an alleyway that hadn't been shoveled. Everything cleared from the walkway, and the street had been pushed into a small mountain here, a packed wall of snow and ice, which could be climbed but was impossible to get through by car.

As cars passed, pulling off the main drag onto the side street, we hurled the small snow grenades into traffic. They smashed onto hoods with a thunderous boom. They rained down on rooftops. Pummeled door panels. They were thrown with the speed of a fastball. I am sure we caused some damage, but no accidents or injuries, thankfully.

Drivers would skid to a halt as we raced in the opposite direction. It was a one-way street, which made it difficult for them to come after us in any direction. It was impossible to drive anything over that wall of shoveled snow. The only option left was to pace us along the street against the flow of traffic trying to clock us in the alley between gangways.

We were home free.

They usually got out, looked over the damage, chased us a couple of paces on foot, and abandoned the hunt. We laughed as we fled, then secreted into narrow gangways alongside a neighbor's garage between yards, falling silent and listening until we were sure the coast was clear.

We covered our escape routes with footprints, back and forth, through every yard. We tracked into gangways, up and down the alleys, backyards, walkways, footpaths, and so on through the snow. It was impossible to know what was stomped down by us in escape.

It covered our tracks perfectly.

When we knew it was safe, we headed out to do it again.

We set our sights on a boat of a car making the corner. There was an old-timer behind the wheel. We assumed the positions. Waited. Unleashed. Hurling snowballs and ice. They smacked the hood, the roof, the side panels, and the trunk. Thud! Thud! Thud! We exhausted our supply and started to run, pulling the sled behind us.

This time, the car pursued. The old-timer raced up the block in the wrong direction against traffic. We split up. Leon, Martise, and I went one way; Tony and Boo went the other. We scattered, making us harder to catch. We raced down a walkway connecting to the alley. The car, still behind us, tried to head us off.

The old-timer abandoned it, leaving the door open, racing on foot into the gangway directly behind us. He was on us only a short distance on our tail through backyards, over fences, across snow-covered lawns and back lots.

Finally, we reached an abandoned garage we'd cased from the outside earlier in the day. A lopsided carport door. A caved-in roof overhead. It was fire-scarred and ruined. The only entry point was a broken window with the glass smashed out. We hurled ourselves through it into the darkness inside. It smelled like a campfire. Everything bent inward on the verge of collapse—broken shelves above a broken workbench. Refuse piled in a corner.

Footsteps crunched through the ice along the narrow passage leading to the alley. We held our breaths. The old-timer paced up and back on the other side of the thin, crumbling wall. Our hearts were slamming in our chests. Outside, he made his way into the alley and around the front.

Overhead, icicles formed spikes dangling from buckled I-beams, some so long they connected the concrete slab to the ceiling remains. It was like being in some deep underground cave surrounded by stalactites and stalagmites—a frozen waterfall through a gaping hole overhead.

We slunk deeper into the shadows. It felt as if the place was going to crash down on us. If the old-timer figured us out, he could have brought the whole thing down with a well-placed hip check to the outside wall.

He made another round or so, walking the perimeter before leaving. None of us made a sound even when we were sure we'd heard him return to his car a block over and drive off.

Fighting to catch our breath, we gulped cold air in silence for what felt like forever. As my heart seemed to return to some normal rhythm, I heard Leon gasp.

I imagined something out of a horror movie as the old-timer faked us out, reaching through the wall to grab him up. I lurched forward in the darkness, half-expecting to fight some grown-ass man.

Then I saw it. A German shepherd frozen to the concrete slab, encircled by a perfect pool. Open maw, as if mid-pant, before expiring. Paws outstretched in a doggy dream, sprawled in a run on its side in sleep.

"What happened?" he asked out loud.

"It must've died here."

"Had to have frozen after, huh?"

"It had to have," I hoped, but I wasn't sure.

We stared. It was the first time we experienced death, so up close and personal. A couple of weeks later, my father was killed.

THE CALL

I remember Mom's scream when she got the news. Anguish and rage. She sounded as if her own life was being ripped away. I never heard nothing like it before or since. The phone dropped from her hand and sprung back on the cord as she followed it down. She toppled into a heap on the floor, hugging her knees to her chest. Sobbing. I remember that.

THE DRIVE

My grandparents drove us to the hospital. The highway was eerily empty. No traffic. Winter storms left cars discarded in snow drifts. The wind spun up blizzards across lanes. Windows frosted.

We were mostly silent. Wipers scraped across the ice on the front windshield. Hot air blew from the vents. No one spoke. We stared straight ahead. Radio silenced.

We sat impatiently in the antiseptic-smelling waiting room, fidgeting on plastic chairs. I'd worked loose a string from my coat and pulled at it until the sleeve frayed. My entire cuff came undone. I'd have caught hell over a new coat like this under any other circumstances. No one paid any mind. I wrapped a thread around my thumb, cutting off circulation.

In the waiting room, I began asking questions that took decades to answer. My feet barely reached the bland, beige-tiled floor as I absently kicked. I was swinging my legs. An occasional scuff from my toe sent out a sharp squeak. Nobody so much as flinched. I would pose some variation of these questions to family, friends, and my father's homies in the years to come, carrying them with me to prison and back, searching for answers.

Bogan eventually confessed. In the weeks that followed, he owned up to killing my father. It was mostly an empty gesture. He was a homeless stickup man already facing a sixty-plus-year sentence for home invasion and attempted murder. Even police tossed the confession as bogus at first. Assuming he was covering for someone.

That didn't stop Bogan from getting the brunt of my blame and rage for the next decade. The first thing I did when my auntie got an AOL account in her house was look up his Stateville prison record. Virtually infinite information was at my fingertips back when the internet was new, but all I could think to do was pull up his image and sit in my hate. For years, I would dial up daily. Wait. Let the image load pixel by pixel on an oversized monitor and stare. I was feeding a scorching hot rage.

Every. Single. Day.

QUESTIONS

In the short stretch that followed his release from prison, before his death, my dad regrouped quickly. He came out hungry and went right to work. That built him up a reputation fast, but it also put a target on his back.

When you get successful, you get haters. Period.

I'd wondered where Dad's friends got to when Bogan says that he seen him crossing the lot in the Dearborn Homes. Only a bit of time elapsed between my father leaving the house with his friends and Bogan claiming to see him over on Federal, where he was found. So he drives fifteen to twenty minutes with his guys on the coldest night on record in Chicago history, and, what, they drop him off to run errands? On his own? On foot? That be like two and a half hours walking distance on a nice night in good weather. It didn't make sense.

Bogan made it sound like it was an impulse. A crime of opportunity. No premeditation. Just a well-dressed guy in the wrong place at the wrong time. Bogan sees my dad bundled in his fur in the thick of "Robbin' Season"—the crime spree spans just before Christmastime on into the New Year—so he goes for it.

Open. Shut.

Except that other details didn't add up.

I spent some time wondering if my dad was set up. If Bogan was used as a weapon and a scapegoat. Maybe his friends put him in Bogan's path on that day.

Bogan never acted alone, if he even acted at all. Dad's guys, who he looked after when he was on the street and, again, once he'd been released, were responsible. Turns out that five men, guys he trusted, were the ones who beat him to death.

King Shorty Freeman, head of the Black Disciples, was locked up at the time of the murder. Other crew members sanctioned the hit on my father without his permission. In the years that followed, Freeman and I would talk about this often. He was very upset my father got killed. He had never intended for that to happen. Freeman would eventually come to mentor me and help me turn my life around, but his willingness to set the record straight for me so many years later may have been his greatest impact. It finally would give me peace of mind.

I never did learn exactly why the hit was ordered.

The truth is that five men, who my father trusted, beat him to death in that entryway. They betrayed him over nothing. It was about jealousy and envy. It wasn't "just business" that got him killed. It wasn't a quick cash grab. It wasn't a robbery. My father was murdered over plain, old-fashioned, run-of-the-mill envy.

Eventually, I would hear these facts direct from others who were there. Men who participated in my father's murder would tell me this firsthand. I would confront my father's real killer in the narrow gangway between buildings. My own crew standing guard a few feet away. A loaded piece wrapped in a handkerchief set in a drainpipe just beneath my palm. My finger hovered over the trigger, and a single nod from me to my guys be all that separated this dude from his own death by beating. That was still some years into the future.

AT THE ER

They cut my father's clothes from his body in the hospital trauma bay. They operated. Trying to stabilize him. The beating was too severe. Head injuries. Internal bleeding. Broken bones. Busted ribs. Swelling brain. He was in critical condition when he arrived in the emergency room. They couldn't save him.

His belongings were gathered together and stuffed into a translucent plastic bag. Button up. T-shirt. Pants. Underwear. Socks. Shoes. Crumpled together and stuffed inside. His bloodied coat balled at the top of the pile. Dark brown fur matted with blood. It looked like roadkill. A dead animal on the shoulder of the highway.

7

STRATEGIES FOR
RESOLVING CONFLICT

Englewood, Chicago, July 2015

My call to Lil' B goes direct to voice mail. Heading back from the gas station, I want to get up with the guys. I want to untangle the robbery with them in person. I want to see how they react. Body language. Nonverbal gestures. Any tells that clue me in on who knew what, if anything, before I share what I learned. I need to see if they are holding out on me. Suppose some of the guys were in on the robbery or at least aware of it. If this thing was done by them, was it sanctioned with Big Folks' blessing or a few guys acting rogue.

At the same time, the debt is settled, and the matter is resolved. In our training material, we develop these formal strategy methods for resolving conflict. Clean boxes on tidy grids organize the complexity and chaos of a situation like this one: "reasoning and consequence," "saving face," "de-escalation," "between-group mediation," "internal mediation," and so on. This will call for an appeal to their better nature outside the emotional charge of the situation. Once I have a fix on the kind of robbery we are dealing with here—the details of the incident—I will better know how to move forward. Let's just put this thing to bed, I'll argue.

Meanwhile, Hot Rod is asking after the light-skinned guy in a beige skully and tan Timberlands who robbed a Vice Lords in the neighborhood. We want a read on this guy. How does the stickup man fit the equation? Who is he connected to on this end? Is this part of some larger move on Big Folks to shake things up?

Big Fella put some of the guys with connections to the Vice Lords, rank-ing members that go way back, onto JB, Zo, and Brian for a little "construc-tive shadowing." Check in with them to see how they are feeling. Make sure things stay cool, and the situation is stable. The vicious cycle of tit-for-tat retaliation spins out when both sides think they have something to prove. Community norms reinforce violence by making it so every victim becomes a perpetrator to guard against future victimization. A binding contract that the only way to protect yourself is to create more victims, who in turn have to make more victims, who in turn have to make more victims, leaving bod-ies on both sides.

I make quick time back up Racine. It's a straight shot now that I don't have to cruise side streets looking for the car. I'm not completely sure where Big Folks and his crew are holed up waiting, but I know the area well enough to camp in the vicinity.

COMMUNITY VIOLENCE

The body count is not the only harm to the community. Trauma and loss rack up on both sides. Psychological casualties. Bystanders exposed. Com-munity Violence Exposure leads to all kinds of traumatic stress responses and physical and mental health complications. It is all the same symptoms of posttraumatic stress disorder, like vets returning from war, but there was never any normal time before. In our community, we just have traumatic stress disorder. It is no post.

Children exposed to violence, just witnessing it, not even participating, are likely to have a harder time in school (behaviorally and academically), abuse substances (drugs or alcohol), act aggressively and suffer anxiety, depression, and a range of other mental health problems.[1]

And people always forget that kids exposed to violence grow up to be adults who were exposed to violence. As adults, substance abuse increases, we are more likely to engage in criminal activity, and those mental health issues deepen—often going undiagnosed and untreated.

Then, more of those "wicked problems" cascade into the community. An overreliance on so-called solutions causes more problems.[2] None of us are any safer in the long run. Policing, arrest, prosecution, persecution, incarceration, parole, probation destroy lives, tear apart families, under-mine economic opportunities, collectively punish, and oppress entire com-munities. This costs $296 billion a year, not including medical expenses or economic losses.[3]

Community violence intervention works to reduce shootings and killings without the oppressive tactics that destroy neighborhoods, families, and individual lives across generations.[4] Organizations like CeaseFire, Cure Violence, and others nationwide break the cycle of violence by working with the highest risk. They are more effective and impactful because they empower communities to address these problems themselves, but police refuse to let up on their choke hold over the public safety domain.

My phone chirps. Lil' B. I thumb the speaker function.

"Where y'all at?" I ask. "I need to holler at you. It's important."

He offers an address about five minutes away.

"We had to get up out of the heat, bro." Lil' B says. "We just chillin'. Playin' video games and drinking lemonade."

"Staying off the street," I say aloud. "Good. That's good."

"Tryin'."

POLICE AND SOCIAL CONTROL

Police were not created to "serve and protect" despite the catchy slogan emblazoned on the side of their squads.[5] They were not designed for public safety in this country. They were not even designed to solve crimes, despite what season after season of *Law & Order* marathons might have you believe. Dun. Dun. Nah. Even police themselves will tell you that it is a myth of the thin blue line that they are there to prevent crime.[6]

It is a fantasy that police spend their time running down bad guys. Even if "bad guys" is a concept you believe in, police spend their time responding to noise complaints, writing traffic citations and parking tickets, and doing routine patrols and business checks. Research of publicly available data showed that police spend only 4 percent of their time focused on violent crime.[7] Four percent.

And they definitely were not formed to prevent shootings and killings.

Police exist for one thing only—social control. Since they were created, they have existed to keep Black and Brown communities in check. They were created to check the poor, immigrants, working-class communities. They were created to shut down social movements and acts of resistance. Through intimidation, incarceration, violence, the threat of violence, and death, the police maintain social control.

BIG FOLKS, MIA

"Yo, Cobe," Lil' B says, "before you get here, I should give you a heads-up."

"What's that?" I ask, turning the wheel and closing the gap between us.

Lil' B sighs on the other end of the line. I hear his breath catch. Hold. Then a deep exhale.

"Big Folks ain't here, man."

I feel a momentary gut punch at the information. An immediate rattling of nerves. My thoughts don't spin out. "Okay." I manage—measured.

"He was pretty worked up, is the thing. Angry. Letting that shit go didn't sit right with him," Lil' B explains.

"Bet."

"I don't know that he is gone and done something," Lil' B clarifies. "Might be just blowing off steam, but I figured you should know."

"You got an idea where he might be?" I ask.

"A few spots that be worth checking."

"How about I scoop you up and we try to run down on him down together?"

UNDERLYING CONDITIONS OF VIOLENCE

Here is the plain truth: police don't prevent violence. Forget what you think you heard. They don't.

Occasionally they respond after violence has been committed.

But they don't prevent it.

And, occasionally, they work hard to prevent us from preventing it, too.

In all my years doing this work, I have seen the police actively try to sabotage this work more times than I can count. They have targeted outreach workers and interrupters in Chicago, making it virtually impossible for us to do our job at times. They promoted misinformation and attempted to frame the staff in Baltimore. In New Orleans, police all but shut down sites, acting on bogus information. It stands to reason since community violence provides the perfect rationale to justify their power to a fearful public. I'm not claiming conspiracy. It is in the interests of law enforcement to resist community violence interventions as a threat to their existence.

They don't address the underlying conditions that lead to violence in the first place: drug addiction, housing, homelessness, poverty, and unemployment. These issues are left to underfunded social workers, mental health professionals, crisis workers, and substance abuse counselors. Community hubs that provide intervention of this kind are often scraped together through private donations, volunteer hours, grant funding, and so on.

I once shared a stage with writer and sociologist Alex Vitale, whose book *The End of Policing* became the playbook for the "defund movement," envisioning a world without police and prison. I was there to discuss how community violence intervention programs work to stop shootings and killings, but Vitale challenged the audience to think bigger. Imagine therapists, crisis responders, social workers, sociologists, doctors, researchers, community activists, organizers, health workers, and change agents providing intervention and support that could lead to real safety and security for communities.

ON THE TRAIL OF BIG FOLKS

I pull up. Lil' B is waiting on the sidewalk, arms folded. On the front porch, I see D-Boy and some of the other guys sitting around.

"You want, I just get in?" Lil' B asks.

"Yeah, come around the side."

The guys come up off the stoop and make their way over.

"Cobe," D-Boy calls, walking up.

He hitches his pants up, high around his hips.

"You want something to drink? Bottled water, juice, soda, or something?"

"Y'all don't got nothing stronger?" I ask, playing around. They all know I never drink. Lil' B looks momentarily confused and then laughs.

"Nah. We're not getting into that today either."

"You staying out of trouble?"

"Tryin'," Lil' B says, squinting. He looks both ways down the block. "Tryin'."

"Maybe even against our best judgment," D-Boy responds.

"True. True. I second that," Lil' B answers back.

D-Boy plants his hand on the side of the car and leans in the open window.

"Why you say that?" I ask.

"Feelin' exposed out here."

"It's like we askin' for trouble by not doin' nothin'."

"Somethin' bad fixin' to happen."

Lil' B opens the passenger side door and slides into the seat.

"You got video games, AC, juice—what more do you need?" I ask.

Timing doesn't feel right to press them about the robbery, but my gut instinct is to do a bit of damage control before I go looking for Big Folks.

"I got up with the guys responsible for this morning," I explain patiently.

"And?" D-Boy pushes.

"It was a misunderstanding."

"Don't sound right."

"It was Vice Lords come through and do this thing?"

I want to explain it to everyone at the same time: Lil' B, D-Boy, Big Folks, and the others. Break everything down in detail. Press a bit about the robbery to see if I can get anything out of that. Mostly clear the air. Set the record straight.

And I can't do that 100 percent without Big Folks around. If I get into it here, without the complete ensemble, maybe I can get these guys on the same page, but Big Folks becomes a wild card. The moment he resurfaces has the potential to undo any agreement. All he has to do is question whether Vice Lords are lying about the whole thing, set this into a tailspin. Better to have everyone on the same page at the same time, ask whatever questions need asking, and arrive at an agreed-upon conclusion together.

Once information is out there, you can't control it anymore. It changes with each listener—shapes, reconfigures, contorts—before it is shared again. A grade school game of telephone passing secrets from person to person along a line until what comes out the other side sounds completely different than where the whisper began—channeled through the lens of their experience, perspective, perception, and mindset. Billiard balls on a pool table colliding with one another all obey the same laws of physics with different results. The rotational spin that comes off the cue can send a target ball veering in another direction. Even on a clean break with a perfectly lined-up shot, all kinds of variables come into play.

Big Folks coming in after everyone else is perfectly aligned is a collusion we can't afford.

My next move is to try to get all three to ride with me. I may as well bring them along. It has worked before.

"Why don't you climb in? We'll get up with Big Folks, and I'll buy y'all something to eat."

"Got food inside," D-Boy thumbs over his shoulder. "I'm fixin' to beat this level, too."

"You hit pause on the game to come out and wait for me?"

"Shit. You can bring food back if you want."

"You be here when we get back?"

D-Boy pops off the car like he is doing a push-up and claps. "We ain't gonna make a move without Big Folks anyhow, you know this, but if he comes back through while you gone saying he wants to ride out and set things right, you know how it got to be, right?"

"You can gimme a call first," I counter. "Look, y'all gave me your word that you'd sit tight on this until I could get you some answers. They gave me their word they want to drop everything, but out of respect, I can't break down this whole thing without Big Folks."

D-Boy shrugs, bringing his shoulders up around his ears, head bent at the neck and tucked into his chest. He looks like he is ducking something.

I look at Lil' B, uncomfortable in the passenger seat. His face has the *test results come in, and they don't look great* look to it. Strained. Tight-lipped in a bit of a grimace.

"Text me y'all food orders," I instruct, putting the car in drive. "Yeah? And what?" I pause. "And, if Big Folks come back, okay?"

I pull off the curb. Text Hot Rod to pop in. I want him to check in on them as soon as possible. Turn out onto the street.

"Where to?"

SAFER, STRONGER COMMUNITIES

Safer, stronger communities are about more than just the absence of crime. Our society has such a hard time getting its head around that concept. It is a failure of our collective imagination that we can't picture anything beyond prevention, prosecution, or punishment. Locked in the binary of black and white, crime and punishment, law and order. We don't envision much beyond survival. We never can imagine a way for the community to thrive that doesn't operate within this outdated narrative according to these rigidly defined lines.

K. Bain, founder/executive director of Community Capacity Development, talks about his Human Justice Network, an equation that combines human rights with human development, as a way to strive beyond the prevention aspects of our work.[8] Human Justice is about surviving and thriving by getting resources to the most marginalized.

Bain started his program in New York with no budget. He would travel from Jamaica, Queens, on his own dime to learn violence prevention techniques before the mayor's office or the state formally recognized his nonprofit. He participated in our training workshops to learn the model *as if* he had the backing of a major organization. He was putting in the work and getting results before the resources appeared.

Mediation and interruption were just a starting point—the survival portion of the work. Bain began to elaborate, iterate, experiment, and refine the model, layering what he refers to as his three-point "Sustainable Growth Plan" on top of it to deliver the thriving aspects of the work. He realized that the highest risk we were all working with lacked purpose, so he built tools for personal transformation into his outreach work. Goal setting, aspiration mapping, bridge building, and other activities to develop a healthier mindset overall.[9]

Community Capacity Development put this enhanced model to the test in Queensbridge, the nation's largest public housing complex, establishing peace agreements and introducing these developmental mindset shifts at the same time. The following year, not a single shot was fired in the Long Island City housing projects.[10]

Bain sees community violence intervention work encompassing more than street-level conflict resolution; it is also making inroads into deeper issues of systemic violence. Economic violence stripped Black and Brown families of intergenerational wealth, investment, business development, and opportunity.

Safe communities are about more than prevention. They are about creating long-term health, well-being, and opportunity for every resident everywhere. It is about security, sure, but it is also about economic investment, financial literacy, and entrepreneurial training. It is about creating support systems. Promoting physical, psychological, and emotional well-being. Creating stable housing opportunities and cultivating community connections. Opportunities for thriving. Opportunities for growth.

8

AFTER MY FATHER'S MURDER

Englewood, Chicago, 1984–1988

After my father's murder, everything fell apart. My mom, who filled the house with laughter, loved to dance, and was often generous to a fault, especially with her kids, changed overnight. It was like a light went out. She started using drugs. I'll spare the details since there are so many stories like this out there; it seems no point in going into specifics. Except to say that with addiction, the pain is so all-consuming it might as well pull up a chair at the dining room table: another house guest, a constant companion, this ever-present grief.

We moved out of the second-floor walk-up. Bounced around a bit. There were guys around, coming and going. Some boyfriends who actually took to playing house for a time. Others just helped pay the bills—*"There go Mr. Electric Bill." "There go Mr. Gas Man."*—making ends meet. Most rarely made an impression.

Occasionally, Mom's fun-loving, playful, affectionate self would re-emerge. It was as if she were coming out of deep sleep. Suddenly, she'd be laughing at the kitchen table. Present for a spell. She did what she could to keep us dressed, fed, and sheltered. When Run-DMC had everyone rocking their Adidas, Mom decked me out head to toe in a sharp branded tracksuit, funky, fresh, and cold, catching everyone's eye on the playground. Trice still talks about me walking around like a peacock in these duds. Whatever it took to care for us, Mom did.

There was a brief spell where she ran women out of the house. It was better, she believed, to have women look after women than some pimp on the corner, who would get rough with them, acting like they were his property. She would provide shelter, food, and a place to sleep in exchange for a percent of what they were earning. Another time, she tried her hand at Dad's trade, dealing out of our place to keep the lights on.

I don't judge or begrudge any of her choices in these years. She did the best she could with whatever she could at that time. She was a single mom without means and three mouths to feed, using whatever skills and resources she had on hand.

Eventually, though, Boo, Trice, and I moved in with Granny. That became my home.

I want to be clear that I never once felt abandoned, either. Even when going back and forth between Granny and Mom, I was never somebody's burden or made to feel that way. No matter how much they struggled at the time. The opposite was always true. I always felt loved. I had almost a half dozen living rooms with aunties and Grams, where I could put my feet up, while my friends might only have had one or two (if their parents were divorced). I had a neighborhood that always looked out for me and more families than I could count helping raise me. It could be easy to get that twisted and feel put out by that living situation, but I flipped it, and no one ever made me feel that way.

GETTING OFF THE BLOCK

Auntie Shirley was so strict that to this day, I jokingly call her the "mean one." She took good care of us kids. The third eldest in the lineup, she was the most disciplined of all my mom's sisters. Mildred popped the whip on the eldest children, Shirley says, referring to Granny, but that ended with child number four. Shirley was the cut off for the kids who got punished and those who, in her words, got a free ride. My mom, included in the latter, was able to run wild, according to Auntie Shirley.

As a result of this upbringing, Shirley ran a tight ship, expecting us to be in the house, at the table, doing homework right after school, no matter what. No excuses. Auntie Shirley helped teach me discipline. I owe her that.

Auntie Hilda was Shirley's counterpoint. She made the best grilled cheese sandwiches I've ever had in my life with the assembly-line efficiency of a short-order cook in a fast-food diner. We would sit at her kitchen table and eat our fill.

On Saturday, after we ate our grilled cheese, she would take us to a movie downtown. It was important to her to get us out of the neighborhood. She wanted to show us that the city was bigger than our few square blocks. She'd pack us onto the train heading to the Loop, an all-day event. I saw *Raiders of the Lost Ark*, *Ghostbusters*, *Superman*, *ET*, *Star Wars: Return of the Jedi*, and other classics of my generation at that theater every Sunday— thanks to Auntie Hilda. Movies are often a window into a larger world, but the theater represented that for us here.

COMING OF AGE IN TIMES OF WAR

Summer before freshman year, Solomon got a brutal beatdown from a grown-ass man. It was 1987. We were boys, barely out of eighth grade. This guy was an adult. The community was changing at the same time we were. We were gathered together at Ollie's house, waiting for word on how he was doing.

"How'd it happen?" Ty asked.

"Don't know," Ollie answered.

"This is fucked up," I said. "He didn't deserve that shit."

"It was GD," Lil' Paris said, balling his fist, "which is really messed up."

"Sol isn't even with anybody, though," Ollie said.

"GD be trying to recruit everybody," Lil' Paris responded.

At that time, dividing lines were becoming more prominent. Moes, the Islamic branch of the Black P. Stones when they turned into El Rukn, were organizing. Gangster Disciples and Black Disciples, two forces we were connected to our entire life, began to splinter. They were building their own armies across the city.

"If ain't GD, it's the Moes," Ty said of the situation. "If it ain't Moes, it's GD."

"What the fuck a Moe anyway?" I said, antagonizing playfully.

"Moes be trying to recruit everybody, too," Ollie said.

"They even recruiting dogs now," I joked. "I saw a Moe trying to recruit a golden retriever."

Everyone laughed.

"Moes, short for 'Moorish Science,'" Ollie answered earnestly. "That's the whole religious thing."

I hadn't asked for real but nodded in affirmation.

"Sol isn't even with nobody," Dog said, repeating Ollie's earlier observation. "I'm seeing more the GD thing around here than Moes. It is out of control."

"Truth."

"This ain't about our little fist fights on the playground at recess, no more," Ty observed, clapping his hands. He was pushed to his feet by anxious energy—got up, paced the floor—which caught our attention. "We ain't no kids no more. If they ask what's our ride, we can't just say the bus."

"We getting to the point where we are going to need to be choosing sides and backing that up," Lil' Paris caught in Ty's frenetic energy. "It's better you make it your own choice than have them put it on you, right? What happened to Solomon shouldn't have happened. It didn't have to happen."

"GD trying to take over the neighborhood. They going around telling everybody they have to be with them or they is gonna fuck you up, you know?" Dog said bluntly. "So, they go and call one of our best friends out, and a grown man is going to stomp him like that? No."

"It leaves a bad taste in your mouth."

"This is that line in the sand," Ty added. "We ain't kids no more. We have to accept that anybody we friend with that go to opposition now—they ain't our friends anymore."

"It doesn't matter you go all the way back—first grade, second grade, third grade, fourth grade, or whatever—if they opposition now, they opposition. They ain't your friend no more. They done for you," Lil' Paris rallied.

This felt like a moment. A declaration. For anyone not born in, this was a deciding factor. Sadar had joined years earlier in grade school after the incident with C-Man on the school playground when Dirty Mike got a mob of D-Boys to show up after class in a display of force. The Freeman Family took him under their wing. He wasn't just a Disciple at that point but part of the family, the same as me.

"I got a lot of guys I'm still tight with living in the neighborhood I won't even talk to no more," I added to the growing sentiment. "Just the way it's going to have to be from this point forward."

By the end of the summer, long before any of us went to freshman orientation, we were officially BD. It was no longer a shorty playing a role, but we were formally BD. If you were on something else, we cut ties.

Solomon pulled through, and the incident somehow emboldened us. You'd have thought it might send us the other way, but instead, we went all in together. That was the call we answered.

THE WAR COMES HOME

Boo waited around the corner, down the hall, as I came home. He stepped out. A locomotive fist chambered and swung, like a piston firing, slammed into my gut. I dropped to my knees. It knocked all the wind out of me instantly. I choked to breathe as Boo walked away without a care.

One constant throughout our childhood was that Boo and I were always into it with each other. It didn't matter whose roof we were under. Trice used to say she had never met two people more at odds about everything and nothing, all at the same time. We fought over dinner portions, sports scores, T-shirts, fall jackets, and what to listen to on the radio.

Boo was a little crazy, a little mean, and always fixing for a fight. For my part, I played the annoying little brother, always knowing what buttons would set him off. I'd try to see if I could send him off with half a smirk alone. If that didn't work, I'd start talking shit.

This was beyond ordinary sibling rivalry.

When I gulped enough air back into me, I pushed to my feet, hurling myself after him down the hall. I tackled him to the floor, raining punches down on the back of his head with both fists as we fell to the ground. We grappled, throwing each other around the wooden floor until we could both get up again.

Boo had size and strength on me, but taking his attacks without reaction could disarm him. It became my greatest defense. He'd clip me with a right hook, and only the physical motion of it registered. I'd look back, staring from a void—tearless and stoic—no pain or emotion on my face. Nothing. Fat lip bleeding. I would throw a punch in response. My eyes gave nothing.

Trice would get knocked about just for being in striking range as if swept up in a storm. We would collide like cartoon cats kicking up dust, Boo and I. Throwing expletives, stars, exclamation points, and swirls as we rolled in combat throughout the room. Trice got swept into the tussle, no matter where in the house she might have been, when the whole thing kicked off. As if carried off by a tornado, she didn't stand a chance to resist.

Her alliances were arbitrary. She tried to give as good as she got. Sometimes, falling in with me. The two of us are going after Boo as a united front. "Why. You. Got. To. Be. Such. A. Bully!?" she'd howl at Mike as we toppled into one another, spilling into the next room.

Other times, she'd pile on in opposition. "I. Hate. That. You. Granny's. Favorite—you so bogus!" she'd scream at me, punching me upside the head.

Occasionally, Trice started swinging on the both of us at the same time.

"I. Am. Trying. To. Watch. *Facts. Of. Life.* In. Here." she'd rage, landing punches wherever they were thrown. She caught him upside the head with a hook and kicked me in the shin at the same time. The whole mess of us tumbling together into the front room, three sets of arms and legs flailing.

Everything and nothing at the same time. Until it was that everything became something. Boo became Boo Stone sometime before high school. He joined Almighty Black P. Stone Nation (BPSN)—leaders of the People, enemies of the Folks—direct rivals of the Black Disciples.

From that point on, it became the only thing we fought about.

In the hidden history of modern gang culture, two groups, both started in Chicago, formed the contemporary American archetype for the street organization. They had at least a decade on the Crips and the Bloods, becoming the template those groups would eventually follow.

Disciples started over on the South Side, spread across Englewood, of course, southern Kenwood, and Hyde Park. Originally as the Devil's Disciples, with a name plucked straight from the Bible calculated to cultivate devotion and stoke fear. My kin was always connected to Black Disciples and Gangster Disciples like it was part of the root system of our family tree. That history is our history. My mom's second-oldest sister, Auntie Cookie, was in that earliest incarnation. Her eldest, my cousin, G-Money, ran with Dad back in the day as his right hand. It was a family business on both sides of the tree.

Originally, Hyde Park and Kenwood were white neighborhoods. In the 1950s, Disciples formed for self-preservation. White gangs were shock troops stalking through the neighborhoods, attacking Black kids. Disciples fought back. Politically, they were fighting for the right of Black families to own property, live where they wanted, and build wealth.

Later, under the leadership of King David Barksdale, Disciples began spreading their influence, recruiting smaller gangs, street organizations, clubs, and crews into the Disciples army. These groups added Disciples to their original names, retaining their identity while expanding territory and growing membership.

In Chicago's Woodlawn neighborhood on Blackstone Avenue, around this same time, Jeff Fort founded the Blackstone Rangers, partly because, as with the Disciples, they needed to defend their homes against white gangs attacking Black families. Eventually, Rangers used the same playbook as the Disciples, allowing street organizations to keep their homegrown identity but adding "Stones" to their name.

Blackstone Rangers evolved into the highly politicized Black P. Stone Nation. It splintered again into an Islamic faction, the El Rukns, which gained true notoriety when the FBI framed them as a terrorist organization and set Fort and others up with Libyan leader Muammar al-Gaddafi and Nicaragua's Sandinistas. The true claim to fame of BPSN/El Rukns was organizing smaller gangs throughout the city under their banner. This is how the People Nation came to be formed. They recruited smaller groups block by block throughout neighborhoods to form under the Stones, eventually numbering in the tens of thousands—my brother among them.

These two armies advanced across the Black Belt in Chicago for decades, expanding territory, growing membership, conquering, and claiming victims. Ultimately clashing in Granny's hallway as Boo and I exchanged blows while Trice tried to dodge them.

"How you go against our family like that, motherfucker?" I wanted to know.

Boo's decision to join the Stones went against everything we knew. Our entire lives, our home, our destinies were connected to the Black Disciples. My father's entire legacy was invested in BD. Our inheritance.

Boo landed an elbow that sent me flying backward, awkwardly, across the floor. I could taste blood in my mouth, feel it on my chin, dripping from my nose.

"I'm a Stone 'cause this family, dumbass!"

I was climbing back to my feet a little wobbly.

"The fuck that s'posed to mean?"

"You the traitor."

Now, we just stood shoving each other back and forth. Trice bowed out by this point. She'd gotten in a few good licks and hugged against her knees in the corner.

"How that?"

He stood back, squared, seething. My guard, up, offset his stance. Circling.

"BD killed our daddy," Boo growled. "You riding with them? They the reason he's not here!"

Boo dropped his guard. He stood in front of me, jaw jutted, challenging, but we knew the round was over.

HOW VIOLENCE FEEDS THE SCHOOL-TO-PRISON PIPELINE

Chicago Calumet High School (Cal High) was over on South May in Auburn Gresham, nearly ten miles outside downtown and a bit of a hike from Granny's. It was home to Stones, period.

Cal High was in Stone territory. GD and BD were not welcome. We clashed constantly. Even if we wasn't at war yet, we clashed constantly. Every day, a fight. On the way to school and on the way back. In the hallways, classrooms, auditoriums, and along bus routes. Navigating blocks between home and school meant constantly testing tensions, pushing territories, posing threats, and making challenges. Urban geopolitics in square city blocks surrounding the institution.

When we walked through the neighborhood, we represented. Back then, cocking our hats to the right and making our way through Foster Park, where they were set up. Fighting took on a new form. It wasn't just head-up, toe-to-toe boxing. You shoulder bump someone on the way to class or knock the books out of their hands, it isn't just the two of you going up against the lockers. Everyone on the sidelines takes the cue, throwing up signs and yelling out the name of their group. They aren't chanting, "Fight! Fight!" but invoking GD, BD, Vice Lords, or whatever. I'm saying entire forces clashed in those halls.

All that friction, grinding out a spark, kicks off a riot. People throw themselves into the fray, not just by standing from the sidelines.

Grade school is a test.

High school is a final exam.

It used to be six on six or, occasionally, six on ten. Now, it would often come to be six on thirty or more. It was only a short time later that fistfights became gunfights. When dealing with those numbers, it isn't long before everyone is strapped. Stakes are higher. Everything escalates. When we were kids, somebody might come at you swinging a stick like a club out of anger, but nobody was trying to do grievous bodily harm. You were throwing down to bloody noses or maybe blackening an eye. You weren't, never trying to kill nobody until it was you were.

We all carried. It wasn't just repping in the park, throwing up signs, or putting tags on a wall. We had serious responsibilities. Banging was a job. Recruitment. Dealing. Before, we'd just been playing parts, all of us, but now we are serious about it. I was building a small army that, in a few years, would amass over a hundred guys.

At the same time, I was failing algebra.

My scene changed, too, as often does in the transition between schools—grade school into high school—and on account of getting older. Some of my guys didn't go to Cal High from Oglesby. We posted up at a house just across the street on South May.

I started hanging out more with my main man, Ty, and his cousin, C-Man, who were both Shorty Freeman's nephews, more regularly. We all went to grade school together, messed around in the back of the class, played during recess, and everything. We weren't tight until later. Ty was a little older, so an age gap that seems huge between third grade and fifth don't really seem like nothing when it's sophomores and seniors. C-Man, Sadar, and I were all in the same grade, but it wasn't until we got older that we really started to jam.

We all became family, too, at that time. C-Man and Ty were already blood-related cousins, both nephews of King Shorty Freeman. Sadar, who joined when he was a shorty, got adopted not only as BD but also as a Freeman after that. All of us, myself included, considered ourselves Freeman as well as BD at that point.

In the morning, we would arrive just before homeroom. We'd wrap our pieces in newspaper and stash them in a mesh garbage can, caddy corner to the southern entrance, across the street. We'd have eyes on them all day. They'd be there when we got back. Across the street, up the stairs, over the threshold, past the metal detectors into the main hallway. We'd assume new identities. Students now.

Shuffling sneakers squeaked on gleaming wax floors. The clang of locker doors, graffitied and tagged. Banners in maroon, white, and blue—school colors—mixed with the palates of People and Folk. The usual crisscrossing of teens up and down the halls pre-homeroom bell that occurs in any school in America, filled by repping between classes. In doorways, on desks with book covers, notebooks, and scribbles on school jackets. Territory staked out. Same as on the streets. We'd negotiate the space nearby or across. Posturing. Flexing. Challenging.

We knew who one another was.

Teachers position themselves against gangs by default. They don't want to make enemies of their own students, but they are in opposition to gangs. This is where the friction starts. Idealistic and hopeful educators, intent on inspiring the next generation, see gangs as opposition to learning. Declaring war on gangs often results in declaring war on students themselves. Divisions quickly form. It may not start this way, but it ends up there quickly. Opposition to the students themselves.

Initially, it is a form of self-preservation. They are trying to keep a couple of students from colliding. They are trying to keep a full-scale war from kicking off in the hallways—keeping the peace—but the divisions deepen. Educators police the floors, becoming stand-ins for prison guards. It may start with the best intentions, but it leads to disciplinary action. Inspiration and education become secondary to social control.

First, in a physical way. Educators try to keep students from clashing. It is no longer in opposition to the concept of gangs but to the members themselves. Then, in an institutional way, pushing out any student deemed troublemaker for defense of the "students that want an education."

This is where the school-to-prison pipeline kicks into overdrive.[1] Miss too many classes, expelled. Get too many detentions, expelled. Mouth off to a teacher, expelled. Start a fight, expelled. In a fight, expelled. Controlled substance in your locker, expelled.

And so on and on the list goes. It does not begin here, but it feels inevitable that this is where it ends up.

I am a textbook case of this pattern. I can't pretend I had any passion for learning at the time. Gangbanging was my education and employment. Fair to say I was a hard case. I was difficult to reach, difficult to teach, and actually represented the threat I was perceived to be at the time.

Fact.

That said, I also can't pretend anyone had much interest in educating me in the first place. The associations were no longer about opposition to the concept of gang and eventually became about opposition to me as a person. I am hard-pressed to recall a single teacher who took interest in showing they cared and trying to put me on the right path. Hate to say it, but there weren't many educators in my experience at the time interested in intervening on my behalf. I'm not trying to put responsibility for my actions on anyone else, only trying to show that this is how the cycle perpetuates.

This is the system at work.

Cal High, like many schools in Black and Brown America, never had adequate resources. It was underfunded, overcrowded, lacked qualified teachers, and spread too thin. Sometimes, all an educator could do was try to keep the peace. It was not just students that pushed them into the role of prison guards but the entire system itself. Eventually, giving the student the boot can feel like a welcome break for both the student and the teacher. By the time I left school, it felt long overdue.

National education efforts have been shown to incentivize pushing out low-performing students, encouraging dropouts, or creating disciplinary programs like zero tolerance that kicked students to the curb for minor offenses. Black students are three and a half times more likely than their white classmates to be suspended or expelled, according to a nationwide study by the U.S. Department of Education Office for Civil Rights.[2] Studies show expulsion increases the risk of arrest, conviction, and probation.[3]

I went back and got my high school diploma after prison. I would go on to earn a bachelor's degree from Northeastern Illinois University (NEIU) in urban studies through the University Without Walls program. At the time of this writing, I am halfway through earning a master's degree in social work. I share these accomplishments not just to brag (okay, maybe a little brag, but I earned it) but more to show that I was not irredeemable as a student. I don't know where I would be or what would have been possible if I had been reached sooner. So many of these national education policies act as if there are no other options for hard cases like mine, but clearly, that's not true.

As a result, I have spent a lot of time in my formal education, throughout undergraduate and graduate school, wondering what could be done to change this dynamic. Research shows a combination of support, including home visits, mixed with effective discipline and behavior modification techniques, can help even hard cases successfully stay in school. A lot of work focuses on policy change, which is important, but we have to focus on services in schools as well.

School-based community violence intervention can offer the same alternatives to the school-to-prison pipeline as community violence intervention programs do in neighborhoods with police and prisons. Having "credible messengers" working one-on-one with students to build them up constructively rather than sending a troubled teen to the dean's office with a security escort or kicking them out altogether. I have seen a successful school-based violence prevention program in Milwaukee turn around one of that city's most violent schools and disrupt the school-to-prison pipeline. The Community Capacity Development's three-point "Sustainable Growth Plan" that K. Bain had so much success with at Queensbridge could easily be a model for education beyond the classroom that helps students to graduation.[4] More work needs to be done in this area to give kids a chance.

In 2013, the award-winning radio program *This American Life* spent five months at Harper High School in West Englewood. That year, twenty-nine Harper High students were shot.[5] My friend, author Alex Kotlowitz, reported on one of the stories and brought me in to consult. Principal

Leonetta Sanders and social worker Crystal Winfield Smith, featured in the story, embody the kind of educators it takes to overcome these challenges. Smith will go out of her way to show students they are valued, appreciated, loved, and seen. She is compassionate and patient and takes the time to connect with students on a human level.

I don't put my choices or experience on anyone, but I know some things can be done to turn it around for kids on the same path I was at the time. I have seen it happen. I wonder if things might have been different for me with that kind of intervention.

9

GETTING UP WITH BIG FOLKS

Englewood, Chicago, July 2015

I scooped Lil' B and drove around looking for Big Folks. Even though I had his word that they weren't going to retaliate against the Vice Lords who had taken shots at them this morning, at least until they heard back from me, Big Folks was having a difficult time being patient. He was worked up and angry. Beneath these feelings of rage, he likely felt threatened as well. Not responding can make you vulnerable to future attacks if someone moves on you. You are perceived as weak. This is what Big Folks was probably feeling right now.

Meantime, D-Boy and his guys stayed out of the heat, playing video games and waiting for Big Folk's word. Whatever their next move, it would be Big Folks' call. I was trying to get somebody with roots in BD over to the clubhouse to sit with the guys, but not having much luck.

The Vice Lords' attack was rouge, launched because one of their guys had been robbed. They assumed it was part of Big Folks crew. They retaliated against the grievance for the same reason Big Folks had a tough time standing down. If the Vice Lords allowed somebody to roll one of their guys, it signaled that they couldn't protect their own. Any of their corner boys could be a target for stickup once word got out.

The biggest problem for me right now, aside from Big Folks gone missing, is that I don't know the stickup guy who went after the Vice Lords. It could be an unsanctioned robbery from one of Big Folks' men, or, worse yet, it could be a calculated move to put Big Folks in this exact position.

"Make a right up here," Lil' B gestures. "Big Folks, stay around the corner on this block."

I follow the instructions.

"You want to run up and check if he's home?" I say, heading down the block.

Lil' B nods. "Y'all find them?" he asks as if an exhale. Having been silent on the subject for the last fifteen minutes, being able to express the question out loud seems to be a relief. "The car, I mean. Were we right?"

I am reluctant to answer straight at the moment. If I confirm that the shooters were Vice Lords, it is information that Lil' B can bring back to the guys as definitive. Now, they *know* who made an attempt. Even though I got Lil' B quite literally riding with me right now, I have to consider all the angles on how this thing may play out. If I can't get to the bottom of the robbery and be able to inform all the guys together of what I learned, this whole thing could cascade like dominoes.

At the same time, providing background to an ally like Lil' B, who is doing his own part to keep a lid on this thing, could help give me more answers.

We reach Big Folks' house in the middle of the block. I pull beside a couple of parked cars and throw on my hazards. Now that we've arrived, I can delay the decision, so I pop the locks, indicating Lil' B run up and check.

He looks over at me.

"Run up and check," I instruct.

Lil' B doesn't push. He throws open the door and slides out.

"I wanna know, though," he says, looking across the passenger seat at me. "Okay?"

I check my texts. No word yet from Hot Rod on the identity of the stickup man. I scroll through screens. I prefer to sit on it until I hear from Hot Rod on any leads he might have.

Big Fella tells me we got someone sitting tight with JB and Zo on the Vice Lords' side. It's chill right now. Everybody is staying cool.

I send a few texts of my own in response. Follow up with Big Fella. Let him know what I am into right now. A status update on tracking Big Folks. Let's get somebody over to D-Boy in the meantime, I suggest.

I send Hot Rod a "What's good?" looking for some news.

Then, I wait.

After a beat, I try to put myself in Big Folks' thinking. Trying to get my head around where he might have gotten to when he left. I firmly believe that how you feel about a situation determines how that situation affects you. It determines your outlook. Our mindsets are a collection of attitudes and behaviors that determine our quality of life.

Big Folks stepped out earlier, probably because he didn't want the guys to see him wrestling with everything. He'd given me his word. That helps him save face, and it is also something he is fixing to honor, but at the same time, I imagine every fiber of his being is screaming out like he is physically under threat. Not taking action feels like he is putting himself in harm's way.

More than that, since it is his call to begin with here, not taking action also feels like he is putting all his guys in harm's way. He is in charge. He is calling the shots. He is responsible for the outcome here. He is responsible if he doesn't do something, and it is on his watch. Understanding this mindset—where he is coming from—gives me the insight I need to try to shift it.

Lil' B comes across the lawn and pulls open the door handle. "His mama thinks he is at his girl's house," he tells me flatly before climbing in.

He looks down the block ahead, then hops into the passenger seat.

"You know where his girl lives?"

"I can find out," he responds.

"Booty call at a time like this," I joke. "Big Folks, whatchu thinking?"

Lil' B's phone on speaker burbles to life with a ring.

"Great stress relief, though," I continue. "I can't fault him that."

Lil' B stifles a laugh as the line trills. I keep at it with quips while he busts a gut, switching gears.

"B, stop being so immature," I rib. "Get it together, man. You aren't being professional." A voice on the other line kicks in with a greeting, and Lil' B is choking back his laughter. It isn't very professional of me, but it puts things at ease for the moment. It also delays having to confirm it was Vice Lords.

We get the address. I punch the hazard button and roll forward.

In all my years doing this work, I have come to learn one stone-cold truth about mindset. Most people don't want to kill. They don't want to kill over respect. They don't want to kill over money. They don't want to kill over loyalty. Despite what you see in the movies or on the evening news, most people don't want to kill.

They have staked their identity, self-esteem, and reputation on these things, so they feel that is all they have. When this is challenged, they feel they must do something. It's what they've seen and what they know, in other words, what they've learned, time and time again.

When you live in a community of violence, self-protection often begins by forming a reputation. This is part of what is driving Big Folks right now. Unpacking the psychological, social, and cultural ingredients that make up this drive is critical to leveraging it. In this community, every perpetrator starts as a victim, moving across that line back and forth.

We get a couple of blocks in silence before Lil' B clears his throat. I know what's coming next. "You get up with them?" he asks.

I keep my eyes straight ahead, watching traffic come to a stop at the light.

"You got any idea why this might have happened?" I begin.

"I said no before," Lil' B fires back.

"What do you say now?"

"It's still no," he answered.

"Anybody that might be mixed up with something you all don't know about?"

"It was Vice Lords?"

"Vice Lords or whoever, you into it with anyone?"

"No. Still no," Lil' B replied.

I nod. "I got up with the guys that own the Caprice, yeah."

"Vice Lords?"

"What do you think they said for why they came at you?"

The traffic light changes. Cars roll forward. I switch lanes. Lil' B fidgets and clears his throat again.

"Man, I am telling you, I don't know."

"You know anyone been robbing over by you? A stickup man hitting corner boys on your crew?"

"Oh," Lil' B says.

He clears his throat again and fidgets in his seat.

"Okay," he says quietly. "Okay."

10

THE PROFESSIONAL GANGSTER

Englewood, Chicago, 1988–1989

Solomon's attack marked a turning point. We'd gone from kids fucking around under the monkey bars to full-scale battles seemingly overnight. Bigger picture, the old guard were all being sent away behind bars. That event activated long-dormant fault lines between factions, like the rumblings of an earthquake. The breakdown of the Gangster Disciple Nation, when they started arresting all the leadership, created splinters throughout the community.

King Shorty had been busted for heroin trafficking. The circumstance is debatable because the law had been watching him for some time, looking for any excuse to put him away.

For years, we'd been building up against the Gangster Disciples and the Moes, recruiting, structuring, and organizing. We sweat them as opposition. We never had the same numbers as they could mobilize, but we made up for it by being scrappy. We built our notoriety on this fact. If you send thirty guys, we'll go up against you with three. G-Free, our chief, used to joke that they can't all be hitting you at the same time. When you are that thick in it, they just end up punching their own guys, so being smaller gave us an advantage.

These tectonic plates were grinding away at each other as the backdrop to my high school education—and Cal High was sending us daily into Stones territory.

UNCLE RAY

Uncle Ray, like his older sister, my Auntie Hilda, tried showing us a bigger world in his own way. Ray was the baby brother of the whole family, the only other son, a bookend to Phil, the eldest son, and his opposite in many ways. He was quiet, introspective, shy, mild-mannered, and smart, while Phil was shit-talking, funny, and larger than life. Ray was tall and lean, built for basketball, with a short, tight crew cut; Phil was built sturdy, wearing his hair long, wild, and impressively groomed.

They complimented and contrasted each other, as brothers do.

Sports kept Ray out of the streets as a kid, even through high school. Mostly basketball. He played on the court from sunup to sundown. He was a live-in babysitter when Granny would watch the kids: me and my sibs, all the cousins, and so on. He was just a teenager but seemed adult to us at that age. He took on the responsibility of watching over us. Ray would line us up and march on down to the park a couple of blocks over to play ball. He took all his nephews down to square off against guys that were older and bigger than us. It didn't matter to him that we were outmatched, out-gamed, and fixing to lose from the start. We lost a lot of those games—fact!—but we played our hearts out against stacked odds. It was a valuable experience just trying to hold our own against that competition.

Later, he enlisted in the army. Ray set his sights beyond Chicago. At that point, he'd seen the streets swallow up friends and loved ones. That wasn't for him.

In the same way, Shirley made our world bigger than the block by taking us out of the hood; Ray opened up the world for us by his example. He spent thirteen years in the service, settled in Amsterdam, learned a whole new culture, married, and started a family.

Ray came back to take care of his parents as they aged. He'd been gone over a decade. And what a world it was returning to here. My mom, his older sister, strung out. His nephews, who he did have a hand in raising, all ganged up: me, Boo, my cousin, Tice.

He was back in the hood, starting his whole life over again. At the same time, he was going through a divorce. Feeling pulled between the family he left here and the one he left overseas. He was trying to do what he could to set things right.

"What's it like over there?" I asked, wiping down the table at a horseshoe booth when he'd popped up at the Lounge one night for a drink.

"It's on the water, on a river, so people live on boats in these canals. They get around by boat," he answered, pulling off a beer, "and bikes, a lot of bicycles, instead of cars. It's how they get around, by bike. Streets are made for bicycles, not cars or scooters."

He'd spent the day rehabbing a house. His hands caked with drywall plaster. He picked at it absently. Then, giving up the effort, turned his attention to the label on the bottle.

"No cars? I can't picture it. Don't know I could even find it on a map."

"They got some cars, but not a lot. Mostly bikes."

I nod.

"How's school? You take geography?"

"Cal High bogus." I smiled at him like there was no point in going there. He laughed.

"We learned to read maps in the army."

"You miss it?"

"Being a soldier?"

"Living over there, I mean."

"Netherlands?"

"Wherever you from, Amsterdam."

"A bit. My family. I do. You got cousins on the other side of the world. How about that? My kids. This is home, though," he answered, setting the bottle in front of him. "Though, if I could, I'd move back down South. I'd love to move back out to Louisiana."

"For real?"

"I got a lot of good memories being out there. Camping, fishing, hunting, horseback riding. That'd be the life."

"I can't picture it. Visiting, sure. Living out there, though. Can't see it."

"It's peace of mind. Buy up a little plot of land, maybe along a river somewhere, with some acres on it, and settle there," Ray let out a deep sigh and cracked his knuckles. "But yeah, you know, someday."

We talked like that in the booth all night till close.

G-FREE'S STRATEGIES

Gregory "G-Free" Freeman—our leader, our Chief—welcomed us into his living room. At nineteen, he was older than us yet carried himself as a leader with poise well beyond his years. He was a strategist mapping out the future of our organization. As savvy as his uncle, King Shorty, and sophisticated. We would have followed him anywhere. G-Free spoke in flowcharts as if a C-suite exec mapping a Fortune 500 empire, setting a vision for the future, which was the same energy he brought out onto the battlefield.

Let's say we were fixing to sit down with a Gangster Disciple clique to divide up comings and goings in a given area. G-Free would try to position all the players in place.

"Doc, you go here. Cobe, Ty, Ima need you up here with me when we talking to dude," and so on, he'd explain.

Moving us into place like we were pieces on a game board. He tried to have everything thought out in advance.

Every little factor.

Every variable.

"Now, if things are going South and I don't like what I'm hearing, Ima do my hat like this, running my fingers across the bill, 'kay? Doc, when you see that, check it, my fingers running across the bill of my hat, like this." G-Free would demonstrate, reaching up to his hat and pulling it down over his forehead, low-like, as if the sun was shining a bit too bright. "I need you to throw a punch at dude on your left, 'kay?"

"That'll give me some plausible deniability for when we need to circle back with them later. I'd rather have it look like I can't handle my guys than that I was pitching the whole deal."

By the end of the meeting, everyone would have some kind of visual cue to watch for during the negotiations. The entire exchange relayed through a series of hand positions—signals and gestures—like how a catcher used to signal a pitcher on the mound back in the day.

"Who is going to remember who is responsible for what?" I joked. "Sadar got a thumbs up. Ty got an elbow scratch. I got 'palms pressed together.' It's a lot to remember."

G-Free loved my clowning. He had a great sense of humor, but he leveled a serious look in response.

"You only need to remember what *you* need to remember, 'kay?'"

It might sound complicated, which is what I was having fun about, but by thinking through everything with such detail, you always knew where you stood and where you were going. Many of the leadership skills that G-Free embodied I still try to practice to this day. They are skills that have come to serve me in mediation work—if someone doesn't hold up their end of the bargain, it is good to have a plan B, a plan C, a plan D, and so on. They are also skills I have brought with me, setting up programs in other cities as we expanded the model across the country. In many ways, it is thanks to G-Free that I am the leader I am today.

The organization was highly professionalized when you got up in rank. We had a treasurer, a chief of security, and structured meetings with detailed minutes. Members reported back. We collected dues, distributed literature, put in the work, and managed finances. Ledgers, report backs, agendas, and plans. We went around the room with updates. Speaking to the status of the corners. Business development, marketing, product design, human resources, and logistics all under a different name.

G-Free was about all that out of a sense of formality, but his leadership style was focused on the collective. We were all in this together and looked out for each other. He was royalty yet didn't carry himself with any entitlement. He made it so we worked together, not as employees but as partners.

We were trending in this direction as an organization at this time, but he really helped us to refine this structure. He helped us to get serious about what we were doing as an organization. It is important to know that all of this was happening at this time.

Now, given who he was, some of our own in the organization didn't take to his method. They preferred to have these rigid chains of command, so just by order of how we were running things, you got friction. That was where the trouble started.

HOUSE PARTY

Sadar, C-Man, Ty, and I rolled through the house party like politicians on the campaign trail, shaking hands and making connections. Furniture cleared from the makeshift dance floor in the crowded dining room. Oversized speakers bumping bass. DJ live on the turntables. Gelled lights set to the beat. Red, blue, purple, green. A disco ball on the ceiling throwing splashes of color through the room.

We were there on official business. G-Free was all about connecting. Connecting. Connecting. Connecting. While other groups might do things dirty, recruiting through intimidation or an outright beatdown, the way Sol was messed over back in the day, G-Free encouraged us to take a more diplomatic stance. The way a civic club might, an armed Rotary International or the Jaycees, if they were slinging dope. I am not saying that BD never deployed underhanded tactics or that we wouldn't get physical when necessary. Still, G-Free was focused on building relationships to bolster our numbers, which suited us fine. It never made much sense to me you fuck a guy up to make him a member just out of fear.

Once we'd made ourselves seen, we posted up in the corner of a crowded living room. Relaxing a bit into the scene. Sadar rolled a blunt, pinching the end of a tobacco-emptied Swisher Sweet. He leaned against the archway between the living and dining room, firing it up. He was more interested in partying than anything else in those days. His hand cupped around the cherry to inhale deeply.

Sadar wasn't one to start something, even when you got a few drinks in him, but he would be first in the mix to finish it if a fight kicked off. Sadar had us covered. He was as fast as he was loyal and a skilled boxer. In those days, though, it was more about the party favors, making the rounds to see what he could score.

Ty found his way into the gravitational pull of a game of chance in a far-flung corner of the party. Gambling was the only thing that could get his attention more than women. Once he heard the clacking rattle of dice, any chance of getting him to play wingman went out the window. He inserted himself into the game faster than anyone could say, "Bet."

C-Man wrapped my chest with the back of his hand. "You know that shorty over there?" he asked, nodding to a cluster of females in a semicircle across the room.

"Who you got your eye on?"

"She cute," he pointed. "You know her?"

I didn't, but that had never stopped me before. I love to get people talking and laughing.

Being silly, making connections, meeting new people.

C-Man would tell you I was a smooth talker who had finesse with the ladies. That was more Ty's approach. He had a way about him and lines at the ready that weren't rehearsed. It was his style. Really, my strength was just not being afraid of looking silly.

Given that Ty was wrapped up in a game, C-Man was looking to me to break the ice with the women across the way.

"I got you," I told C-Man.

I started across the space, hamming it up. I walked to the rhythm, waving my arms, playful and offbeat, between dancers on the floor who really knew what they were doing. When I made it over to the semicircle on the other side of the room, they could see me coming. This was all part of the production. I learned early on that there is a certain kind of charm in being over-the-top ridiculous.

"How you doing?" I asked when I reached Paulette, who'd caught C-Man's eye, standing with a group of her friends.

There were four ladies in all. You could sense a collective eye roll. I introduced myself anyway.

"I'm Cobe," I said with a smile, shaking hands. "You know me?"

Paulette shook her head. "Do I know you?"

"Yes. Do you know me?"

"I don't think so. Nah. No. I don't know you."

"You see my Mella over there?" I asked, pointing over my shoulder at C-Man.

Paulette wore a faint smile but really wasn't having it. She shook her head.

"You know him?"

"That guy over there?" she asked, pointing.

"Yes. My Mella. You know him?"

"No."

"Then why you staring at us?"

"What?"

"You are making him uncomfortable checking him out like that," I told her. "You gotta be cool about it. Subtle, like me. I came over here to tell you that."

"Oh Lord," Paulette responded with an eye roll and laugh. "Oh, Lord."

Her friends fell out laughing, smiling ear to ear. They looked over at C-Man.

"I mean, I can provide you an introduction."

Paulette was shaking her head back and forth. Her girls were giggling at the spectacle.

"I'll call him over," I said, waving C-Man over.

He started across the floor. Paulette shrank. Her girls laughed.

"He needs your help. He got one or two moves to his name. It's hopeless. You have to show him some moves," I tell Paulette. "Can you do that?"

"No," she laughed in response. "No."

"See, you can tell just by how he is walking over now he needs your help," I said, laying it on thick. "You've gotta help him."

Everyone in the circle laughed as I talked shit.

Paulette slapped at me playfully. "You're goofy," she said.

I turned to C-Man as he got closer, shouting, "This Paulette. She can't dance. She only got but one or two moves. She needs your help to teach her a thing or two."

"I can do that," C-Man grinned back at me.

I winked at Paulette as he led her out on the dance floor. She rolled her eyes back at me, joining in the laughter. The group of us pushed the two of them out on the dance floor together.

They ended up dancing together all night and many nights after. Nearly four decades later, they are still married.

I should tell you that Paulette remembers this whole thing differently. She knew G-Free and Ty for years beforehand and recalls being introduced to C-Man as a "family thing." She jokes that it was really more like an arranged marriage. I am still taking credit for them getting together, though.

That is how I remember it.

GOING ON OFFENSE

In October 1989, a Cadillac, candy-coated apple green, the color of a waxed Granny Smith, with tinted windows, pulled up across a street littered with fall leaves. It was a sight to behold. Shiny, brand-new, shimmering with bright chrome rims on whitewall tires.

Doc and G-Free couldn't do nothing but admire it—the kind of car you want to caress hood to tail—in adoration. They were so enthralled, in fact, that they didn't notice the rear window roll down until the AK was already blasting from the backseat. Doc had been carrying since he was fourteen. Might have been one of the first among us, though, by then we all had a piece, but truth was we never really engaged in gunplay.

The machine-gun fire tore into G-Free's gut, sending him flying back off the curb. Doc dove into the lawn to take cover as the Caddy raced off down the street. We were into it with the Bogus Boys but would have never suspected that ride would be used in the call of duty. It was a Trojan Horse.

G-Free pulled through at the hospital. Surgery was needed to patch up the damage, and his stomach was stapled. The shock waves, though, ran deeper. When you are coming under fire, you start to shift from defense to offense.

THE LOUNGE AFTER HOURS

We met at the Lounge during off-hours after Granny's guests cleared out. One of the perks of working there was always having my own keys. It was fully stocked. I knew my way around both sides of the bar, and it was a chill place for all of us to unwind. At house parties, we were on official business.

At the Lounge, we could unplug and be on our time. We weren't punching the clock, so to speak.

Sometimes, I would help clean. Break everything down. Sweep the floors, wipe down tables, put the chairs up. Get everything straightened up for the evening and leave out with the rest of the staff. I would circle around the block, only to open everything back up once the coast was clear letting my guys in through the back. This was a good party spot for new recruits. Giving the guys who worked for me a place to blow off steam.

One night, the Lounge was closed up early over a holiday break. I went through the motions. Ushered out all the regular customers. Tidied up. Broke things down. Locked the doors. Reopened them. Got my crew back inside and got the party started. It was a revolving door of festivities, except that this night, my Auntie Shirley was driving past.

Out of all my aunties who might have been passing by the Lounge that night after hours, it would have to be Shirley. If it had been Hilda, she might have taken over the DJ booth. Cookie, if she was living in the area at that time, probably would have kept right on rolling, but it was Shirley.

Auntie Shirley—the "mean one," the disciplinarian—sees the lights on and people inside. She hangs a U-turn at the corner and circles back. She pulls up in the alleyway, cuts the lights, and carefully approaches the back door. Auntie Shirley had her own set of keys as well. She unlocks the back door, makes her way inside, thinking the place is being robbed or something. She is going to catch the culprits in the act—I am not sure what she had in mind to do next if she caught them.

Inside, music is playing. Drinks are being poured. Celebration. Dancing.

It is like the scene in a movie where someone comes through the door, and the record scratches. Everything falls silent and still. We all having an "oh shit moment" together. My guys are thinking, *Who is this coming in the joint like she owns the place?*

Shirley, probably thinking, *What the hell is going on here?*

And, me thinking, *Of all the aunties it could be it got to be Shirley? Well, it was a good run, but I am busted now.*

She sidles up to the bar, looks at me across the counter, point blank. "You are supposed to put parties in the book. I didn't see no party listed in the book."

I know, I tell her. I didn't put the party in the book.

Auntie sits for a minute or two, making me sweat, and then she goes, "Pour me a drink."

I do.

"You know, I thought the place might be getting robbed."

"I'm sorry, Auntie."

She took a swig of the drink.

"Turns out it's just you stealing."

"Don't be like that, Auntie," I plead.

She drained her drink, set it on the counter, and motioned for another pour by tapping the rim.

"If you want me not to tell Granny, you are going to have to promise to pay for everything you drink."

I nod, imagining Granny would be heartbroken if she knew I was using the Lounge after hours like this. "Sure thing."

"And you got to pay for everything I drink, too" Shirley says, taking another swig.

I laugh, putting my hand out.

"You got yourself a deal Auntie," I said, shaking her hand.

She blackmailed me from then on, expecting an invite whenever I brought the guys out. She'd come over after hours, sometimes alone, or occasionally with friends, "supervising," as she put it, hanging out with us all night.

ACTS OF WAR

That year, 1989, November was unseasonably warm for Chicago. There were T-shirts and shorts days throughout the calendar that month. Only a few weeks after G-Free got caught in a drive-by and a week before Thanksgiving, on November 13, it was getting into the seventies and sunshiny. It was the kind of out-of-place weather that felt like the entire world flipped on its head.

A few years earlier, Sol getting rolled by a grown man had been a wake-up call. We knew after that event that neither our neighborhood nor us would ever be the same. It marked our transition from grade school gangbanging to grown-up gangsters. Now, the attempt on G-Free was a follow-up lesson. Reverberations, shaking not just our crew but throughout the entire city.

With King Shorty locked up, it had become common that BD factions squared off against BD factions in sprawling brawls in public parks throughout our neighborhoods at this time.

For years, we'd been squaring off against the Gangster Disciples and the Moes. Now, we had to worry about our family coming apart at the seams. All that mass collapsed under its own weight as Shorty was behind bars.

At Lowe Park, a small rectangular patch of green at the northernmost edge of the Norfolk Southern Rail Yard complex, those seismic waves began to tremor on a Monday afternoon. Trains rolled through the far end of Lowe, metallic scraping as they switched between tracks, plunging deeper into the yard. Barbed wire–wrapped concrete cinder blocks and stacks of creosote-soaked rail ties fenced them off. That day, even over the ruckus of two dozen or so BD clashing in the park, those freight cars grinding along the railway artery behind a grumbling engine could be heard.

That Monday in the park was slated as a rematch. The same factions had been going rounds in the street a day earlier, twenty-some-deep. G-Free, Doc, and two members of our crew working under him ended up pitted against a mob of nearly two dozen. G-Free still with the staples in his belly, Doc oblivious to whatever it was they were even into it over, and his guys, Al and Big Melvin, just happening to come by as all of this transpires, hop the fence to run up on that mass of bodies throwing down on one another. There were so many guys throwing punches that they couldn't even tell who was hitting who anymore. Eventually, though, they were outnumbered and overpowered. They got the best of us.

That weekend, G-Free spent rounding up more guys to head to Lowe on Monday.

Doc was strapped. He lifted his shirt to show G-Free, tapping the grip with his fingers.

"Whatchu doing?" G-Free said calmly as they neared the park. "Put your piece up, brother. These BDs, we going to fight. We don't need to be armed. We all BDs."

Doc protested. "Better to have a gun and not need it than to need a gun and not have it. Am I right?"

"These BD, though," G-Free replied. "Families fight, 'kay? That's the way it is sometimes. We are going to settle this the old-fashion way. Head up. As men."

That didn't sit right with Doc, but G-Free was chief. He put up his piece. They continued to the park.

Things resumed as they had the previous day—in a melee. Two factions of BD into it with each other, throwing hands and catching fists. If you have never been in a clash like that with twenty-four bodies hurled at each other with brute force under their own momentum, consider yourself lucky. It feels like a car crash. Everything happens with immense speed and in slow motion at the same time. Disorienting. Shouts and obscenities at a deafening pitch. Elbows flying, punches thrown, mass crashing against mass.

Everything is moving herky-jerky, like something is wrong with your vision. Images gone wobbly on the one hand, and on the other, you are catching more details than you'd ever see otherwise. Clumps of dirt kick up from the lawn as your homie runs alongside you. Numbers on the battered freight car idling yards away on the train tracks across a field beyond a fence as if it was clear as day printed on a piece of paper in front of you. Things you might have no other way of knowing suddenly fix your attention.

Then, maybe you catch a hook upside the jaw and another jab as you tumble. Adrenaline is kicking so high that you only feel the way your body is ragdoll tossed by the punches rather than the pain itself. You catch up with your stagger, bracing yourself mid-fall before hitting the ground.

Homie, who was right next to you, is now up against a chain-link fence hammered by a couple of dudes. They got him blocked in like he is against the ropes in a ring, pounding away with body shots and head blows at the same time.

You break off from your opponent to bum-rush one of the guys who is double-teaming your friend. Tackle the one dude to the ground. Start swinging on him, giving homie enough space to claim the upper hand over the remaining opponent.

They didn't have the numbers to overpower us this go-around. We were so evenly matched that Doc, still sore from the beating days earlier, and G-Free, healing from the gut wound the previous month, stepped to the sidelines to catch their breath.

Then the temperature dropped in an instant. Suddenly, everything runs cold. Doc says that he sees three guys wrestling just across the battlefield. In the same way that you can zoom in on the numbers of that battered freight car yards away, Doc can tell that the action with this trio seems different than anything else going on in the park.

That's when he makes the gun. At the same time, one brother peels away from the other two, leveling the pistol in search of a target. Doc sees it. He says he looks back at G-Free, like, "See, I told you." Then he gives the chief a shove, hard, to make a break for it. Shots rang out.

Four total.

Doc watched those bullets pop out of the fabric at the back of G-Free's shirt as if it were happening in stop motion. Even as he watched G-Free topple backward to the ground, part of him didn't believe what he was witnessing.

Those shots drown out the idle engine, the scraping of metal on metal along the tracks, and the shouting of the guys as they scattered, fleeing. The park emptied in an instant.

Our chief was laid out.

It wasn't until the ambulance had come to take him off that Doc fully understood what had happened.

G-Free was dead.

II

ALL OUT WAR

THE STICKUP MAN

Englewood, Chicago, July 2015

"You know anyone been robbing over by you? A stickup man hitting corner boys on your crew?" I ask.

"Oh," Lil' B says.

The utterance has volume over the engine as we roll onward, looking for Big Folks. It is not just audible over the mechanics of the car: rattling exhaust, tires over asphalt, whirs of belts, slamming pistons, grinding, groaning of the vehicle moving, but also seems to occupy the space.

As if the "oh" in exhale, balloons in the interior, expanding throughout the car. It is an "oh" with mass.

Lil' B clears his throat again and fidgets in his seat.

"Okay," he says quietly. "Okay."

I had been reluctant to share that information—that someone had been robbing up around the area where Lil' B and his crew operate—until I had everyone together. Vice Lords who had opened fire on Big Folks, Lil' B, and their crew did so in retaliation for one of their guys being held up at gunpoint. A stickup man ripped off the shorty, so the rogue Vice Lords took action on his behalf.

I originally held back from exploring this with Lil' B because I wasn't sure if the stickup itself was one of Big Folks' own guys. If someone in Lil' B's crew was breaking rank to line their pockets, the act could be an impulsive money grab, or it could be the first step in a coup over Big Folks.

I had wanted to get everyone together, Big Folks, Lil' B, D-Boy, and the rest, in a group, in one place to see how the information landed. It had felt right, just now, to go back on that with Lil' B, who was working with me to keep a lid on things and loop him in to recognize his cooperation.

His response, the presence of this "oh" that Lil' B offered as if in revelation, which had its own mass, implied he might actually know something.

Lil' B and I were heading toward Big Folks' girlfriend. We had until the evening to sort this out before they escalated. T, a member of their crew with a car, got off work at that time. He was fixing to pick up Big Folks and the guys to run down the shooters. Big Folks had given his word that he would wait on me until before they took action, but I only had until T got off work.

Now, Big Folks was missing. The whole stand-by-and-wait situation was making him feel vulnerable, so he had ducked out. We checked with his guys, we checked with his mama, and we were heading over to his girl's place to check with her. So far, Big Folks was nowhere to be found. I had his word that he would wait until that evening, but I couldn't be sure that he hadn't gone in search of trouble.

Or, that trouble might still try to find its way to him. Vice Lords had given me their word that nothing more would be done on the matter. At least until I could confirm one way or the other that Big Folks' crew weren't responsible. I'd even paid off any outstanding debt to Vice Lords, so that they could feel the matter was settled. I couldn't control for anything that might happen if they ran into one another.

"You think one of us did this thing?" he asks.

The question comes across as genuine. It feels honest. It seems clear at that moment that Lil' B had no idea of the robbery. I don't know for a fact, but he seems to be processing in real time, weighing the inquiry. It doesn't let everyone off the hook, but at the very least, I can tell Lil' B is being straight with me. He likely wasn't involved or knew about the incident before I told him.

"I'm not accusing anyone," I tell him. "Just asking the question. It could be it came from someone in your crew."

Lil' B begins to play absently with the phone. Slowly turning it in his hands back and forth. He is not engaging with the screen so much as toying with the object itself. He rotates it back and forth in a toss, right palm to left and back as if tossing a ball he is fixing to throw.

I flick on the turn signal to make a left across traffic at another light. I veer into the far lane as the rhythmic tick of the blinker sounds. In the space following my explanation, the tick sounds like a kitchen egg timer, indicating the passing moment.

"Who, though?"

"I was hoping you could help me with that," I respond, enlisting him in the process.

Lil' B stares out the window. We roll through the intersection. His gaze absent. He resumes fidgeting with the phone as we drive on in silence. The turn signal snaps off without the same satisfying buzz of "times up" on a cooking clock.

"Ain't D-Boy," he replies.

"Wouldn't think so."

"If it was D-Boy, he'd have told me outright," he says confidently.

"That's what I would assume."

"Truth be told, if it really was D-Boy, I would have been involved myself, I figure."

"I figured as much myself," I responded.

He looked from the passenger window over at me, studying me as I kept focused on the road ahead. After a pause, he clucked his tongue.

"All right. All right. You think this bigger than a robbery?"

"I'm not sure," I tell him honestly. "I don't know. I'm just trying to play this thing out."

"You thinking someone might, you know, could use something like this to make a move on Big Folks?"

"Right now, we consider possibilities—that's all. You and me just talking things through, right?" I don't let the question hang. "I seen it before. In the past."

If there was one thing that I had learned from G-Free, our chief, back in the day, it was to try to entertain every possibility and have a plan for each. In those days, we were doing it to navigate war. Threats were coming from opposition, police, internally, externally, and everywhere in between. You can't predict and plan for every variable, but you can identify enough patterns in the possibilities to protect against them.

I've heard it described as six-dimensional chess. I don't know enough about the game to know if that is fact, but the concept tracks. Things come at you from every direction. When you respond to an event, you have to be prepared to set something else in motion. Actions cascade, resonating outward and building on one another, or set off a cycle that pulls you deeper and deeper.

I have done my best to carry this same mindset into my mediation work—and to train others to do the same as well. Interruption means considering all the variables. Trying to anticipate triggers that might derail negotiations. *What can set someone off even after an agreement has been reached? What happens if one person violates an arrangement? What happens to plan when emotions kick in to hijack a situation?* I can't tell you how many times we've reached common ground between two parties after days of conversation, negotiation, airing grievances, processing emotions, and doing all the things that need to be done, only to have everything come undone in seconds when an auntie, a homie, a girlfriend, or a friend asks the wrong question in the wrong way: *"Oh, so, you just going to forget what happened?"*

If you can anticipate these things, then you can correct them in advance.

"I don't think it is T, either. That dude got three jobs anyway. Where he gonna find the time to moonlight as a stickup guy?"

"Facts."

"Ain't T."

"What about the rest of your guys?"

"Big A?"

"How about Big A?" I press.

"When this thing happen?"

We make our way onto side streets aimed at Big Folks' girl. As we close the gap between location and destination, I start working the mental arithmetic on how to bring Big Folks in on the conversation once we reach him. It may backfire, putting it on his mind that the move might have been a breach of trust. Bringing him in on the conversation needs to be done in a way that acknowledges we don't really know nothing.

This is all exploratory.

I break down the timeline with Lil' B when everything transpired. Big A had an alibi. He'd have been out of town during the episode. It wasn't Big A.

"How about Lil' Guy?"

Lil' B laughs and shakes his head. "Nah."

"Okay, so ain't Lil' Guy, you saying?"

"Nah," he responded. "Lil' Guy wouldn't do this thing."

"He somewhere else at the time?"

"I don't remember where he was, but he just wouldn't do that, I am saying," Lil' B answers. "He wouldn't be going against us like that."

"Okay."

"Gotta be someone who don't have that kind of loyalty to Big Folks," Lil' B ventures. "Or, worser yet, someone who is trying to make a move on Big Folks."

"You know anyone fits that description?"

"I mean . . ."

"Anyone that would want to take him down?"

"There are guys that talk shit, but, you know, there always guys who are going to talk shit. I don't think anyone would actually pull anything like that," he responds. "Even the guys that are talking shit are just talking. They may disagree with a decision here or something there, but they still respect him. You know what I am saying?"

I nod. I did. That made a world of difference.

We reach an apartment complex. I have to wind around the block once, searching for a space. I pull off to the side to double-park out front of the building.

"You going to want me to run up?" Lil' B asks.

"Let's finish this first," I tell him.

"I don't think that attack came from us," Lil' B answers flatly.

He stares out across the parking lot. His fingers scratched at his chin absently, then he begins chewing at his nails. Gnawing at the cuticles of his thumb, then he snaps his fingers, followed by a wrap on the dash.

"In fact, truth be told, some of our guys been held up over the last few couple months."

"Y'all been robbed?" I ask.

"Not our crew, but some of the shorties in the neighborhood we know been robbed."

"This was in the last few months?"

"You got a description?"

"Stickup man?" I reply. "He's a light-skinned dude. When he jacked the Vice Lords' shorty that kicked this whole thing off, he was rocking a tan jacket and beige Timberlands."

Snapping his fingers again, Lil' B lets his jaw drop.

"Bro, I know that dude, for sure," he responds.

Nodding again.

Another snap of the fingers.

"For sure," he repeats. "For sure."

Pausing a moment for effect or sincere contemplation, I don't know, Lil' B goes back to scratching at his chin. He swivels in the seat to face me. His knee propped on the center counsel.

"I can't say this same dude did all these robberies, but I can say I know who fits that description."

"For sure?" I play.

Lil' B gets ready to repeat but catches on that I am having fun with him. He rolls his eyes a bit.

"Yes," he pushes. "And, Cobe, Bro, check this out, dude isn't even from around here. He don't even live in the neighborhood, but I know who dude is."

"Where he stay?"

"I don't know. Suburbs, I think. Harvey, maybe? I don't know."

"You know it's him?"

"For—yes! Yes. I know it is him."

"You got a name?"

Lil' B relays the identity of beige Timberlands.

"You know how I can get up with him, you think?"

"His uncle stay near us," Lil' B responds. "I can tell you where he lives."

I nod. The puzzle pieces were beginning to look like the picture on the front of the box. I needed to check in with the team at the office. We had to adapt our strategy, organizing around the new information. I wanted to sit with these details a minute. Play out these scenarios to keep anything going sideways.

"You mind running up to check on Big Folks, G?"

Lil' B nods as he pops the lock and hops out of the car.

I can't get up with Big Fella, but leave a message as Lil' B makes it across the lot. I text Hot Rod the identity of beige Timberlands. I know he's been asking around to see if he could find out anything about him.

Whenever new information emerges, we have to relay it to the team to adjust our strategy. In this instance, China Joe, over on the West Side, has come at these events from the opposite end. Joe was a national leader of the Vice Lords at one time. He still has sway with membership and, as a part of the Englewood CeaseFire office, was checking in with JB, Zo, Brian, and the other Vice Lords, who had been in the Caprice this morning.

Even though the guys had given me their word that they would consider the matter settled, we were working from every angle, chess in six dimensions, as I've been told, to make sure that they held their end of the bargain. China Joe would physically pop in on them in person to follow up.

While Joe wouldn't relay Timberland's identity, he would make sure to clarify that the initial robbery, the one that kicked off this chain of events, didn't come from Big Folks or a BD faction at all but some independent operator from the burbs that had nothing to do with nothing. Clearing the air on that fact would go a long way toward letting the matter settle, especially as I already reimbursed any money they might be out.

Meanwhile, our guy, Head, out of the office, had been following leads on the Gangster Disciple end of things. He'd be doing this just in case we had bad information to start with, and it was GD that came through, not Vice Lords. We now knew that was not the case, but I was still trying to keep a lid on things, so I hadn't had the chance to fully brief everyone involved.

Hot Rod hits me back. He knows who Timberland and his uncle are, but he don't really know them. On the second-floor landing of the wraparound patio, I see Lil' B making his way back solo. No sign of Big Folks. I scan the parking lot and land my gaze back on the screen.

I text Rod that I am with Lil' B and trying to get to Big Folks but that I could use his help closing the loop with Big Fella and trying to locate Timberland. Rod agrees. He's on it. Thumbs-up emoji pings on my screen.

Lil' B is moving fast across the lot. He isn't running, but his gait is wide, and he steps quickly. There is enough urgency in his stride that I roll the window down before he gets to the ground floor.

"What's up, B?"

"Big Folks got a car, homie. He's already on the move."

12

AT MY FRONT DOOR

Auburn Gresham/Englewood, Chicago,
July 1990–1994

On a warm summer evening, a few weeks before my birthday, I headed out for the night. I was still living at Granny's place, but it felt more like I was a tenant, like Uncle Phil before me, than a dependent, like the wards Grams looked after. Before hitting the door, I did a routine inventory, patting my pockets: keys, wallet, money, gun. I didn't go anywhere anymore without a piece on me at all times. Then I turned the knob and stepped out onto the front porch.

The block was peaceful save for the hum of some distant traffic and seasonal cicadas buzzing. A couple of weeks earlier, fireworks were a constant. A prolonged Fourth of July celebration beginning in late spring stretched on through the holiday and a little beyond. Bottle rocket whistles; heavy percussive eruptions; explosions of stars and stripes in red, white, and blue; arcs of metallic silver and gold in sparkler bands kicking off daily at sunset. They'd tapered off in recent weeks. The street had a calm about it. Moths fluttering around the dusky orange haze of streetlamps, the only activity.

Suddenly, I paused. The hair on the back of my neck crackled to attention with a static charge. Something in the air shifted. Then, what seemed like a pack of Black Cat firecrackers tossed in a metal trash can sounded. It was a brrrr-rat-tat-tat noise. Only when the hail of bullets began hitting the porch did I realize it was machine-gun fire.

Bullets ate into the wood. Splinters burst around me. They lodged in the door frame and boards on the porch. I could see the white-yellow light explosions from the muzzle. The shooter was posted up in the neighbor's shrub. He emerged in slow motion, moving across the lawn, sending that spray, swinging the gun right, left, and back.

I dove from the porch into the lawn. My body hit the ground, and I dropped low, rolling. Out of my periphery, I could make out the underside of the porch within arm's reach. Pressing against the Earth, I crawled forward until I took refuge beneath it.

As soon as I was shielded, I pulled free my own piece. Kept moving forward, flat on my stomach, toward the center of the deck. I held back from returning fire so as not to give away my position. Once I got clear of the barrage, I pushed up the best I could in the cramped space.

Shooter came up the gangway to the walk. He was firing the whole time. Reached the curb, keeping that spray active. Stepped out into the street, blasting. Completely in the open, beneath the streetlight, he exhausted his clip. It was only metal clicking on metal as his ammo ran dry.

My breath was a steady pant as my whole body flooded with adrenaline. I caught my air up in a gasp and held it. My heart slammed in my chest. I fought to curb the tremor that coursed down my arms, spilling into my hands. Stabilized. Upped the pistol. Fired.

I lurched forward, pulling the trigger. Hammer pounding, bullets firing. I moved until I got clear of the porch myself. Stood. Firing. Ran across my own front lawn. Firing. Past the gate on the chain link fence, past the sidewalk, the curb, on into the street. Firing. I kept my finger on the trigger and kept pulling until I was running up the street myself into the night.

Only when the gun was firing empty did I quit. Standing in the same place the shooter had been, I looked down the street in both directions. Empty as it had seemed when I first stepped out on the porch. The street had returned to its stony silence. Moths circling lamplight overhead.

Down the block, lights came on in windows. Curtains pulled back as neighbors peered out. The evening started to come to life with a bustling like it was midday. A siren split the silence with a single piercing whoop.

No lights flashed yet, but seemed clear police were close.

I walked to the front gate. My hand purchased the top rail, and I pulled it toward me, closing things up. Flipped the latch and shut tight the front yard.

My energy was leveling out, and it was getting near I needed to make myself scarce before the police arrived. I looked up the street again in the direction the shooter had run, with a single thought cycling through my mind: *"I was finally successful enough for someone to want me dead."*

A HUNTING PARTY

Some time passed before Ty came to scoop me at a gas station a couple of blocks away. I walked over and gave him a call, trying to get off the block and clear of the area before the cops arrived. Even at this hour, they'd be knocking on doors. Neighbors would be out. Shell casings collected. Squads blocking through traffic. I wanted to be gone.

C-Man was sitting in the passenger seat, Sadar in the back. He scooted over when he saw me, popped the door open, and gave me space to hop in.

"Man of the hour," Ty said in celebration.

Everyone laughed.

"You got some idea who was come at you?" C-Man asked, getting right down to business.

"I got some ideas," I responded.

"In front of Granny's place," Sadar said. He shook his head back and forth in disbelief, clucking his tongue in disbelief. "Shit ain't decent."

"That's not the half of it," I told him, taking a swig of cranberry juice I'd bought to make change. "This motherfucker was posted up in the bushes across the street waiting for me."

"Where at?"

"Across the street. He must've been sitting up inside that shrub for—how long?—I don't know."

"Hiding in the bushes, though?" Sadar said. "That's for real."

"Like it's a deer blind or some shit," Ty murmured.

"Ain't decent," Sadar repeated.

We were driving now. A hunting party of our own, moving through the night. Riding down on clubhouses in search of the usual suspects. It was dark out and happened fast, but I was pretty clear on who was responsible. We all knew the laundry list of enemies we were racking up in those days. There was the inherited opposition: Gangster Disciples, Vice Lords, Stones, of course. Conflicts that were going back in some ways before we'd been born. While at the same time, other BD factions were vying for power.

We ran through a list of names.

"This Vice Lords," I said as we drove onward to Racine.

"GD been talking a lot of shit 'bout you in particular," C-Man said, glancing up at the rearview to make eye contact.

I was pretty sure it was Vice Lords who made the move. I told them as such. We were already into it deep with them, and it seemed only a matter of time.

We managed this situation the same way I would years later if it were a mediation. We kept an ear out for rumors, had conversations, asked questions, followed up with anyone who might know anything about the shooting attempt, and got into it with dudes who weren't even involved.

I couldn't believe the audacity that someone would move on me at home and put so much effort into making it happen. There was a sense of pride, the residue of that initial revelation that I was big enough that someone wanted me dead, combined with a feeling of exposure that came with an attack at home.

It is a different feeling dodging bullets between parked cars on a street near the clubhouse, on your way to the store, or out and about in the neighborhood than it is to get hit at your house. A move in the front yard where you used to play as a kid, bullets embedding the door frame behind which you sleep, adds another dimension altogether.

Shooter didn't brag about the attempt, probably on account I was still above ground. He didn't want to give away his position in the same way I didn't take those initial shots from the porch to keep myself concealed. If they'd capped me, there'd be a billboard advertisement announcing it, but fact I was still breathing meant the shooter needed to keep it under wraps.

It also meant it was likely he was going to make another move.

"They must think you real important, homie." Ty cracked. "Going through all this trouble."

"I'm King Cobe, of course, they got to come at me!"

Everyone laughed.

"You hit your head under that porch?" C-Man asked, needling me. "King Cobe."

"Hit his head? Man, I'm surprised his head fit out from under that porch in the first place, it got so big," Ty quipped.

MAKING PREPARATIONS

On the living room table, Ray had laid out cleaning supplies for a 9mm: gun bore cleaner, lubricant, wire brushes, and a silicon cloth. After the attack, my uncle began advising us on security issues. The man who managed the impossible by not getting ganged up throughout his high school career, even though most of our family and many of his friends were affiliated, who had moved halfway across the globe, over four thousand miles, to spend over a decade as a career soldier, was helping the Black Disciples clean weapons and fortify our surroundings.

We began with landscaping. In the days that followed the initial attack, we removed any cover in the neighborhood that someone could use in an ambush, asking neighbors to remove the hedges out front. We had motion-detection lighting installed off the alley and along the side of the house so we'd get a notice on anyone creeping in from around back.

Now, Ray was teaching us basic maintenance, training us on care, and cleaning our weapons.

"This is important to keep your guns from jamming," he began, holding up a nylon, phosphate bronze, and stainless-steel brush in one hand and a semiautomatic in the other. "You don't want to be in a situation where you are taking fire and can't defend yourself."

"Set up everything you are going to need first. Before you even get started, you put out your cleaning kit, your materials, your solutions, your bullets, your weapon."

"It's like in a restaurant," Sadar responded.

"Right, your mise en place," Ray continued.

"I was thinking more like a hamburger joint. How you put out your tomatoes, pickles, onions—all that before you turn on the grill."

"Right, same thing, having all your ingredients measured and cut, pans prepared, mixing bowls, tools, and equipment set out, and everything."

"Just say that, then."

"It just means 'putting in place.'"

"In English, I mean."

"Same as what I said," Ray continued, "Make sure your pistol is clear. Check the breech. Make sure there isn't a round in the chamber. Then, you disassemble it."

We'd had guns jam in the past, usually just tossed the piece and kept it moving. After the attack, though, it wasn't a chance we were willing to take anymore.

"Remove the magazine from the well. Find the slide lock lever—here," Ray said, demonstrating the part by turning the weapon to display the side of the piece, "and rotate it clockwise into a vertical position."

We listened closely. Paid attention. Took notes.

In the weeks that followed the incident, we were no closer to who made the move on me. They'd gone in hiding, knowing both that we were going to be coming back on them and that they needed to keep a low profile if they were going to make another attempt. Our ears to the ground, there was rumbling. Something was coming.

My birthday was approaching in a couple of weeks, so we half expected something might go down in August. Birthdays, memorials, anniversaries, celebrations, and ceremonies are often used to make a hit. The expectation is that people would be having a good time—drinking, smoking, getting high—celebrating. They'd be messed up, their guard down, so it was easier to go after them.

We were putting preparations in place beforehand.

"Find where the spring meets the barrel—the spring is under pressure, right?—so you have to be careful removing it."

We were all springs, coiled. Contents under pressure. Wound tight. Compressed energy, ready to explode. Somewhere, Vice Lords were legit gunning for us. We didn't have a name yet but knew enough to say who was responsible.

For years, Stones, GD, and BD had been moving behind the scenes, building up armies. We were recruiting small factions under large banners, tacking on our name, absorbing these splinters into legions, carving out kingdoms in a patchwork of blocks.

Now, as the hierarchy was crumbling after law enforcement went after leadership, alliances that held together these citywide territorial armies were falling apart. In the disintegration, we even had to look over our shoulders at our own.

These preparations gave us something to focus on.

"After removing the spring, the barrel is just free to slide out. When you push the slide forward—like this, okay—toward the barrel," Ray demonstrated, "it'll just slide right off the front."

Ray continued with each step, introducing brushes, dowels, and push-rods. He demonstrated the activities in detail, showing each step in the process: breaking down, cleaning, lubricating, and reassembling.

In the attic, we built a sniper's nest, propping a rifle just beside the window. We kept a shotgun in the coat closet just off the foyer. Pistols were wrapped in rags, concealed in a drainpipe, or stashed in a gutter.

When Ray started doing rehab work on the house next door, which Granny purchased to flip, we stashed weapons in the basement. We cached guns in the walls and tucked them behind vents, which we could access easily in case anything went down. If someone somehow got the drop on us, managing to get us disarmed, we were always only a few feet from a backup.

If someone was coming down the one-way street to do a drive-by, we rigged traps on the block and in the alley out back. We designated parking spaces on either side of the street. These were permanently ours, so we stashed a car in each space with keys nearby. It was a narrow space, a single lane on the city street for a vehicle to come through so our cars could mobilize into a choke point. If someone was racing up the block firing, we'd get a car from either side to come at them. It would be like a demolition derby on Aberdeen, we'd box them in, pin them down, and open fire.

In the alley, we did the same with garbage cans. We could jam up the cars by pushing trash bins under the axles. That be enough to get them stalled out, and we could move on them. There were booby traps set throughout the yard, the garage, the house, and the neighborhood.

This is the psychology of a coiled spring. Trying to manage every threat from every direction is like trying to hold a bicep in flex indefinitely. Eventually, a muscle is going to have to give under strain and exhaustion. It can't not.

That spring is going to need release, eventually.

We were guarding against Vice Lords, but Gangster Disciples, Stones, and even factions under our own banner were coming, too. We were fully engaged in the retaliatory tit-for-tat.

The street took notice; it had my name. Once that happens, police are close behind.

⓭

HOW THIS COULD'VE PLAYED OUT

Englewood, Chicago, July 2015

"She didn't know where he was going?" I ask Lil' B as he hops into the passenger seat.

We just learned that Big Folks borrowed his girlfriend's car. For over an hour, we've been running around the neighborhood looking for him and barely kept up. He was on foot, and I'd missed him by a good minute at his homie's house, his mama's place, and now, again, at his girl's apartment.

Letting things slide hadn't sat right with him, so he'd gone off to clear his head. That restless energy pushed him to get mobile. I was worried. This morning, two things prevented Big Folks from riding down on the Vice Lords that shot up his corner: giving me his word and the fact that he didn't have wheels. Before, he had to wait for his boy T to get off work before he was mobile.

Now, only half that statement was true.

"He didn't say, or she isn't telling," Lil' B replied.

"Any ideas? You think he'd ride down on them himself?" I ask, meaning the Vice Lords that he was itching to retaliate against.

"I don't think so," Lil' B answered, "but I don't know for sure."

I'm formulating a plan. Trying to tap into Big Folks' mindset. Years ago, when I had been in the life myself, Vice Lords had made a move on me at my granny's place, where I was staying at the time. I'm not sure how I'd have responded to someone like me, a violence interrupter, but I can tell you that when I got the slightest hint where I might be able to catch up with them, I would have taken it.

I'd been fueled by rage to find anyone responsible. While Big Folks didn't come under attack at home, he would still feel that residual threat. That dogged fear of vulnerability could only be put to rest by taking action. For us, without knowing who came at me, it was setting up defenses around the house and going out searching for someone responsible. For Big Folks, who was holding back while I tried to get to the bottom of the events, sitting in a basement with his homies playing video games wasn't enough to restore a sense of control.

"Call D-Boy, see if he checked in with any of the guys," I tell Lil' B as I crank the ignition.

If I were in his headspace, the way I used to think myself in these situations, I would cruise into Vice Lords' territory. I would make it as though I am joyriding and pop up at a clubhouse, a favorite spot, a restaurant, or a gas station. Act as if I were just picking up a meal or filling my tank, while really, I was making myself out to be a decoy, ready to come under attack, leaving me with the only option but to defend myself.

I reasoned Big Folks might head to the gas station where I had first caught up with Zo, JB, and the guys. He knew they might be there, and he could save face with me by claiming that he was just coming through to fill the tank when the guys came at him. The more I thought on the scenario, the more I thought that might be what was happening.

"Any word?" I asked Lil' B in his attempts to get up with D-Boy.

Lil' B shook his head. "Nah. Straight to voice mail."

I nodded, further entertaining my hunch. I reasoned it wouldn't make much sense to ride over there with Lil' B in tow. If I was right, I was actively putting him in harm's way by heading over there with him. If I was wrong, I'd still be putting him in a potentially dangerous situation, not to mention testing the Vice Lords crew, who just gave me their word to let it go. How would it look if I came rolling through with their opposition as if I were saying, *"Hey y'all, just testing to see if you would hold up your end of the bargain."*

"Try someone else, Big A, maybe, or if you can get up with Lil' Guy, just check," I encourage Lil' B while maneuvering out of the parking space into the street.

My hope is Lil' B can sync up with one of them first. I text Hot Rod to see where he is at, considering he might be able to head over to the gas station himself to check. I also let Big Fella know what is happening. If he can get up with China Joe or anyone plugged in with the Vice Lords, maybe they can use their influence to temporarily get them off the street. Even having one of our guys take them out to lunch would provide some temporary cover. Once again, all we are doing is trying to buy some time.

If an opportunity presents itself, it seems likely Big Folks will take it—even if he is going to manufacture that opportunity himself. Anyone going through a shift in mindset—kicking a bad habit, say smoking, or trying to learn a new skill—goes back and forth in their thinking between states of being. In this sense, Big Folks' situation is not unique to him—he could be any of us, really.

Outreach workers, violence interrupters, conflict mediators, and other community violence intervention experts throughout the country practice motivational interviewing techniques to help people resolve ambivalence about behavior change.[1] At this point in my career, I've trained well over a thousand workers on using these methods. Back then, on the front line of these mediations, I practiced it nearly a dozen times a day. As a social worker, I've also spent a lot of time understanding the mechanisms behind the method and how it works in Big Folks' mind to help him turn a corner.

The approach started in the 1980s as substance abuse recovery.[2] Therapists found that the more they pushed their clients to make a change, the more they resisted. They might make a little progress but then back off all the way or have a setback and just relapse entirely. I'd seen it happen with my mom and other substance users. Friends who had addictions over the years. If they were pushed from the outside, someone using external force, a minor slip-up could lead to a major relapse.

Motivational interviewing tries the opposite approach, creating space to help patients find ways to change themselves. Basically, work alongside them, presenting information and opportunities to resolve any ambivalence.

After the approach had initial successes with addiction recovery, it began to get applied to other areas of behavior change—medication adherence, weight loss, diabetes care, health behavior (exercise, diet)—with amazing success. It worked by increasing a person's motivation for change, hence the name, while leveraging their commitment to it.

In community violence intervention, we began to apply it on the street to prevent homicide. The field has a hard time thinking of violence as behavior. It is so weighed down by the ethical, social, theological, and cultural elements that understanding violence as a pattern of social programming threatens our understanding of humanity. As a result, there has been some resistance to the idea that using mental health techniques, especially at the street level, might have any success.

Also, I think the model itself seems counterintuitive. I hear all the time from detractors debating this work: *"What are you going to do?"* An academic criminologist might front on a panel about deterrence and prevention: *"Ask a Latin King not to shoot someone?"* And the answer is *"Yes."* We will ask them not to shoot and kill someone, but it is obviously so much more complicated than that.

Eddie Bocanegra, who appeared with me in the documentary *The Interrupters*, went on to earn his master's degree in social work, policy, and practice from the University of Chicago and introduced cognitive behavioral therapy as a method for behavior change alongside motivational interviewing.

Eddie grew up in Chicago's Little Village neighborhood and worked at CeaseFire at the same time as me. He has gone on to be the executive director of a number of youth violence prevention programs over the past decade and a half, eventually becoming a senior adviser in the Office of the Assistant Attorney General to oversee community violence prevention, even guiding the White House policy on community gun violence reduction.

READI Chicago, an innovative violence interruption model that Eddie helped create after CeaseFire, takes the mental health intervention even further. READI Chicago, which has since grown into a national model, has been highly successful at connecting young men at high risk of experiencing violence with mental health support, paid transitional jobs, professional development opportunities, and other services. Their efforts build off the motivational interviewing approach to use a broader range of mental health tools, including cognitive behavioral therapy. According to early results from a randomized controlled trial, READI has been shown to significantly reduce arrests for shootings and homicides.

Youth Guidance, also based out of Chicago, developed the BAM program, which stands for Becoming A Man, as a school-based counseling program for young men from seventh to twelfth grade. It operates by teaching participants to internalize and practice social cognitive skills. Mikey Davis, my mentee, who also appeared in *The Interrupters* documentary and worked alongside me at Cure Violence, ran youth groups for the program.

Today, he is focused on bringing these techniques for impulse control, emotional self-regulation, social cue recognition, and interpreting others' intentions into street-based work to teach guys on the corner a similar mental health model.

Lil' B and I return to his homie's place, where I first scooped him up. He has rung through his guys only to end up in voice mail. Big Fella confirms that China Joe can get some of the guys—JB and Brian—temporarily off the street. I am thinking on next steps as we round the corner and see Big Folks on the stoop with his guys.

It is Big A with him out front as we roll up.

"We got to worrying you'd gone after them yourself," Lil' B says, leaning from the window as we pull up.

"Y'all get to worrying too much," he responded.

"When your girl said you took her car, we didn't know what to think."

"When you talk to my girl?"

I parked the car, and we made our way up the walk. I came around the front bumper from the driver's side and up the curb across the lawn.

"We stopped by earlier looking for you." Lil' B jabbed a thumb back at me as I reached the sidewalk in front of the stairs. "Cobe learned some things, is why."

"Whatchu learn?" Big A asks.

"Whole thing has been a misunderstanding," I say with a clap. "They were thinking you were someone else."

"Course they saying that now when they been busted out."

"You hear anything about a robbery?" I ask.

"Yeah, it's the robbery got me," Lil' B says to back me up. "I was on the fence with what's what, but you remember a while back how one of our shorties was robbed in the neighborhood by dude, who I think stay out in the burbs, but we couldn't get up with him?"

"Okay," Big Folks say flatly, "what that got to do with this? They the ones that rob him?"

"No. No," Lil' B responds. "One of their guys got robbed, too, is the thing. A bit later."

"They thought it was you," I added.

Big Folks runs his hand across his chin, down the front of his neck. "So, lemme get this straight, some guy from the burbs been sticking up both our guys, 'cept they don't know that. So, when they hear one of their guys got held up around our place, they figure they blame is on us—and that is why they come through this morning?"

By now, his hand has run a course from chin to chest, where he pauses and thumps his fingers a digit at a time.

"That's what's up," I say.

Silence. Slow nods from Big A. Lil' B leans all the way up the stairs along the rail, holding his weight against it, suspending himself over the stairs. It is the kind of fidgeting around my kids used to do when they were younger and had to wait in line for something. Burning off nervous energy. Big

Folks himself stays stoic. It is a default setting that he doesn't let show what is on his mind. I can see the wheels turning but can't really make out the direction.

"So, you're gonna tell me we should let it drop?" Big Folks levels with a point in my direction. "Since it's a case of mistaken identity, we just gonna let bygones be bygones? Ain't worth pursuing?"

"They still did what they did," Big A reasons, backing Big Folks. "Seems something should come back on them for that."

"Nobody was hurt though," Lil' B notes. "Just saying."

"And it was all over a robbery that y'all may have been victims of anyway," I tell them. "I met with the guys who came through this morning, settled up any outstanding debt, encouraged them to drop it."

"How much?"

"What's that?"

"How much they taken for in the first place?"

"Shorty was robbed for $50."

"Daaaamn, they came through like that over $50? I figure each of us is worth at least $500."

"I think it was more the principle of the matter," I clarify, "and I imagine you'd probably have done the same if you were in that position."

"Facts," Big A exclaims. "Shit, I might pop a motherfucker for $5 if he catches me on a bad day."

"So, you think you can leave this alone?" I ask.

"What about the robber?" Big Folks asks.

"You think you can let it alone with the guys in the Caprice first?"

Big Folks is silent, but after a long pause and a deep breath, he nods his head once.

"I suppose I can let this shit go," he responds.

"See, we are all becoming bigger people," Lil' B replies, pushing himself off the railing and back to standing. "Now, what you think about dude in the Timberlands?"

It stings for a moment that Lil' B, who has been backing up my plays all day, circles back to the loose end first. It is probably because he has been backing my plays that he feels he has to bring it up again. I get it.

"Y'all know what I am thinking," I laugh. "How about you tell me what's your mind, huh?"

"I'm saying if we catch dude, we going to have to put him on notice."

"He shouldn't be robbing around here," Big A adds.

"At least not our guys, yeah?" Lil' B says. "At least not without giving us a cut."

We laugh, but Big Folks holds back his opinion. I press in and needle him a bit.

"How about you, Big Folks?" I ask. "This guy even worth it?"

He weighs his response a beat before he speaks, same as before, knowing the weight of his words. His hand runs back under his chin.

"We see him, we gonna fuck him up," he says with a shrug, "but I don't see it makes much sense to kill a motherfucker behind a few bucks."

I nod. At least he wasn't going to "kill the motherfucker." Progress. Slowly. One mediation at a time. We all shake hands.

I pop for lunch. We break bread. The room feels like a collective sigh of relief, though that shared exhale goes largely unnoted. We talk about life, things in general, and things in the neighborhood. Share a few laughs. The only violence is on the video game play in the corner as Big A and Lil' Guy move through missions in a digital war zone.

This whole thing would have gone down differently if it were the police running it. Big Folks' crew would have been out on the curb, like they perps for taking fire. They might've even been put on their knees and zip-tied. For sure, their names would've been run. If they got a ping on some outstanding warrant, it'd be cause to run one of the guys in.

Or, as I've seen happen a hundred times or more, they figure Lil' Guy, D-Boy, or Lil' B as a possible suspect in something else. It don't matter if this thing—say, a home invasion, carjacking, stickup, or what have you—happened a couple days earlier is real or imagined, they figure our guys for it. They scoop 'em up, one or all, bringing them down to the station for questioning over some incident or another. And, remember, this is all because they themselves were taking fire.

I recognize I am trafficking in hypotheticals saying all this about what might've happened, but this is how it went down for me years ago.

In this instance, police chalk that up as a win. They respond to a shooting, and maybe they put a possession charge on Lil' Guy and an outstanding warrant on Big Folks. They figure D-Boy as someone who knocked over a fast-food joint a few weeks back, never mind, he wasn't there. So, on paper, how it looks is that they responded to a shooting and arrested three bad guys.

Ain't that cause for celebration? Forget they don't have a lead on the shooters and ain't doing nothing to resolve the matter at hand. There is no unpacking the issues that led up to it, no effort made to resolve the matter one way or the other and put it to rest. Misunderstanding, miscommunication, and misinformation amplify into full-scale war, leaving a trail of bodies behind it.

In this scenario, let's say Lil' Guy, Big Folks, and D-Boy have all been rounded up with Big A, Lil' B, and T still on the streets, forming up a hunting party as nearly transpired in the real world. They head on out in search of the Caprice and maybe catch up with the Vice Lords at the very same gas station where we met up. JB, Zo, Brian, and the crew, blazing like they were, high on adrenaline and weed, kicking by their parked car out back, suddenly dodging bullets as our guys pull through.

Now, one of the Vice Lords lay dead, another in critical condition in this hypothetical, so, of course, they will have to come back on them hard, right? It just keeps going around like that.

One of the challenges I always encounter setting up shop in a new city is trying to demonstrate a homicide that didn't happen. Sure, we can point to statistical models that show reductions in shootings and killings in service areas. Community violence intervention programs have reduced violence by up to 60 percent in communities where they have been implemented properly.[3] Cure Violence Global measured significant reductions in shootings, killings, and retaliatory homicides with twenty-two scientific studies, reports, and evaluations in fifteen cities worldwide, as much as a 90 percent drop in violence.[4] READI, which is now a national model, showed a 33 percent overall reduction in shootings and homicides and 79 percent fewer arrests in Chicago through a randomized controlled study, which is the gold standard of research.[5] Youth in the Choose to Change program have 48 percent fewer arrests for violent crimes than their nonparticipant peers, also in Chicago.[6] In Los Angeles, the Gang Reduction and Youth Development program from 2011 to 2016 had 58 percent of participants seeing such a significant reduction in risk level that they were no longer eligible for services.[7] I could go on and on, but my point is that these models work.

This is what it looks like in action, and all these guys I been talking about—Lil' Guy, Big Folks, D-Boy, Big A, Lil' B, T, JB, Zo, Brian, and so on—are alive because of community violence intervention programs like this one throughout the country. That is the real talk behind the stats, data, and percentage drops. That is what it looks like for a homicide not to happen.

When the "defund" argument comes around, stories start making the rounds that Black people want local police presence. They'll point to Black communities and say, "See, citizens want us there. It is only the criminals that want us out." Elderly women in floral print Sunday dresses and straw hats with pastel-colored ribbons and lace will be paraded out to argue for training and reform of police rather than overhauling the system. I get it.

Jumaane D. Williams, a former New York City Council member, political organizer, and activist who worked to create a citywide gun violence task force in 2010, is quick to point out that, of course, ordinary citizens fearing for their safety are going to say that if they aren't presented with any alternative. If they don't know about community violence intervention work or violence prevention strategies in general, mental health or social work options, or alternate solutions and if that is the only option on the table for keeping you safe, they will take it. This is a false choice, though, because people aren't being given all the facts.

And, here, I am just talking about police playing the game the way it is designed to be played. I am talking about them actually performing their duties as assigned and playing things mostly by the book, but that isn't how it actually plays out in real life. I have experienced firsthand how police can instigate and antagonize both sides in a situation like this one. Officers throwing gasoline on a fire already raging might let slip when they got Big Folks and crew seated on the curb that they know where the Vice Lords are heading. I'm talking cops who literally put it in their ear where opposition can be found.

This happened to me more than once when I was coming up. Police even put me and C-Man in the back of the squad to drive us over into rival territory. In this instance, it be like they threatening Lil' B and D-Boy with arrest, but when they throw them in the back of the car, they cruise on to where JB and Zo hanging and drop them off unarmed. I mean, literally, a curbside delivery, as they throw them out of the car gift wrapped in enemy territory.

That's how they did me.

14

ESCALATIONS

Auburn Gresham/Englewood, Chicago, 1990–1994

Vice Lords had just taken a shot at me out front of this very house. Whoever was responsible had gone into hiding, but that hadn't kept us from regular skirmishes. We were into it now. The machine-gun fire was the opening declaration of all-out war. Every day, it seemed we'd go hunting them or be on the defensive, expecting them to come back through after us. The fact that no one, in particular, had laid claim to the attempt on my life meant that they were likely plotting another move.

In the meantime, we were still clashing regularly with the opposition. Gangster Disciples, Stones, and Black Disciples had spent my lifetime organizing ourselves, growing our numbers, swallowing up whole sections of the neighborhood, and bringing up under our banner every smaller clique and faction. We three were the archetype of the contemporary gang dividing up the city. The war we seemed to be preparing for most of my life was kicking off.

It felt like the walls were closing in constantly. I'm not claustrophobic, but it did seem that the spaces we moved in were getting more and more constricted. Everything narrowing around us. Tighter and tighter constraints. We were all feeling that way.

My movements felt like walking across freshly laid asphalt in the summertime. Every step sticky over the surface, giving your feet a little drag. As kids, we used to do it on a dare, betting one another to make it across the street. Hot tar melting your heels. You'd have to be careful not to lift your foot completely, or it would slip right out of the shoe. Orphaned sneakers on some hot, slick surface between lanes, glossed in heat vapors, a landmark of my childhood.

On top of this, my gang, Black Disciples, which I had been loyal to my entire life, was now experiencing friction internally. Our structure was beginning to fray. Factions pit against factions in a civil war that created another level of threat we hadn't anticipated.

Now, police started coming down on us harder than the opposition.

A couple of uniforms showed up at the game room. I was hanging out front with some of my guys just messing around. I was strapped and didn't want to get caught up on a weapon's charge, so I fled.

"Yo, come here!" one of the cops said. "I want to talk to you."

I broke off and raced inside. My guys formed a human shield to slow them down a bit while I scrambled through the crowd toward the back. I could hear footfalls from their polished leather shoes behind me. They made it past my guys. Now, we're moving through the bustle inside. The crackle of static on their microphones let me know they were just a step or two away from me, but they kept pace. Close behind.

When I reached the back room, I removed my piece and stashed it up under the couch we kept back there. I'd done this same maneuver before, stuffing the weapon into the underpart of the sofa, where the fabric had already come away from the rest of the material. I heard the whisk of those polyester slacks coming down the hall a few moments later.

"Goddammit!" the burlier of the pair growled. "You didn't hear me or something."

I kept my tongue but itched to spit back *I heard you just fine.*

"What you running for, Cobe?" snarled the lanky cop, coming up behind his partner.

"Y'all, motherfuckers get against the wall!" Burly howled to the room and then to his partner. "Toss the place."

Lanky nodded, pulling back seat cushions on the recliner. They checked a table we kept back there. Opened cabinets and rifled through drawers. Lanky tossed furniture and eventually thrashed the couch, peeled it back, and found the gap in the fabric. It was only a minute later that they found my piece.

"What do we have here?" Lanky asked.

"That looks like a firearm, which I'm betting ain't licensed," Burly said.

"Looks like the registration even been filed off here."

"You file off the registration, Cobe?"

I remained tight-lipped without so much as a nod. I stayed facing the wall, silent. They patted down the guys and came through, trashing the place. Even after they had the piece, they radioed more cops. Police had probable cause now, and they wouldn't let it go to waste.

"We got you on possession now."

"Ain't shit you can do."

Burly slapped the cuffs on me and yanked me around by the chain, laughing. He hauled me over to the center of the room and spun me to face him. I was looking into his eyes. He wore a snarl, like a pit gnawing at a bone. In an instant, he cocked his head to the side as if he were studying me. Again, not unlike a dog. His snarl dropped to a grimace.

Then, he threw a jab, smashing my nose. It was a flash of white-hot pain as my head rocked back. As soon as his fist collided, I could feel a break in the cartilage. The sensation, what I imagine scalding knitting needles, jammed up each nostril. My nose burst like a garden tomato hurled against concrete.

They waited until they had me in cuffs, arms behind my back, restrained before they threw a punch. Blood was running down my face and over my chin. The front of my shirt was covered. I couldn't even pinch the bridge to cut off the flow. The police looked on and laughed, then they perp-walked me out of the place like I was a trophy.

And they called us thugs.

Police had what they would consider a "clean arrest," at least how it would appear on paper, so I was pretty confident they'd just run me down to the station. I didn't think there would be any detours into GD's hood or that I'd be taking any more blows, hands cuffed behind my back, unable to defend myself. The possibility always existed, of course, but it seemed more likely they'd just read me my Miranda and take me in.

Grams and Auntie Shirley came to bail me out later. Auntie Shirley, hands on her hips, drew a breath, about to launch into a signature lecture.

"I don't know what kind of nonsense you're getting into out there, but," she began strong, but when she saw my face, still a bit bloodied, and my shirt stained, her speech tapered off and ended sharply. "Boy, what did they do to you?" she asked. Her tone softened to a hush.

My eyes were swollen and puffy, both blackened from the break. I could feel a knob on the bridge of my nose that wasn't supposed to be there. The shape of my face felt different. There was a purple discoloration on each of my cheeks.

"What happened, Cardy?" Granny asked, reaching out to hug me as she touched at the bruises with her fingertips. I winced a bit, but it didn't show.

"He got into it with some guys in lockup," the desk sergeant snapped. "Came in hotheaded, swinging on some of these guys. Ain't that right, Ricardo?"

I didn't say nothing in response, staying silent until we were back in the car. Even then, I didn't want to talk about my injuries. I was more interested in showing gratitude for Granny and my family. I was happy they'd bailed me out, and I wanted to get my version of events on the only record that mattered.

I was still that nine-year-old at heart, wanting Gram's approval, hating like hell I'd disappointed her.

"Cardy," Granny said sternly, addressing me by her pet name. "We won't keep going around like this again and again. I'll get you out this time, but if anything happens again, I'm going to have to leave you behind bars."

She made eye contact in the rearview to let me know she was serious. Her gaze looked hurt and severe at the same time.

I caught my first case a short while later.

Ty, Sadar, and I were pitching quarters on the corner with a few guys from the neighborhood. There were six of us in total, lined up just in front of a brick wall, standing off the curb facing it. How the game is played, each of us takes a turn tossing a quarter at the wall from the same fixed distance. We anted up real money in a small pot set beneath a brick. It wasn't just we were playing for change. The objective is to pitch the coins as close as possible to the wall to win the pot.

I pitched by putting a little spin on the quarter like a tiny Frisbee. Pinched between my fingers, pointer, and thumb, I squeezed the coin. Hold the position steady. Then snap my digits—pop!—like keeping a rhythm, flinging the quarter. It would sail through the air with a zing, plunk off the concrete, landing just in front of my neighbor's change. Tail side up. A fraction of an inch shy of where I'd landed.

It was mostly friendly. I was talking shit at full volume, as I do. "You don't fuck with the King!," but there was the usual spot of tension that comes when all the money and luck seem to flow in one direction. Mostly, everybody kept it light. Laughing even through gritted teeth.

"Bro. Bro." Dude came up the block looking rocked and ratty with glazed eyes and a fist full of bills. "Y'all holding?"

I waved him off.

"Don't be like that, my man. I got money."

Our distribution had gone out already. We were big enough that our crews put the work in on our behalf. We didn't have to hold our own to keep the product circulating.

"Man, I'm just looking to score," Dude said, bug-eyed and desperate.

He held out a wad of cash. Hands outstretched and grasping. Glassy gaze wavering over each one of us to the next, like he'd gotten lost on the way over and needed one of us to point him to the bus.

"I'll take this fool's money," my guy quipped, scooping the whole stack of bills from his hand and pocketing them.

"Oh, man. Oh, man. Oh, man." Dude moaned, his whole body back and forth. "Don't be like that, man."

"Get the fuck out of here," my guy urged, waving him off now.

"You got my money, though."

"We're in the middle of something here, motherfucker. Get gone."

Dude seemed to suddenly come aware that he was out of money. He started pushing at us, growing panicked.

"Oh, man. Oh, man. Oh, man."

"Get outta here, or we're going to fuck you up," my guy threatened.

What was done was done. This Dude coming around waving money like that was begging to be robbed. That was our logic in the day.

Dude lunges aggressively.

My guy steps out of the way and swings a bottle. It smashes across his face. Shattering upside his head and claiming an eye. Insanity ensues. Dude ups a pistol. Now almost completely blinded by broken glass, stumbling. Tears of blood streamed down his contorted face. One hand slapped over his vision, trying to staunch the blood flow, while the other hand whipped the gun around randomly.

Then, Dude started firing. Busted off a round that ricocheted off the wall we were playing quarters against.

Blam. Blam. Blam.

Dude fires again through a window. A second bullet goes astray. A third hits a tree.

It turned out Dude was a cop. A drug addict with a badge looking to score, but a cop nonetheless. We were all rounded up on that one. Police claimed that he was an undercover narc looking to build a case. They insisted the whole thing was a drug bust that went sideways. Despite all of these claims, they never pressed charges. They knew how it looked. A druggie cop up to no good, so to avoid the bad PR that was sure to follow, they let me get bonded out. They didn't want to go to trial. The case was dropped.

TRANSITIONS

The girl Sadar had been messing with had gotten pregnant. Amid every-thing that was happening, it put a lot on his mind. He was reevaluating his life, beginning with the fact that he'd have to sneak across town just to see her since she lived in enemy territory. Even that, on the face of it, seemed crazy. Not that he had to put himself in harm's way to be with this girl, but that there was even a harm's way in the first place was madness. This whole world we had grown up in wasn't making sense anymore.

"I always promised myself that when I had a kid—when I became a father—I couldn't be in this anymore," Sadar said, measuring his words carefully as he spoke. "I don't think you can be a dad and be out in the streets gangbanging."

We were in the clubhouse chatting. It was the three of us occupying this space. Sadar was on his feet, wringing his hands and pacing. Ty, on the couch, set forward and upright. I was closer to the door, moving about but tuned in, listening.

"What are you saying?" I asked, turning toward him.

Ty just tsked. He was seated on the couch and gestured to Sadar to grab the recliner across from him.

"I'm out of here, man," Sadar responded. "I have to be."

The entire time his girl was pregnant, a child growing in that belly, these notions of getting away were taking root. Every night, hunting parties. Ev-erywhere we went, we were on our guard. That fine line between paranoia and precautions started to erode, one bleeding into the other until you are an exposed nerve end, frayed, raw, and explosive to the touch.

Now, this child left him feeling he had no choice.

Sadar hadn't come up as a Black Disciple the same way Ty, G-Free, C-Man, and I had. He was not bonded to the BD initially. His father was a gambler, a grifter, and a pool shark. He'd been in debt throughout Sadar's childhood, always trying to get one over or to just get by but not really mak-ing anything of himself. For most of Sadar's formative years, his father had been behind bars for shooting a cop in a botched robbery. At that time, he knew his dad only through stories and passing impressions. He was deter-mined not to be that kind of dad.

Sadar would be the first to tell you he was drawn to power. Throughout childhood, Dad told the story of the time he had been on an elevator with the King of Kings, David Barksdale, founding father of the BD, who passed his reign to King Shorty. Through a series of misunderstandings, as Sadar's old man put it, he had somehow found himself in possession of stolen goods that belonged to Barksdale.

It was not a good position. Others had been killed for less. In his old man's telling, Barksdale boarded the elevator, flanked by some twenty soldiers all lined up. He could do whatever he wanted at that moment. No one would say a thing so much as blink.

That day, Barksdale showed grace. He let him go with a warning.

Sadar had heard this story a hundred times growing up. It was one of the few things he'd gotten from his father. The takeaway was clear. Don't be like him; be the one with the power. It had driven most of Sadar's decisions until that point.

When he formally joined, it had been in response to seeing that power on display. He had become a member of this family. Not in some abstract sense of brotherhood but adopted and fully embraced kin.

Now, he was walking away from that.

"And, go where?" Ty asked.

"I don't know," he responded. "I can't be putting my life in jeopardy no more, though. I'm out here. I'm thinking of her."

"That's just where you don't want to be," Ty answered.

"Anywhere but here," Sadar retorted.

Ty let go a tsk again.

Ty had gone to the hospital to pick up Sadar after baby girl was born. He pulled into the receiving bay as an orderly wheeled out Sadar's girlfriend, swaddling the child in a bundle, swathed. Sadar let mom and daughter into the backseat and came around to climb in on the passenger side.

In the dark interior, Ty swiveled to see Mama and baby girl. "Let me see," he instructed, flipping on the dome light. Everything went illuminated. Ty took in the scene, then came slowly back to look at Sadar, nodded, and flicked the light off without a word. He didn't say a word of congrats or well wishes. They just drove on to Sadar's place in silence.

Ty hung his head and shook it. Staring some time at his hands. Sadar made his way around the side of the recliner and situated himself in it, up close, appealing.

"It's got to be this way," Sadar said. "I'm thinking Vegas. I don't have a record, so I can get a straight job. Might even make a go at being a pro boxer."

"That's the way it's got to be?" Ty said, questioning.

"I got to be looking out for my family, bro."

"She ain't yours, though," Ty replied coldly.

It was an emotional gut punch. Sadar winced when he heard it. He'd had enough time to do the math and knew the baby girl wasn't his biologically. He knew for some time the truth Ty was speaking aloud. It didn't matter. When he saw that child, she was a little angel, who he needed as much as—if not more than—she needed him.

Sadar let out a sigh as if he were deflating. He got to his feet and walked out, leaving a short time later for Vegas.

15

HOW THIS COULD'VE PLAYED OUT, PART II

Englewood, Chicago, July 2015

Timberland, the stickup man, had an uncle who stayed in the neighborhood. Lil' B put me in tune with him on the DL. He didn't want to advertise that he knew where Timberland stayed when he was in the city. Just in case anyone in the crew had a change of heart about leaving him alive after a string of robberies got BD and Vice Lords alike—that almost got his guys shot this morning—Lil' B thought it best to keep that knowledge under wraps.

Hot Rod checked in from back at the office for an update. He had Timberland's given name and some details about the situation. Timberland was a free agent, so it didn't matter who he knocked over as long as he kept it moving. He bounced between the city and relatives out in the southwest suburbs with frequency. Until now, no one had really been able to get a fix on his identity.

I gave Hot Rod an update as well on how things were left with Big Folks and the guys. Lil' B, in particular, had been helpful in sorting out the mess, which I made known. In many ways, that was more a display of norm change in action than almost anything that transpired throughout the day. Lil' B was doing his part, making contributions to resolve the conflict without violence. That in itself was remarkable.

"I'm down if you want me to go with and check up on them later this week," Hot Rod said.

"I think it be good to keep tabs on them a little while," I responded. "I don't think anything will flare up again, but it would be good to stay in the mix."

"Keep on the pulse," Hot Rod affirms. "At least with Big Folks."

"Right," I respond. "And Joe is working with Zo, JB, and the guys."

"Great."

I reached the uncle's house and signed off with Hot Rod as I headed toward the door. Through the glossy side window, I could see him coming up the hall. He was an old-timer with a ring of gray hair around his bald head and a bit of a shuffle to his step. I didn't suspect he had a clue.

He seemed a bit confused to see me when he answered the door.

"I help you?" he asks, almost in accusation.

I reach out to shake his hand, introducing myself.

"I'm Cobe, an interrupter with CeaseFire. How you doing?"

Old-Timer nods his head as if that is a response to the question. He pauses a moment, but before I can continue in the silence, he says, "What do you need?"

"You got a nephew stay here sometimes?" I ask.

"Sister's kid."

I say Timberland's name.

Old-Timer gives me another nod.

"He's in a bit of trouble," I tell him.

Old-Timer nods.

"It seems like some people figure him for ripping them off," I say, trying to let Timberland save a little face with his uncle on account I don't have much proof and I am not fixing to get any. My entire goal is to warn Timberland off of the area, for a while at minimum, or indefinitely. It isn't my place to make judgments or accuse anybody of anything, but I am trying to keep him safe.

"Okay."

"So, might be good for both of you if he stays in the burbs for a while."

I get another nod.

We both stand silent a moment.

"You think he do this thing?" Old-Timer asks.

"I do."

"He in danger 'cause of it?"

"He is."

"Best he stay away—how long?"

"Tough to say."

"If you had to guess."

"Forever."

"Yeah," Old-Timer responds, looking heartbroken. He gives a long, slow nod. "Okay."

I shake his hand again. "Thanks."

"He's my sister's kid," Old-Timer says. "He been pretty messed up about a year now. He saw his friend killed. I think it put him on the wrong path. We try with church and stuff to make things right, but he got to work through some things himself."

To be a stickup man on your own is a certain kind of reckless. Even if you do spend most of your time outside the neighborhood, you are taking some pretty extreme risks in self-imposed isolation. Nobody got your back. Everybody is out to get you because you are into it with everybody. It is a suicidal lifestyle.

It was my turn to nod.

I fish out a card from my pocket and hand it over. "You can have him call me. Maybe we can get him some help." I am not expecting a call, but I hope Timberland steers clear of the neighborhood and gets the help he needs.

If he rings me, I might get him assigned to an outreach worker, refer him to a social worker, or try to coordinate support.

Old-Timer and I part ways on the porch.

Addressing violence in this way, before it breaks out, changes things not only at the street level but everywhere. It resonates throughout the community, the courts, social services, and the prison system.

We often say one bullet can shatter a community. You see families torn apart over grief and loss. Children raised without a parent. Parents mourning the loss of a son. A presence suddenly becomes an absence, like a cancer grows, among those left behind. Dark spots expand. A deep well of violent emptiness situated in the middle of lives and lifetimes. That loss casts a shadow over everything that follows.

In response, a retaliation, just one, let's say, a second bullet amplifies this pain. The loss, the darkness, the grief, the grieving, the mourning, the emptiness. The absence expands. Shooter gets rounded up and sent behind bars. Now, his life, too, shattered. His people mourn. He won't be able to come out from under this thing he did. It affects his life, lifetime, and livelihood for the rest of his days.

Expand that out to the community. Held down by trauma. Unable to elevate itself out of this suffocating spiral. Shops that have to shutter early. Investments that don't take. Businesses that can't flourish. Property decreases in value. Everything spun down, down, down as if circling a drain. This stretches out across neighborhoods over generations.

Trauma and violence activate a downward spiral that swallows up lives and lifetimes, individuals and families, and entire neighborhoods in the fallout of a single event, but I believe the opposite is true, too.

One direction's spiral is another's cascade, rather than vanishing, expanding ever outward. Conflict mediation can transform the whole system. A chain reaction that affirms instead of destroys. Mediators, interrupters, mental health providers, crisis responders, social workers instead of beat cops, uniforms, SWAT teams, and detectives. Researchers talk about the justice ecosystem, which encompasses school systems, social services, housing, health care, reentry services, job training, and support.

We need to think of the underlying factors that create and contribute to violence.

16

A SHOOT-OUT AND A FRAME-UP

Auburn Gresham/Englewood, Chicago, 1994–2000

When the staccato rat-tat-tat rang out into the quiet summer evening in front of Granny's house, it set in motion a number of events. Some took years to unfold. While the shooter who attempted to assassinate me had gone into hiding, our clashes with Vice Lords escalated. We were already into it, but now a day didn't pass without some kind of skirmish. It got so you couldn't even pull to a traffic light without fear of getting shot by the car next to you.

Even everyday activities had an ominous tone. It didn't matter if you were going to the mall, getting groceries, hanging with your boys, or heading to the club, you had to look over your shoulder for whatever was coming at you next.

On top of this, my run-ins with the law were becoming more frequent. They often had less to do with my activities than my reputation. Police were already fixing to put something on me; whether or not it was a crime I actually committed was just a matter of timing.

After the shooting incident with the cop, I stopped carrying a piece. I was facing charges now, so having a weapon gave me too much heat. The few weeks I was going around without a gun made me feel exposed, but I was already being scooped on the regular and refused to give them anything to go on.

It was a hot summer day. We'd just picked up flavored ice from a corner store and were making our way down Racine. Trying to stay cool. Another group was coming from the other direction, staggered on the opposite side of the street, about a block or so down. They seemed an equal number to us, just messing around.

I don't remember if we made them first or vice versa. There are specific details emblazoned in my mind, as vivid as anything happening right in front of me. Sun-drenched rooftop on a parked sedan, dark maroon in color, refracting light as if it were the strobe-bulb pop of a camera, blinding white. Blue cherry flavoring of the ice cone wrapped in waxy paper, sticky, sweet, and cold to the touch. The fact that I was a couple of steps, a sidewalk square and a half, from the momentary shade of a tree, which I was looking forward to as temporary relief from the heat.

One group upped their pistols. I couldn't tell you who. Someone pulled a trigger. Someone fired back. I recall seeing the glint of sunlight reflecting on the metal of the gun as it was pulled, flash, then the muzzle burst in orange, like the wheel in a Bic, trying to strike the flint without flame. Next thing we knew, we were in a firefight.

Vice Lords were shooting; my guys were returning fire. We were firing; Vice Lords were shooting back. I don't know. Some details I can see in my mind exactly as they transpired. Others are impossible to recollect like an old-fashioned videotape used one too many times, images layered over images, smeared by static.

We ducked behind the parked cars, hugging the side of the road. Glass shattered around us and rained down. We hustled toward the corner, staying low under cover. A bullet clipped the brake light of a Dodge Ram just beside a bumper where my head was tucked. Red plastic shards shower across a bright green patch of lawn.

I can tell you for sure that I wasn't strapped.

A couple of the Vice Lords broke from their group, rushing out ahead into the middle of the street. They were closing the gap between us quickly. I gave up on the corner, scrambling for cover in a nearby alleyway. The five of us were spread out along the block on the west side of the street—half of us pinned down a little way up the block and the other half trying to make it into the temporary safety of the alley.

In equal numbers, they had about half their guys in the center of the street along the median strip in broad daylight blasting away. Then, about half a block behind or so, the other half of their ranks came up on the east side of the street.

This positioning is important for what happened next—and, as much so, what didn't.

A Vice Lord in pursuit, in the middle of the street, catches a bullet in the backside. They drop right there. There is no way that it could have been one of my guys that did it. They were firing in the opposite direction.

A rearview mirror took a shot and shattered reflective glass. Bullets punctured a door panel and a front tire.

Then the Vice Lord screamed and spilled to the ground. The shooting stopped for an instant, giving the whole group of us a chance to break into the alley at a run. We reached the next block at a steady pace. Putting distance between ourselves and our attackers. We were good, slightly rattled, but overall unharmed.

Police scooped me a little while later to put another attempted murder charge on me.

"You had yourself a pretty eventful day, Mr. Williams," a mustachioed detective grumbled after leaving me in interrogation for hours. I was fidgety, thirsty, and had to piss.

He flipped the pages of his notebook dramatically. "Kid you shot is going to make it, but barely."

He probably figured himself looking like Magnum PI, but he really came off more like Captain Kangaroo.

"I didn't shoot nobody," I responded flatly, folding my hands in front of me, still cuffed at the wrists. They made a jangling clatter against the table.

"We got witnesses, two of them, says you did," replied Kangaroo's short, squat partner.

"Just tell us what happened."

I went through the events from earlier that day. I didn't know the "kid" who "barely" survived had been shot in the ass yet. Even if you had doodled a quick sketch of how the firefight played out, it would have been obvious I couldn't shoot anybody in the back from where we were holed up.

Never mind that I wasn't armed and that we were boxed in.

If they'd gathered the casing or looked at how the event occurred, it would've been pretty clear that Vice Lords shot one of their own, but they came in wanting to put charges on me.

"Let's go over this again," Kangaroo sighed, staring at the pages of the notebook.

"Just tell us who you are into it with to help clear things up."

They leaned pretty hard on me to give up names.

"Come on, they just tried to kill you—why are you protecting them?"

I wasn't about to give them anything, not even the name of the opposition. I'd known who had done the shooting and who it was that got shot, but I wasn't about to tell them. They had me run through everything again in detail.

"That's not how the witnesses say it went down."

"I don't know nothing about no witnesses, but how I say it happened is how it happened," I repeated.

"Nope."

"No."

"Tell us your version of events again."

I repeated my account of the event. When it was pretty clear they weren't going to get me to ID anyone involved, they changed tactics.

"When you saw them coming up the street, you made them from a block away and pulled your gun?" Kangaroo asked.

"I didn't have no gun," I repeated.

"How's it you shot first, then?"

"I didn't say I shot first."

The squat detective nodded.

"We know you did," he said.

"I didn't," I repeated.

Kangaroo sunk into his notebook pages. He flipped through them.

"You knew who they were?" he asked without looking up.

"Not at first," I explained.

"When did you recognize them?"

"I'm not sure I did, not until after the shooting started."

"Who all was there?"

"I couldn't say."

"You can't or you won't."

Kangaroo nodded. "They shot at you, and you returned fire."

"I didn't have no gun."

Around and around like this we went, circling like the hands on the clock until hours passed. The adrenaline flushed from my system at that point. I was starting to feel exhausted. Repeating myself again and again. The frustration I felt took on a kind of friction, eroding me from the inside out. I started to numb to the whole experience—the repetition of it all.

I can understand how false confessions happen. More than a quarter of the 365 people exonerated for crimes in recent decades had initially confessed to their alleged crimes.[1] A combination of psychological pressure and manipulative questioning takes a toll on anyone. Hours of this they actually had me second-guessing my own experiences. I was sitting there thinking, *"Wait. Did I do this thing?"* after a time. I know I hadn't carried for a couple of weeks, but could someone have handed me a gun before this whole thing went down? Did we shoot first?

I felt hazy about the details. A kind of hypnosis follows the lull of repetition. The way they ask the questions has more to do with how they want them answered than any fact-finding. At one point, they started feeding me names to get me to repeat them, but I remained tight-lipped, giving them nothing. It seemed to frustrate the squat detective to no end that I was "protecting" the same guys just trying to kill me over putting my trust in them.

"So, you are saying you were shooting just to defend yourself?"

They plant little details from their version of events into the interrogation. The only way you can get some relief is by answering the same way they asked. There is a certain kind of madness in how it feels.

"I didn't have no gun, though."

"Witnesses saw you with a gun."

"I didn't have no gun."

"Look," I said, finally, ending the interrogation after hours of cycling through details. "I didn't shoot nobody. If you all got witnesses against me, say I did just charge me—or just let me go—but the bottom line is I didn't shoot nobody." I pushed away from the table. "Now, let me call my lawyer."

Police are trained to interrogate in this way.[2] They watch behavior for signals of anxiety or deception. They are studying body language for cues that a suspect isn't making eye contact, or they are slouching away, folding their arms, and so on to determine they are lying. Then, the questions come rapid-fire, focused on the event. This is considered a formal interrogation— they ratchet up the queries—so fast your head starts spinning. They make accusations and dismiss denials. Round and round, it goes. All the while trying to connect with the suspect, looking for an empathetic way in, like they are looking out for you, acting like somehow, they are protecting you.

"You were just trying to defend yourself, though," the squat detective responded. "I can understand that."

"Anybody in that situation would do the same, right? I'd try to protect myself, for sure," Kangaroo said.

On and on like this it went. Police wanted me off the street; this was the way to do it. They never did get a confession from me, but not for lack of trying. In my mind, I was already warping my memory to fit their version of events. Those distortions made a certain kind of sense.

Even after I learned the facts, that the Vice Lords had shot their own from behind, I was still stuck trying to understand how I was in this position. I rationalized that even though I wasn't guilty, there was certainly enough wrongdoing I hadn't been caught up on to justify the charges.

It was a fair trade, I reasoned. I was just being sent up for the wrong thing. This is how I made peace with going away for a crime I didn't commit.

There is an irony to the fact the police had the same logic. Well, we haven't actually gotten him on anything, but we know he's guilty, so we should put him away for this thing he didn't do all the same.

In any case, I was now on my way to prison with two attempted murder charges.

III

PATH TO PEACEKEEPING

17

HISTORY REPEATING ITSELF

Stateville Correctional Center, 1995–2004

My son, Latrell, was three years old when I was sentenced. He was in the courtroom. Guards came to bring me back to holding. My child let out a wail that shattered my heart and flooded the room.

"I want my Daaaaaaaddy!" he howled. "I waaaaaaaaant my Daaaaaaaaddy."

I felt my heart seize with a breath caught in exhale. Tears were burning in my eyes before I even noticed them falling.

"Hold it, officer," the judge said, making eye contact with me from the bench. "Give him a chance to hug his boy, okay?"

It was a rare display of compassion in the system. One that should be a given, not an exception. And, unfortunately, one so rarely afforded. Honestly, for all the talk of reform among police, prosecutors, justice, judges, jail, prison, and probation, the simplest, most human, most humane efforts might have the biggest impacts. I know I've been forever grateful for that moment. I credit that instant as the beginning of my transformation.

The guard didn't say nothing but undid my restraints temporarily. He let me drop down and hug Latrell. The boy buried his face in my shoulder, sobbing.

"Daddy! Daddy! Daddy! Please don't go."

I stood up. Ready to be ushered into the back. My stomach was a swirl of sick. I was Latrell's age around the time my father was sent away to Stateville.

That night, police came to my grandparents' house for my father I was Latrell's size, the living room awash in blue and red, all those years ago. It also sunk in at that moment: here I was, being sent up on my daddy's heels, shipped off to the exact same location.

My boy, even at that young age, had been the spitting image of me. His tiny features were like miniature versions of my own. I met his eyes but didn't dare speak for fear I would come apart. Instead, I hugged him, clinging for life.

Before the age of twenty-two, I would end up serving two charges for drug possession and two charges for aggravated battery.

I dried my eyes with the back of my sleeve and steeled myself. I numbed my emotions as the guard shackled me back up. I knew the PA was piped into the cells in the back broadcasting the episode. Everyone still in waiting, who had either just had their hearing or was waiting on one, would have heard the outburst.

As I was led through the halls into the pen, I was sure they'd all be inspecting me for a show of weakness. Any display of emotion, like blood in shark-infested waters, might whip up a frenzy. I was ready for it. I expected someone to say something.

And I'd kill a motherfucker if they did.

LIFE ON THE INSIDE

Stateville is a max-security men's facility between Chicago and Joliet, nearly fifty miles south and west of Englewood and just under five miles north of Joliet. When I first set foot on the campus, I'd already had years of preparation. Childhood memories of visiting my father were immortalized in pictures around the home. Family visits there were a staple of my formative years.

By the time I was being sent away, I had seen family, friends, and friends of the family rotate between the streets, prison, and back again. The Lounge had more homecoming parties than I could count. This wasn't some shameful secret kept under wraps. Stateville was a likely destination, the way an alma mater is an expected part of a life journey in another family from one generation to the next. Once I'd come of age, it was my friends being sent off. Doing your bit was a rite of passage.

Ty was the first in our crew to serve any real time. He found himself in the wrong place at the wrong time. Ty got locked up for murder. After the shooting incident with the hype posing as an undercover cop, it was only a matter of time before we were all caught up on something.

Behind bars, we fell in together without missing a beat. The first part of my stint overlapped with the last half of his sentence. We served time together for a few years. We got to pitching quarters and playing cards, just the same as we would on the outside.

Our cells were close enough that we could lie on the floor and speak through the vents. I would speak in a whisper, then cock my head to the side and listen with my ear to the ground. Our conversations carried through the dark long after lights out. We spoke for hours between guard rotations. We all passed news through the block that way, discussed what was happening outside these walls. We entertained futures after our release.

The prison was overcrowded from the jump. Throughout its history, it swung between extreme punishment (experiments with twenty-four-hour lockdown) and reform-focus (classes and education), but it was never a picnic. There were bodies packed in against bodies in tight confines with sadistic guards and unsanitary conditions. That was consistent no matter the ideology in place.

Behind these walls, time passes and pauses simultaneously. Inside, life is routine, moving from morning to night. Meals. Rec time. Classes. Letter writing. Bed checks. Lights out. Sleep. Wake. Repeat. If you are doing it right, you keep busy, fitting your own activities in the cracks. A mix of hobbies, habits, games, gambling, reading letters, getting visits to break the monotony.

Outside, life moves quickly. In a way that you only really notice when you are absent from it. In the same way, you realize someone put on a few pounds when you haven't seen them in a while, though you wouldn't notice if you saw them every day. I watched Latrell grow through photographs sent by post. I couldn't stand the idea of someone else raising my son.

Your family grows older, kids grow up, people get married, loved ones pass away, and life moves along without you. You are a ghost haunting the fringes of your own life, just outside the margins. Present and absent, walking through memories you would otherwise share. Between is the cycle of holidays, anniversaries, graduations, weddings, births, birthdays, deaths, and funerals. An empty chair with an empty place setting without you. Monumental life events X-ed out on the calendar. Gray days behind bars. A tally of all the celebrations, meals, and gatherings where you'd otherwise be.

Trice came to visit regularly. Bringing with her the outside world in Pola-roids and magazines. She'd give me care packages and updates. Filling me in on what everyone was up to out there. It provided much-needed warmth and laughter.

Dispatches from the Lounge: an episode where a regular embarrassed himself on the dance floor after too much to drink.

"He dropped to the floor like he thought he was James Brown himself."

"He feels good."

"So, good."

"And, we hear a *rrrrriiiiiipppp*."

"No."

"Yes! And, he's not wearing no drawers."

"No."

"And, he can't get up!"

"From the floor?"

"Yep. Bad knees."

"Can't be doing splits with bad knees."

"Right? So, his guys come over and pick him up off the floor. His ass in these too-tight polyester pants all split down the middle. Everything hang-ing out. They walk him off the floor with Auntie Hilda, the whole time yell-ing, *"Don't you be sitting your bare ass on our chairs!"*

We fall out laughing.

Updates on aunties and uncles. Updates on Mom and Grandma. Updates on nonsense that our brother Boo was getting into in the streets. These up-dates make you feel momentarily part of the world again. Trice named her son, Cobe, after me. She brought me pictures. In between, I scribbled let-ters to Auntie Cookie in Seattle, Granny (of course), family, and friends—anything to keep the words flowing and contact fresh.

In the same way, your time doesn't belong to you; none of your space is your own, either. Your existence is caged in concrete and steel. Six by eight, windowless, soulless, and cramped. Privacy, alien. Can't choose your cellie. Can't shit, shower, or shave in peace. You are under constant surveillance, especially in an institution like Stateville with eyes everywhere. You've no agency over the lights or the temperature.

If I felt restricted in my last days of freedom in the community, boxed in, pinned down, looking over my shoulder as the clock tic-tic-tic-'n toward me being under lock and key, it was only a dress rehearsal for this main event.

The feelings of constraint on the street are nothing compared to actual confinement behind bars.

And, of course, just as you don't own your space and time, your body is the property of the Department of Corrections—and they never let you forget it. You don't have a choice over what you eat, where you go, or how you get there. Physically, you've no more domain over yourself as a stapler, a stick of gum, or an old boot has over their presence.

Over the years, I made the rounds to seven institutions. Besides Stateville, there was Hill, Illinois River, Shawnee, East Moline, Western Illinois, and Pinckneyville, in that order. To make that circuit in a drive covers over 1,191 miles. At the furthest point, they locked me up downstate, nearly four hundred miles from Englewood. For the most part, each move pushed me farther out of the city, cutting me off from friends and family. It'd be a six-hour drive for visitation to the Shawnee Correctional Center. Other locations throughout the state were only marginally better.

I won't give prison any credit for the changes I made. Collectively, these institutions are not in the service of justice and rehabilitation. They are designed to warehouse and punish. While I had a lot of time on my hands, alone with my thoughts, reflecting on my actions, prison does not get props for the conclusions I reached. I am convinced that I would have reached those conclusions through other means without the heartache and psychological trauma inflicted by these institutions or the system as a whole.

AN INVENTORY OF CONSEQUENCES

Word reached me that my main man, Ty, was paralyzed from the waist down in a shooting. I didn't believe it. He had been released when I was about halfway into my sentence, and the word probably came to me first through those same vents where we used to talk. Now, I was being told outright he would be in a wheelchair for the rest of his days. I couldn't let that reality sink in.

Everything became a kind of inventory of these consequences. I'd think of G-Free's murder. I'd think of attempts on my life. I'd think of being locked up for an incident I didn't have no part in. Over and over again on repeat, I'd think on these things. This wasn't some healthy contemplation, putting the pieces together to understand how I got from there to here. It was some dark days processing all of that. If I started thinking on it too much, I would just have to push it out of my mind just to keep moving.

Prison seemed to push the brakes on life, and all these consequences were catching up. I couldn't do nothing but sit with them all day.

When Ty visited me for the first time after his spinal injury, I saw him come up the ramp through the doors into the visitation room and couldn't believe my eyes. Even with what I witnessed right there in front of me, I was in denial. Some block in my brain wouldn't let me accept that this was for real. I thought, okay, he'll be up and about by the time I am out. It was some kind of magical thinking, not based on the facts before my eyes, that made me deny what I saw.

I had gone into prison with a certain mindset, but it had begun to shift. There was this mental transition into a different way of thinking that operated behind the scenes. It was a conversion into another self altogether.

In motivational interviewing, which I knew nothing about at the time, they talk about the five stages of change.[1] There is pre-contemplation, contemplation, preparation, action, and maintenance. In pre-contemplation there is no intent to change your behavior. That was my thinking on the streets. The attempts on my life, the shoot-outs, the clashes with cops, my broken nose, and, finally, the frame-up all felt like business as usual. This was part of the life I had chosen. There was no point in even trying to alter it.

Contemplation is where I was while behind bars. It occurs when you become aware that there is a problem. This was the shift in my thinking when my boy cried out in the courtroom. It hits you the way it did, Sadar, that something ain't right. You know it can't go on the way it has been but you don't know what to do about it. There is no commitment to act yet because you have no idea what action to take. It just sits with you something ain't right.

In the preparation stage, you are intent on taking action but still a bit fuzzy on the direction. It is the conviction that you will make a change no matter what. Action comes next. This is where you are actually changing the behavior, doing something about it. Finally, maintenance comes after you've made the change, but obstacles and challenges come up against this new you that have got to be figured out.

They aren't an exact blueprint for transforming your life—no clear markers set for the move from contemplation to preparation or preparation to action—but a pretty good map for making change. In reality, you can flip back and forth between these states, like channels on a TV, being of both minds at the same time and neither all at once. That first moment in the courtroom had put in my mind a change was needed. Now, years of seeing where this behavior had gotten us were driving that intent, fixed in the preparation stage, but I didn't know how to move to that next level.

The TV in the rec room was tuned to WGN, a local news affiliate, which broadcast what seemed to be a nightly parade of misery. Gangland murders. Grandmothers living in fear. Residents too scared to walk down the street. Little kids, unable to play Double Dutch. If you live in Chicago or, really, anywhere, USA, then you know these stories, which become so much background noise when you are living it.

Worse than that, there was a period where these stories, rather than being background noise, registered different. I'm not proud of this admission, but for an instant in a gangster's career, making the evening news is something of a badge of honor. Transmitted from the portable at the back of the game room, something we were caught up in made a broadcast it was bragging rights. This is warped psychology. Police blotter was like carrying your clippings as a celebrity. If we'd been in a shoot-out later shown on the set behind the bar at the Lounge, that was a boastful moment.

Inside these walls, it no longer seemed like background noise. It no longer seemed boastful. It was like watching these segments for the first time was bearing witness to the psychology of a community under siege. It seemed unimaginable that the full scope of these stories fell on prideful deaf ears.

In this same period, some Black Disciples living in the hundreds, out in the Roseland neighborhood, made us "public enemy number one" for a good minute. It was virtually impossible to take pride in the kind of stories that suddenly catapulted our lives onto a national stage.

Robert Sandifer, an eleven-year-old foster kid nicknamed "Yummy" for his love of cookies, had been more of a mascot around the gang.[2] He was a little over four and a half feet tall with cornrows and a foul mouth that talked a good game at a blue streak, making it simultaneously easy to forget he was a kiddo and good for a laugh when the notion hit you. I never got a chance to know him or any of the crew he was running with starting at the age of eight, but I also be lying if I said I couldn't identify with the pint-size shorty trying to make himself bigger than he was and older than his years.

Yummy bounced in and out of foster care. His short life was marred by violence and abuse almost from birth. It was his granny who brought him out to Roseland, where he stayed when it seemed his mother couldn't support him no more. He started running with BD in the area, doing petty crimes out of survival. Breaking into homes, stealing cars, and other jobs that benefited from his small stature. It is hard to separate what the press sensationalizes from what was really happening, but the criminal life of a shorty was rare. Most of the time, youngsters were off-limits, so everything that happened next is likely more nuanced than how it came to be reported.

Over the summer of 1994, when Yummy was eleven, an already heart-breaking story took a series of even more tragic twists. Depending on who is doing the telling, Yummy was asked, ordered, or took it on himself to do a drive-by, which accidentally took the life of a fourteen-year-old girl, Shavon Dean, a bystander who caught a stray bullet riding by on her bike. As a result of the attention brought by police looking into the little girl's death, teens Cragg and Derrick Hardaway, ages sixteen and fourteen, both BD, assassinated Yummy with two shots to the back of the head beneath a railroad underpass at East 108th Street and South Dauphin Avenue.

If that parade of nightly misery had a grandmaster of ceremony, it was likely Sandifer, who made the cover of *Time* that year becoming a national symbol for gang violence. These events also briefly made Black Disciples the most notorious gang in America.

Now, when WGN broadcast, it seemed I was looking at them through a new lens. It was no longer so much static, murmuring in the background. When I watched these segments, I thought of Granny. Her face, in my mind, superimposed over these women, who seemed fierce and fearless in floral print. They'd take the correspondent's mic. In a wobbly voice, they'd say they were tired of living under threat. It clicked for the first time that it was Granny's porch that had been riddled with bullets when they came for me. Suddenly, that larger-than-life moment was darkened by this reality.

I recalled fondly how Granddad liked nothing more than chilling out in that front yard, relaxing, which community residents in tearful voices said seemed impossible now. Too much violence for them to let their guard down like that.

I imagined Latrell in place of these kids, unable to go to the park to play anymore. On camera, a small child in cornrows was talking about how he was afraid at night that bullets would come through the walls. He and his brother would sleep on the floor in the center of the room to be safe. I imagined Latrell facing the same fate as a wave of sick washed over me.

How my actions affected my mom, Granny, uncles, aunties, friends, and neighbors started weighing heavy on my conscience. I realized that I was a part of the problem.

As the anchors behind the broadcast desk switched to somber reflection, as they always did at the end of a segment, it began to sink in how I contributed to this madness. There was always this moment before moving to sports where the newscasters wondered aloud, as a stand-in for the viewers at home, how it had gotten so bad in our city. In these moments, I'd recognize the role that I had come to play in everything.

I was beginning to take accountability for my contribution to this assault on the community.

These long stretches of reflection moved me from contemplation to preparation in lockup. Making the leap to action was something I was going to need help with if I was going to be successful.

And I would find that help in the most unlikely of places.

18

WILD WILD

Englewood, Chicago, 2017

Wild Wild, as his name implies, can be unruly. It's been this way since he was a youngster, and as Lil' Ty, the son of my main man, I've known him his whole life. Lil' Ty is a strong leader, just like his father. He is a clever, creative, and inspiring individual, but the name Wild Wild still suits him better. On a good day, he is a bit hotheaded, impulsive, and impetuous.

This is not a good day.

His family asked me to look in on him, knowing he will listen to me most of the time. This is on account of who I am to him, though it is not going well today. We are at his place. I am sitting on a couch in the living room. Wild Wild bounces up on the balls of his feet, animated by frenetic energy like he is doing circuit training in a CrossFit gym. A Glock tucked in the belt of his saggy jeans.

His crew is in the next room, standing a few feet away, ready for war. They are locked and loaded. A ragtag military outfit waiting on Wild Wild's command. It is nearly impossible not to see an echo of my younger self standing in rank. Wild Wild is an absolute reflection of his dad decades earlier, so my mind is a time machine, occupying past to present rather than moving between them.

I hear the soldiers next door moving about absently. Scattered energy and clattered weaponry sound. They are eager for orders and a sense of direction. Moreover, I can feel the heat of that unfocused energy burn through the walls, so I try to keep myself from getting emotionally hijacked in the moment. Staying stable, steady, and focused. Concentrate on Wild Wild, here, in the present.

"I can't, Big Homie. I can't—I can't—I motherfucking, can't," Wild Wild rages.

He throws hard slashes through the air like he's throwing punches at invisible enemies. This rage isn't aimed at me, but it don't have nowhere else to go. He avoids eye contact. If he meets my gaze, I fear all that rage might come out in tears. We talk crosswise to one another. I'm being eaten up inside, too, by pain, both past and present, but trying to keep myself together, working a fine line not to give in to anger or sorrow.

"I hear you," I say. "I hear you"—sometimes that is all you can say.

Only a couple hours earlier, Gregory Johnson, Little Greg, Wild Wild's cousin, G-Free's son, had been shot in the shoulder and arm after a fight at the Super Save on 67th and Halsted. The gas station, dubbed the most violent in America, claimed another victim. Little Greg was pronounced dead at St. Bernard Hospital.

His auntie called me to break the news—and ask that I get up with Wild Wild. It is now well after midnight.

Little Greg was arguing with a group of guys hanging at the Super Save. Nobody seemed to know what it was really about. Those guys were fighting heads up with him toe-to-toe. Greg got the upper hand, taking down one of his opponents with a few well-placed jabs. He made quick work of the second. As he seemed about to best a third, one of the guys upped his weapon, opening fire.

Police later claimed some thirty evidence markers, most of which were shell casings, scattered between the pumps. Shooter set to spraying and didn't stop until he'd dropped Greg right there.

In my time machine mind, I recognize some three decades ago, when Little Greg was still in diapers, that his father died much the same way in Lowe Park when an old-school fistfight gave way to a shooting. It is almost too much to bear at that moment, so I can only imagine what Wild Wild is going through.

"Homie, let's you and me just have a chat, 'kay?" I begin cautiously. "Put up your piece a moment, yeah?"

It is late. We are tired. Emotionally drained. Completely exhausted. At this point, I have done dozens of mediations, large and small, intervening with individuals and mediating between groups. I can't say for certain, but it is safe to assume this has spared hundreds of lives. In the countless conversations, negotiations, mediations, interventions, and resolutions that have to achieve these results, few stand out as vividly as this one.

They all get to you in one way or another, but a handful have the personal impact and emotional complexity as this one. I had a homie once who lost his three-year-old baby girl to a bullet meant for him. That was a nearly impossible interruption to navigate. This one felt as powerful, as painful, and in deficit on the losing end from the start.

Wild Wild nodded. Hesitant to speak, it seemed, for fear he might not be in control of what came out.

Still, the nod was enough to encourage me to continue.

"Y'all know what it is your daddy meant to me?" I ask him. I'm not clear why I start the thread here.

Instinctually, it feels right.

Another nod. Wild Wild still seething gives the go-ahead. He had seen my relationship with his dad over the years. We'd fell in together after I got out of prison just as it had always been. It was one of those friendships that picked up right where it left off, no matter the context. We were the same when we got locked up together as we were when we'd run the streets, seamless, as if we'd never missed a beat. When no ramp was available, I'd transport his father from his chair up into my home, refusing to let the chair slow us in any way.

We used to say we *were* our brother's keeper as a mantra when we were in the streets. When Ty and I were both out, I did my best to live that way. I was my brother's keeper. I'd visit him in the hospital and rehab, where he had to work specific muscles. I never saw this as a chore. It was what was expected of any family caring for one of its own. And I promise you, he was as charismatic a wingman as ever, even in those days.

"Y'all know what it is, your uncle, G-Free, Little Greg's daddy, God rest his soul, meant to me, as well?"

Wild Wild vocalizes this time, giving more than a nod, with an expression between a grunt and a whimper. It is an affirmation with stifled emotion. Hard-edged, wordless, and all he can muster at the moment.

"So, you know, then, what it is you and Greg mean to me?" I ask.

That question warbles with the inflection at the end, a car with a warped axle pulling to the right, everything threatening to careen out of control with the slightest of movements.

Wild Wild gives another nod, holding his own alignment steady, for fear of words.

"So, you know, y'all family, your great uncle, King Shorty, had more in-fluence over my life than just about any man ever outside my own daddy, and at times in my life, your daddy and G-Free were brothers to me, you understand?"

Wild Wild looks on with weary fatigue. Wrath and despair battling it out on his features, which now seemed they couldn't hold much of any expression anymore, gave over to exhaustion.

"So, you know then that the two of you are nearly sons to me," I said with a faltering lilt.

"Y'all be my boys almost as much as my own boys. Do you understand me?"

This time Wild Wild murmured, "Yeah."

"How do you think it be then for me or your mom or your auntie if we lose you both in the same night, yeah?"

We sat together in silence because sometimes all you can do is sit together in silence.

THE GOLDEN HOUR

In trauma medicine, the "golden hour" is a concept that refers to the critical sixty minutes necessary to intervene after a car crash, gunshot, or accident of some sort. It is a general rule that paramedics and emergency care providers use to quickly move a patient from the site of an incident to the trauma bay to save their lives.

The first twenty minutes stabilize the patient on the scene. The next twenty transport them to the hospital in the back of an ambulance. Another twenty are required to move the patient through the trauma center, evaluating them with X-rays, CAT scans, neuro exams, and so on to make an assessment. The last twenty minutes is when the trauma surgeon goes to work.

Anything over an hour and the life expectancy for the patient starts to drop.

When community violence intervention programs began working in hospital centers to slow the revolving door of trauma, where a shooting incident leads to more trauma through retaliation, we adopted this framework. Starting the intervention as soon after a shooting as possible to increase the opportunity for success.

Around the country, trauma docs would tell you that you could set a watch by the consistency of victims connected to the same event. It was a pattern that played out with enough frequency that staff in the emergency department would teach it to residents informally. They'd see a gunshot victim come through the trauma bay, and before they were even out of surgery, a member of the opposition would be wheeled in on a gurney with similar injuries. In Chicago, it was a couple of trauma surgeons who started the first hospital-based program. Dr. Steven Salzman, who seemed straight out of central casting as a doc on Granny's stories, attended a grief support group for moms who had lost a child to gun violence. Salzman recognized most of the patients being talked about in that room. He'd worked on almost all of them. He felt compelled to do something somehow, so he began to look at models that could fit into the trauma team at the hospital. Just the same way the school-based program began to interrupt violence on location in high schools to disrupt the pipeline to prison by basing resources in the institution. Salzman had seen too many impossible situations where grief in the waiting room gave way to anger, requiring a security response that punished patient families for their loss. They needed to create a middle way, partnering with CeaseFire to make that happen. The "golden hour" seemed to fit interruption work just as well as it did with physical injuries. An intervention was most effective when the work began just as soon as a retaliation started percolating. Sometimes, that meant being on-site in a waiting room to talk friends and family of a patient down after they'd just passed. In other instances, it meant working in tandem with community partners to get ahead of something before it had even broken out.

Most of the time, interrupters are plugged into the whole social work system supported by the hospital. They become part of the trauma team, not an extension of it but an integral element, alongside anesthesiologists, nurses, surgical staff, social workers, and mental health providers.

There are nearly fifty programs throughout the country that have some form of this approach being offered. They are hands down most effective when the work in the hospital happens in parallel to work in the community. You can't have one without the other and be successful.

In community violence intervention work, the "golden hour" provides a window of influence. In the immediate aftermath of a loss or just after a shooting, sitting down in person to direct behavior toward a more positive outcome is critical to saving lives.

Wild Wild's homies knew the guys responsible for killing Little Greg. They were ready to take action. These conversations started in a waiting room while the guys gathered for word on Greg's status. I got a call from family to ride down on them after the news broke. I showed up at Wild Wild's just as he and his boys headed out. I needed to work in that small window to get through to him before they took an action that couldn't be taken back.

VENGEANCE AND GRIEF

Wild Wild deposits himself opposite me. He collapses into a sofa seat with a sigh, locks onto his hands, and hangs his head a good moment. He clears his throat a bit. After sitting a spell, he speaks, eyes down at his feet.

"I just can't believe it, man."

It was my turn to nod. "Me either."

Little Greg was a good guy. My surrogate nephew, my surrogate son. It was disorienting to think of him in the past tense.

"Not too long ago, we were just talking," he added. "I mean . . . *just* talking. How this going to go happen?"

I nod again.

"I feel that."

"I'm going to miss him, homie."

"I know it," I respond. "Me, too."

A stillness came over the room as the edge of his words softened slightly. The shock and denial more prominent now. Rage and grief are often a couple of clicks apart on the emotional thermostat. Uncalibrated, they switch between one another in moments, back and forth, until a calm emerged.

"It's late. You're tired. There is a lot to process." I begin, wading back into the mediation again, gently.

"Let's call it a night, yeah? Send the guys home for now. I'll hang. We'll talk for a while. If you want," I continue.

"'Kay. I can do that for tonight."

"It's all I'm asking," I reply. "I'm here. I'll stay. We'll talk. Tonight, though, let's put up our piece. Can you do that for me?"

"For tonight," he answers.

It was near 2:30 a.m. Wild Wild sent his guys home. I arranged with the office to have someone check in with them over the next few days. I'd be doing the same with Wild Wild. This would be top priority.

Given who Little Greg was—not just to Wild Wild but to the Black Disciples as a whole—staying on top of this was essential. If the mediation spun out, it was a natural disaster-caliber catastrophe for the community. I kept everything even keel at this hour, but the ground beneath my feet felt unsteady.

If anything went south, it could drag everything down with it.

19

CHICAGO'S HIDDEN HISTORY
Englewood, Chicago, 2002

King Jerome Shorty Freeman, a founding father of the Black Disciples, was crowned in 1978. At one time, his soldiers numbered in the tens of thousands throughout Chicagoland and across the country. That same year, Folk Nation was formally established as an alliance across gangland nationwide. Initially begun behind bars at Stateville, the Nation was a loose federation that originated a decade earlier as a political movement that connected the biggest gangs in Chicago history with the Black Panthers, Jesse Jackson, and civil rights movements well before my time.

It is tough to say it had any real merit in keeping the peace since by the time I was coming up, a lot of my enemies were under the same banner, and these bygone origins were long since forgotten. Still, Freeman, who'd lived it, felt it was important enough to give me this context. By knowing what had come before, we had a better chance of planning for what was ahead.

Even to someone with my status back in the day, Freeman remained an icon. Proximity didn't make him any less larger than life, legendary. No other man, except my father, had as much influence over my life as he did.

By the time Freeman was seated in my passenger seat, giving directions to a neighborhood BBQ that was bringing together competing factions from three gangs, the King was onto new business.

"I buried enough kids in caskets to know when it is time to call it quits," he told me.

In 2002, I got out of prison. I had a similar mindset to Freeman. Tired of the shooting and the killing. I was ready for a new direction. I wanted to be a father to my son. My main focus was to stay out of prison, keep clean, and make an honest living—Freeman had bigger plans for me, though.

"We gonna keep each other out," he said, gesturing to make a left at the corner up ahead. "And, this, how. We gonna give back to the community we took from. We were part of the problem; now, we are gonna part of the solution."

The system doesn't prepare you for life on the outside.[1] There is very little done for a formerly incarcerated individual to be successful after they've been released. Institutional support is usually limited to ongoing control. Parole keeps tabs without much assistance to get you work, resources, housing, skills, and legit means of making due. Still, there are plenty of penalties if you can't make these things happen on your own. It is a rigged game. The law imposes additional barriers on where you can live and how you can work while adding more and more hoops to jump through.

The moment you stumble, it isn't a safety net to catch you as you fall but a trap to bind you up all over again.

A lifetime after you've paid for your crimes and served your time, you are still answering for experiences decades in your rearview. Stigma dogs you everywhere. Employment opportunities are limited when branded with a record. Even when trying to go straight, your options are few and far between. Those that are available offer low wages, barely enough to keep a roof over your head.

Freeman got me work. He hooked me up with a gig. I drove a delivery truck. On a part-time basis, I did canvassing for a community-based nonprofit. More than half of the formerly incarcerated aren't as fortunate. Released without support, they can't find stable employment within their first year of return. Even just landing a steady job is a wing and a prayer. Not surprisingly, three-fourths are rearrested within three years of release. If Cure Violence Global and assorted community violence intervention programs have accomplished nothing else, they provide a reliable means of legit income to help keep guys clean.

It helped, too, that Granny was keeping a roof over my head. Health, housing, skill development, mentorship, social networks, and collaborative support improve the likelihood of staying out. In yet another example of the system adding challenges, formerly incarcerated are ineligible for public benefits, public housing, student loans, or education opportunities. We are literally blocked from the very things that would set you up for success.

And, if you hoping to change any of this as a formerly incarcerated person, best of luck, since you aren't allowed to vote.

Informally, over the decades since Freeman took me under his wing, I
tried to pay it forward for dozens of prisoners coming back into the community. Throwing some money their way, plugging them into a steady job,
providing additional support, finding housing or a halfway home, and so on
whenever possible. I've done this for my homies and past enemies alike.
Most of this work, like Freeman before me, falls under "other duties as
assigned." I do this outreach in my spare time, with expenses coming out
of pocket.

We take care of our own. As community violence intervention work
continues to evolve, however, having a formal mechanism to engage newly
released ex-offenders is essential to the future success of this work, including one that helps expunge records and reinstate rights. READI includes
reentry programs, such as transitional employment, skill training, and
job readiness, as an extension of the street-level interventions conducted
through outreach and interruption work. This aspect of the model helps
ensure more opportunities for going straight.

"Make a left at them railroad tracks up there at the corner," Freeman
gestured.

I nodded while putting on my signal.

"These guys all agreeing to sit down together is impressive in itself," I tell
him, maneuvering into the turn lane.

Coming up in the era that I did, it seemed nothing less than a miracle
that GD, BD, and Vice Lords could gather in the same park without pointing pistols at one another. Freeman educated me on a history where all
those forces once worked collectively for the good of the community. Now,
getting everyone together for hot dogs had taken weeks of conversation,
preparation, negotiation, and two Costco runs to pull off.

"We all going to break bread," Freeman answered. "That might be
enough. Just getting them to this place, sitting down face-to-face, that
might be enough."

Freeman was talking about an informal meeting. We weren't addressing
any specific grievance. No conflict is being resolved. We are just trying to
get members from opposing groups to connect without any violent occur-
rence, laying the groundwork for future efforts.

The whole community had been invited out for hot dogs and burgers on
the grill, a mix of potato and macaroni salads, assorted greens, fruit salad,
picnic dishes, desserts, and other goodies. This was an effort overall to show
the neighborhood a good time. Try to bring people together peaceably

getting them to see one another. Meeting publicly as something other than adversaries. That was just as true for gang members as it was for residents to relate to one another without tensions.

Any spare time that I had, Freeman packed my schedule. He wanted me fully occupied to keep me out of trouble. We were on a mission everywhere we went. There was some kind of service to the community with every activity. The strategy underlying these experiences were more than making social calls.

BBQs like this one built community relations. They fostered connections. We often contributed to the spread, donating food and drink alongside local church groups, aldermen, politicians, and so on. These activities helped CeaseFire programs and other community violence intervention work build a presence in the neighborhood. It was a public declaration of what we were about. It also brought everyone together, including Black Disciples and GD factions, to build inroads.

In the early days of CeaseFire, before we had a formal process, intervention was a mix of preaching and negotiation. We didn't have the evidence-backed approach. Our mediations were not as structured. The intent was there, along with some of the same techniques, but they were not refined. Before motivational interviewing techniques and cognitive behavioral therapy provided a format to guide these conversations, we went off instinct and intuition. This was the art before the science.

Freeman and I went to homegoings and funerals. Sometimes the deceased was family or friends. Other times, we knew them only by reputation. Young people coming up my generation or the one just behind gunned down in their prime. They'd have been brothers-in-arms, part of the BDs, associated only through our loyalties to the gang, as well as past enemies. We knew that the grieving all too often made for targets, while eye-for-eye would be plotted between hymn and prayer.

In those early days, just out of prison, these instances felt a bit like walking into the lion's den. Sharing a pew with a Vice Lord or Moe who, only a few years earlier, was exchanging gunfire with me was tense.

Here, we meted out condolences, handshakes, and half embrace. It was not easy in those early days. My spine stiffened, entering the flower-perfumed chapel space of the funeral home. I bristled, hugging a former adversary, at first. My central nervous system on overdrive. Everything registered as a threat. We'd say our good-byes and wish well the gathered, put in our time, pay respect no matter past friend or foe.

"What are we even doing here?" I'd asked Freeman during a particularly tense ceremony.

We worked our way through the receiving line of mourners, shaking hands met with too tight a grip, offering condolences to grimaced features of former opposition.

"I been to way too many of these," Freeman groaned.

"I know it," I responded, "but I don't think we are welcome here."

"Who you was ain't welcome, but this is how we stop these things from happening. Showing up, showing our respects, showing them you different now," Freeman instructed. "That can't be done by sending a card."

In those days, even while I was in the situation, playing the part, my mind was not completely won to this new way of thinking. I had to remind myself what I was doing there and why.

Funerals are often the scene of retaliation. Even in a house of worship, emotions can get out of hand as grief gives over to anger. I've seen it where people throw hands or open fire across the aisle; carried away by their pain, they give over to violence. Drive-by shootings unleashed on mourners pouring out into parking lots, cemetery-bound for a final farewell.

"They need to see us, to understand what we are about," Freeman continued. "We can't lead by example from the sidelines."

Loss creates a "golden hour" opportunity, similar to the kind we act on in the hospital where in the mix of pain, grief, and mourning, there is an opening to intervene. Those complicated emotions, all stirred up, provide a window. We are on hand to present options. Even saying a few words from the pulpit might put another thought or two on their mind instead of revenge.

Aside from BBQs, picnics, wakes, and funerals, Freeman would have me going to softball games, sporting events, cookouts, political rallies, and so on. Anywhere we could conduct outreach, connect, and catch up with guys, we'd go—sometimes all on the same day. Giving back to the community we had taken so much from was much more than a full-time job with bankers' hours.

We'd be on call at 2 a.m. if necessary. We'd show up at these events to make more than an appearance but to actually connect. The only way to prove that you are not on bullshit is to show up, be present, and do the work.

"It wasn't supposed to be like this in the first place," Freeman continued. "I mean, not in the first place, you know?"

I turned left at the tracks, en route to the BBQ, driving through an industrial corridor carved into the middle of the community. Vacant lots and loading docks behind razor wire–topped chain-link fences. Empty warehouses with busted-out windows three stories high for blocks on end. Sun-bleached, ashen-gray asphalt streets, pockmarked with potholes, housing empty truck trailers and littered with broken glass.

We drove.

"Originally, it was about protection," Freeman said matter-of-factly as we made our way down the block. "White gangs formed to keep decent, hardworking, Black families out of the neighborhood. They come into the communities hunting us. It wasn't just that the law looked the other way, but they gave their blessing."

I'd heard some of these stories from others. Original gangs were all about survival. Hearing them directly from Shorty, though, was a whole other matter. I was getting history direct from history itself. Freeman had lived these experiences. He was an encyclopedia of times past firsthand. Long-forgotten lore, intentionally hidden from common knowledge.

"History sometimes acknowledge that gangs were formed for protection in the early days, but they never talk about protection from who. Chicago likes to think that it's better than the South, somehow, that there is a difference between these goons who came after us back in the day and the Klan. That's just a distortion.

"It gets implied that we were always just arming against one another; in fact, it was white mobs first that we had to arm up against. We couldn't go nowhere else to get protection—we had to rely on ourselves."

We drove. Until the warehouses and factory buildings gave way to bungalows and three flats. Residential stretches with green lawns. Eventually, the fenced-off rail yards yielded to playgrounds. Ball fields and basketball courts.

Freeman needed to share this history. I was unlikely to hear it anywhere else. In those early days, these drives schooled me not just on violence prevention but also a history of how that violence came to be in the first place.

The park up ahead had banners. People milled about beneath a picnic pavilion. Grills fired up. Smoke climbing skyward. We closed the gap by a block and a half. The smell of burgers and dogs in the air even at that distance.

A line snaked along out front a couple of repositioned benches weighed down with aluminum trays filled with food.

Early white gangs in mixed Chicago neighborhoods hid their identity as "athletic clubs." They enforced imaginary Jim Crow boundaries patrolling the streets with bats and chains, Freeman explained, reviewing the long-distorted history rarely taught in textbooks. A shock troop contingent enforcing the redlining policies of politicians to maintain an invisible geography of a racially divided city.

Devil's Disciples, the precursor to the BD, organized to defend against these groups. Auntie Cookie counted herself among its members.

I said as much.

Freeman smiled.

"That was survival, but by the time we were organizing in the 1960s, everything was political," Freeman said.

We made our way to the pavilion. "That was not just a sign of the times, everything was political in those days, but being a gang was an act of resistance."

We crossed the clearing clustered with picnic goers holding piled-high paper plates of grilled food. CeaseFire table skirts decorated the plastic folding buffet tables beneath the pavilion. Banners decorated the beams overhead promoting church groups and community organizations. In those days, the CeaseFire logo was a chalk-outlined body riddled with bullets, accompanied by a messy scrawl in a blood-red font with the organization's name. It grabbed attention.

Freeman first introduced me to CeaseFire as the community group that organized anti-violence marches while I was still behind bars. They were some of the first positive stories I'd ever seen cut through the nightmare. Watching CeaseFire mobilize in neighborhoods, host demonstrations, and lead candlelight vigils was an inspiration. These scenes put a different spin on the community-under-siege story. Instead, they showed self-reliance, self-determination, and autonomy as neighborhoods took action to change those circumstances.

I wanted to be a part of that.

Alfreda Williams (Cobe's mother). Photo from the author's personal collection.

Arthur Hoover Jones (Cobe's father). Photo from the author's personal collection.

Cobe WIlliams, 1990s. Photo from the author's personal collection.

Cobe WIlliams, 1990s. Photo from the author's personal collection.

Cobe Williams and his wife, Angel Williams, at an awards ceremony. Photo from the author's personal collection.

Cobe Williams with Joakim Noah at the Inaugural Peace Tournament in Chicago. Photo from the author's personal collection.

Cobe Williams with King Jerome Shorty Freeman. Photo from the author's personal collection.

Cobe Williams with Mildred Williams (Granny). Photo from the author's personal collection.

Dre (Cobe's son). Photo from the author's personal collection.

Latrell (Trello) Williams (Cobe's son). Photo from the author's personal collection.

Nay Nay Williams (Cobe's daughter). Photo from the author's personal collection.

Quinn (Cobe's son). Photo from the author's personal collection.

Nova Marie Williams, aka NoNo (Cobe's grandaughter). Photo from the author's personal collection.

Quintus Pascal Collins, Jr., aka Peanut (Cobe's grandson). Photo from the author's personal collection.

Williams family at Mildred's Lounge, owned by Mildred Williams (Granny) (left to right): Mildred Trice Williams (sister), Michael Boo Stone Williams (brother), Alfreda Williams (mother), and Cobe Williams. Photo from the author's personal collection.

Miracle Nevaeh McCallister, aka MiMi (Cobe's grand-daughter). Photo from the author's personal collection.

20

REVENGE IS HARDWIRED

Englewood, Chicago, 2017

Wild Wild is back on ten. I can feel his anger on the other end of the line. Following the homegoing for his cousin Little Greg, he is spinning out again. The whole Englewood Office mobilized for the memorial days after his passing. We worked around the clock to keep things calm. Connecting with Wild Wild and his guys, checking in with them, talking them down when necessary.

"I can't let this go, Cobe," Wild Wild told me in a menace-edged whisper that evening.

His voice was broken. Grief-drunk and alcohol-fueled. I could feel his pain through the phone.

"I hear you," I answered softly, matching his hushed tone without the hostility.

It had only been a few hours earlier we had parted ways at the cemetery. I half expected the day of mourning to unleash anger that evening. When numbed emotions—here, drowned in Hennessy, blunted with herb—collide with big talk among the crew, the results are volatile.

My phone was on. Kept close, waiting on this call.

"You home?" I ask.

"He didn't deserve this, homie," Wild Wild replies, ignoring my question.

"It's not fair," I affirm.

"They were fighting heads up. How you are gonna open fire?"

"It's not right."

"Bitch ass punks," he murmurs, almost to himself, momentarily forgetting I am on the line.

"Where you at?" I attempt to circle back.

Silence.

"You home?"

It's a positive sign that Wild Wild called me at this moment. The impulse to act in retaliation weighs on his mind. It could easily go another direction. A few digits difference, he'd dial his boys instead to come to scoop him up. They had an idea who it was that gunned down Little Greg in the gas station. It was an act of will that Wild Wild called me instead.

The fact that he'd called was something positive, even as he argued with me.

"Sit tight," I tell him. "Ima swing by."

"Something got to give," he replied.

"I'll grab something to eat," I respond. "I can be there in thirty-five to forty minutes, okay?"

"You coming over?"

"I'm going to pop by," I repeat.

"Come over," he affirms. "Good."

"Bet."

It goes back and forth in the weeks following an event. Sadness rolls into a rage. Emotions on a thermostat that won't dial right. Anger, a natural part of the grieving process, gets complicated by violence. Especially when processing pain. Without a positive outlet to vent your grief, it gives over to wrath.

Sometimes the best thing you can do as an interrupter is listen. Let someone process their pain. I hit the drive-through en route to bring over a meal. We set up in the living room. I put out offerings with a little mix of everything in a spread on the table. If you can be in their ear, offering something more constructive than vengeance, sometimes that is alternative enough.

The food counters sickly sweet smells of hard liquor and stale smoke. A slab of ribs slathered in BBQ sauce on a bed of french fries. I hope the food is enough to soak up the booze. I open containers, releasing aromas to fill the space. I've over bought to meet those needs. Side dishes: mac and cheese, mashed potatoes, sweet yams, and coleslaw.

We dive in.

"When Greg was younger, my mom was taking us to the zoo or something," Wild Wild says between bites.

"We getting in the car, but Greg don't want to sit *bitch*, on the bench in the middle, jammed between us kids, so he goes *'I call left'* like he is calling dibs."

"Okay," I respond, encouraging.

"So, it ain't like he's calling passenger side. He putting dibs on *left*. We don't none of us know what that means, but being kids, since Greg wants it, we all want it. So, everybody busting out dibs on *left*, whatever that means.'

"*'I get left! I get left!'* We all yelling and raising a ruckus."

I lean in, listening.

"My mom don't play, as you know. We aren't even in the car yet—all these kids yelling—so, she go, *'Greg, you're oldest, you get left,'* but Greg don't move.

"So, my mom is like, *'Go on. Get in. You got left.'* And he go, *'Okay, Auntie, which one is left?'*"

We both bust out laughing harder than it is funny until we can't catch our breath.

"I miss him," Wild Wild says when he gets himself under control.

"Me, too."

"I can't believe he's gone."

"Me, too," I say. "His dad been gone almost thirty years, and there are times I still feel the same about him," I reply, then add, "It does get easier."

How it is the grieving process, under any circumstance, unfolds is messy. One minute laughing, next on the verge of tears. A heavy weight sits in the middle of your chest, a lump in your throat, a burning in your eyes that feels like it will turn tears to steam if they begin to flow. Our evening passes this way.

This is true if you are processing the loss of an old-timer who lived a full life, passing peacefully in their sleep. It is true when you are processing the loss of someone in their prime, tragically robbed of years before their time, through some violent means. It is also true when the life of a little one is lost before it has even begun to be lived.

Emotions don't ebb into one another in clean stages through the process, but instead, like a sea in a storm, they crash into and over one another. Waves capping waves, slamming into a shoreline. Shock, denial, disbelief, giving over to sadness, sorrow, and guilt. Anxiety, emptiness, and fear are overtaken by frustration, anger, and rage.

Then, all this flows back again.

We swap stories about Little Greg into the evening long after we've finished the meal. Some sidesplitting. Others celebrate Little Greg's charm.

We talk about traits that he seemed to inherit from his father, even while G-Free had passed when Greg was still in diapers. There are war stories that might not seem appropriate to the situation yet acknowledge who he was as a leader.

There is no right way to grieve, but there is certainly a wrong one. When you stifle the feelings by numbing, they tend to come back even harder. When you try to check out of the experience in a way that doesn't let emotions be fully expressed. When you don't allow yourself to be present with the pain, it has a way growing bigger over time.

When you are raised in a culture that sees any emotion other than anger as a sign of weakness, it is difficult to deal with it through anything other than violence. I had spent more than a decade stoking a rage after my father's murder. I fed that anger daily, like tending a fire, which burned so hot in moments it might have consumed the whole of my life. When you amplify that out across all these men and women in communities that don't know any other way to manage that pain, it can't get anything but out of control.

"I can't let this go, Cobe," Wild Wild says after we've been at this for a while.

"You in pain," I respond. "That is understandable."

"I don't want to let it go," his voice wavers and cracks. "Motherfuckers got to get got."

We sit silently across from one another for a long minute.

"How is killing somebody gonna set things right, though?" I ask.

It is *the* question, really. One that I went years without asking, even of myself. One that I went years without having been asked. The answer always seemed emotionally self-evident. If you've been hurt a certain way—lost a loved one, a father, mother, brother, sister, cousin, son, or daughter—then hurting back *feels* like the right answer.

Revenge is hardwired into us.

The question sits center of the room as if I placed it in the middle of the table in front of us. Most of the time, I can feel my way to the answer, knowing that lashing out at the moment may give that emotion direction, but it creates bigger problems down the line. It ignites the cycle of retaliation, but more than that, revenge opens a larger wound. It feels impossible to come to some kind of peace after what is done is done in a way that processing the loss can put it to rest. That's a different kind of hurt.

Interrupters all got some kind of situation that makes it hard to answer that question. When it involves children is a big one for most of us. Providing the right answer there can sting a bit because, with a child, no one wants to say, "Let it go." Especially when a kid has been killed and you are talking to the parent.

It is hard when you are talking about your own family, too. All those personal feelings kicked up into it. As I sit in this space, asking it of Wild Wild, more than a decade in on making peace, a part of me is seeking to contradict what I know. Especially as it is Little Greg that we lost. I feel some deep sense of injustice because it is not fair what happened. I feel some complicated, unresolved, mixed-up mess of feelings about G-Free coming on up to the surface.

Wild Wild is quiet for a moment. He levels a gaze that burns skillet-hot mixed with pain. That look is an answer unto itself. The moment stretches out like a rubber band, frayed in the middle, fixing to snap. Neither of us speaks into the space between us. Keeping our eyes fixed forward, we let the quiet pain speak for itself.

"I don't know what to do," he says softly.

"It's okay."

"I want to do something."

"I know."

A lot of time, it feels like you are saying a whole lot of nothing when it comes to grief. In between the memories, you sit in silence. In a moment, emotion punctures the space. There tends to be in the nonsense of mourning an impulse to avoid the obvious. I've seen people try to keep from naming the loss, like saying the thing might come to make it real, so they try to talk a berth around it. Even when you say nothing or when nothing is being said, stay with it rather than try to turn the conversation away.

"Fuck this, man!" Wild Wild says suddenly, pushing to his feet. "I. Can't. Just. Sit."

"I know this is difficult."

"I want to do something."

"I know."

We go around and around like this all night. The repetition isn't wheels trying to catch traction on a slippery slope. There is a sense of progress as we work through this conversation, even in the repetitions. Daybreak splits open the sky with a sunrise: red and gold.

Eventually, Wild Wild turns in. First, dozing a bit on the couch. Then, he heads off to his room to crash. He agrees to give me a ring when he wakes.

I head home to shower and get some sleep myself. Dazed. In my feelings and stretched between these moments past and present.

Most mediations about a slight have clear markers of where they begin and end. They are negotiated around a point, contingent on a handshake contract, resolved in some agreement. Money is owed and money is repaid. A debt settled. A grievance resolved. Whatever needs be talked through is done so, air is cleared, moving on to a peaceful outcome. They are clearer cut.

When a loss is involved, these steps are blurred. It isn't so much a negotiation as a processing of emotions. We ride anger spikes together, then accompany a dive, down deep in despair. It is more unpredictable.

I call the office to check in for an update. I know that this evening will be repeated many more times before it is resolved, but the alternative leads to more death.

Once on the E-way heading home, my mind turns to the first time I recall being asked *the* question: *"How is killing somebody gonna set things right?"* It was posed by Shorty Freeman, Wild Wild's uncle, over a decade ago. Answering it honestly felt like one of the hardest things I'd ever have to do.

21

THE START OF SOMETHING

Englewood, Chicago, 2002–2007

In the early days of my release, I began volunteering for CeaseFire. Freeman would call between shifts at work to have me help with a mediation. He'd ring me and say, *"You know so-so used to stay over on such-and-such?"* Most often, the response was that I did know so-so, such-such—and their cousins, too—but it had been a minute.

Shorty would respond with an address. *"How soon can you get over here?"* It was an informal process in those days, more art than science, but we were learning as we went. It felt like we were really building something. In between the mediations, we made the rounds out and about in the community, attending events, BBQs, and so on. He had an endless passion and energy for the work. It was inspiring.

"This is what is going to keep us out for good," he always said.

This is how most of us start, as volunteers doing mediation as a side hustle. We are just released and eager to turn over a new leaf with a foot in both worlds. We try on our new mindset. It is a tightrope walk between being legit and still thinking street. Mediation work is another test in a long stretch of challenges. On the one hand, it fills you with purpose, which helps you handle setbacks in a way you might not otherwise with just any straight job. Purpose don't pay the bills, though.

Even when you are on new business—a new mission with a new mindset—you are going right back to that old life. Everything tests you. It is

a constant temptation. A user entering a party sober for the first time kind
of temptation. Habits poised for relapse at the right trigger. Old patterns
always circling in the back of your mind.

On top of these tensions, everyone *remembers when*. Your homies re-
hash tales of days gone by, your enemies still nurse a grudge from your life
before, and all the decent people caught in cross fire between, still look at
you sideways to make sure you don't fuck up. In the violence prevention
training I do across the country, we dedicate a whole module to life after
the streets. It is essential learning for doing the work. I don't know if I could
have made it through those early days without Freeman's encouragement.

THE DOC

Gary Slutkin, aka Doc, an infectious disease specialist with the World
Health Organization, used to tell this story about his time in Somalia. It
was in the thick of a cholera epidemic during his first post in Africa. They
were burying more bodies than they were saving. A local warlord told Doc
that he had a "solution" to save the whole village. It was simple. His soldiers would kill everyone. If no one was left alive, there'd be no one left for
cholera to infect.

America's response to the violence epidemic, with its reliance on mass
incarceration, militarization, and state-sanctioned violence, wasn't much
better, Doc would observe. (Note: Doc is not to be confused with the Doc
I came up with on the streets; my boy Doc's given name, Dre, grew up back
when rapper Dr. Dre was emerging as an icon, earned his nickname when
NWA was a thing, whereas the Doc is an MD, hence the name.) He started
CeaseFire in Chicago around 2000 after five years of research with three
employees, including my friend Norman Kerr, a researcher who would
eventually become Chicago's first violence prevention czar. They worked
in a couple of borrowed offices on the tenth floor of the School of Public
Health at the University of Illinois at Chicago medical campus, seeking
saner solutions.

Around the same time the tragic death of Yummy Sandifer had pushed
Chicago violence into the national spotlight, as I was beginning to reassess
my life behind bars, Doc was coming home to look after his parents. He
began thinking that lessons from public health might be applied to violence
prevention. A "credible messenger" strategy from his time curbing a tu-
berculosis outbreak in San Francisco. Social norm change efforts from his
HIV-AIDS work in Uganda. Frameworks that had served him in Central

and East Africa. He incorporated these components into a vision for violence prevention. They spent five years developing a strategy before putting worker number one on the streets.

HIDDEN HISTORIES

In between mediations and outreach, Freeman spoke on our shared history. It was an education as important for him to share as it was for me to learn. Originally, street gangs were organized to defend against racist attacks. By the time Freeman was coming up in the 1960s, they'd become more politically organized.

"They were keeping Blacks out of the trades," Freeman explained, "so you had all this construction going up in and around our neighborhoods and on sites downtown, but no Black workers on the job sites. Multi-million-dollar opportunities going up in our backyard. We were barred access. They'd claim we didn't have the skills, then they blocked us from getting access to the trade schools to get those skills, see? They'd say it's cause 'the unions,' then they'd block us from joining the unions."

I listened intently. Over the years, I heard fragments of this history. Picking up bits and pieces, here and there, from friends and family. Freeman was an education unto himself, making up for the years of schooling I had missed, as well as the years of schooling I had actually had.

He was a big believer in Black rights and political activism. Even in the early 1960s, Freeman led study groups with BD members on radical movements and Black nationalism. In 1966, when Dr. King visited Chicago to march for access to fair housing, gang members provided security. It was gang members that shielded MLK from racist attacks in North Lawndale when neo-Nazis threw bricks and bottles. BD gave the protections police wouldn't.

David Barksdale was tight with Fred Hampton, a Chicago Black Panther Party leader, in the days before the Rainbow Coalition, a citywide anti-racist organization. They attended political rallies and helped organize alongside the Black Panthers. They formed a citywide gang truce as an economic mission organized around principles of self-governance.

"So, check this out: we all—Vice Lords, Stones, and Disciples—joined forces under the name LSD, meaning Lords, Stones, Disciples, L-S-D. I don't know who it was to come up with that one—funny! We went down to the site, over a hundred of us organized, demanding they give us construction jobs," Freeman continued.

"We told them outright, you need to start hiring Black workers. They said, *'we don't have no trained Blacks,'* so we told 'em, *'you best train some, then.'*

"And they did!"

Freeman talked about Marcus Garvey, Malcolm X, and the Black Panthers. In the period that followed the truce, L-S-D set aside the violence and implemented positive changes in the community. Food pantries, community kitchens, restaurants, stores, businesses, beautification projects, and gardens. They organized politically. Registered voters and provided educational support in the community.

Simultaneously, Fred Hampton and the Panthers connected with neighborhoods on the North Side, unifying the outcasts in the city. They recruited Young Lords, a Puerto Rican gang in the Lincoln Park neighborhood, and the Young Patriots Organization in Uptown, building a diverse network throughout Chicagoland.

"Don't get me wrong," Freeman said. "I don't want to romanticize it. There was still gangbanging back in the day, we were still going back and forth into it, but overall, we were on something bigger, too."

This history was invaluable. They flipped the script, even on what I had come to believe. Kids are walking around carrying nearly six decades and several generations into combat without context. None of us had any idea it was set against this backdrop.

"So, you know what it was they had to do when we were on something bigger, right?"

I shrugged.

"They had to put an end to that shit."

A CHICAGO MIRACLE

In 2000, Doc and Kerr launched CeaseFire in West Garfield Park, one of the city's most violent neighborhoods, with funding from the Centers for Disease Control and Prevention and the Robert Wood Johnson Foundation. They had eight workers covering a handful of beats. Shootings went down by 68 percent.

"That's the thing with miracles," Doc joked. "Soon as you perform one, everybody asks you to do it again."

They did.

Over the next couple of years, more CeaseFire teams covered six areas in the city. These were the segments I saw on the evening news when I was locked up. Candlelight vigils for the fallen. CeaseFire leading marches through the neighborhood. Orange jackets sporting the chalk outline on the back like an insignia. By 2003–2004, shootings were decreasing by an average of 30 percent.

Other groups were hitting on the same idea around the same time. In 2004, AT Mitchell—a Brooklyn-born community activist and longtime collaborator—launched Man Up! Inc. after eight-year-old Daesean (Dae Dae) Hill was shot and killed by a stray bullet. Dae Dae was well known and well loved in the neighborhood. His loss left a deep wound on East New York. AT, who had been conducting informal mediations on his own, just the same as Freeman and I, since his release in 1991, saw the tragedy as a moment to organize and act.

In boroughs throughout New York, similar groups were forming organically. There were groups all up the East Coast. Boston. Baltimore. Philadelphia. They followed similar patterns of gang members transitioning into peacemaking.

Around the country, activist preachers opened up church basements to formerly incarcerated gang members to host mediations. Storefront community-based organizations added violence prevention groups. Organizers linked up with street activists to sponsor peace marches and reclaim neighborhoods.

Similar gang violence prevention initiatives were sprouting through the Midwest as well. In Minneapolis, some guys I'd come up around from Englewood were now doing community interventions. Cincinnati and Cleveland, Ohio. Indianapolis, Indiana. St. Louis, Missouri. These groups were small, informal, and loosely organized. They were community-based operations in hardscrabble pockets, often mixing political organizing, food pantries, recovery work, and violence prevention out of the same shop.

In California, activists made up of Crips and Bloods signed a truce to keep the peace between warring factions in the aftermath of the Los Angeles riots in the early 1990s. In the decade that followed, those former gang members became organizers, activists, mediators, and peacekeepers themselves. They held the line to keep the truce intact by mediating skirmishes and negotiating conflict.

Stan Tookie Williams, who cofounded the Crips, went on to publish nine books on gang violence prevention, including a protocol for peace, from behind bars. In the summer of 2004, the protocol was used to form a truce between two warring gangs in New Jersey.[1] There had been

thirty-four murders in the four months leading to the peace treaty negotiations with bodies on both sides. Tookie's protocol was used to broker a
peace between hundreds of members that continued long after a truce was
established.

Tookie oversaw this from death row less than a year before he was executed. The protocols are still influential in some violence prevention circles
over a decade later. Imagine what could have been accomplished if he had
been allowed to live out his years.

I say all this to say that CeaseFire didn't create nothing that wasn't already in the works. I'm not trying to take anything away from anybody.
Even some of the community groups that CeaseFire was partnering with
throughout Chicago had been doing some variation of violence prevention
already for decades. They were political outgrowths of L-S-D organizing
on their own turf.

By the time the model was cobbled together and getting results on the
Chicago streets, a movement was already percolating across the country. It was happening organically at a hyperlocal level. Block-by-block,
beat-by-beat, it occurred without being networked up, under the public
radar. Street activists were working without any kind of program or formal
title; they were just getting the work done in their own way in their own
backyard.

I'll give Doc props on adding the health framework, the public health
model, and, with the backing of the university, a level of professionalism the
movement wouldn't have otherwise. They were providing that credibility to
pave the way and put the program onto the public radar.

After those early successes, when Freeman was recruiting me, CeaseFire
doubled its sites in Chicagoland and then doubled again. At its peak, it was
operating some twenty-five sites throughout Illinois.

In 2007, the model was expanded to McElderry Park in East Baltimore
under the name Safe Streets. It was being replicated in other areas of the
city and getting the same results it had been in Chicago.

A year later, Kansas City, Missouri, added the Aim4Peace program, a
fledgling CeaseFire replication. Based in the East Patrol section of the city,
one of the most violent areas, it quickly got results. More sites were added,
and the program grew.

Behind the scenes, things were getting under way in New York as well.
This was all still just the makings of a movement, though. My role in that
was yet to come.

THE WAR ON GANGS, CIVIL RIGHTS, AND MASS INCARCERATION

How it was that they put an *"end to that shit,"* meaning having the gangs unified, organized, and political, began with the assassination of Fred Hampton by police in December 1969. It has been speculated that his citywide gang truce was the reason. The FBI tried to undo the peace agreement for over a year. They'd spread misinformation that Hampton was planning to kill Jeff Fort, leader of the Stones, that year, planting that seed of mistrust. They put spies in Hampton's camp and attempted to undermine his credibility in the community.

"Attack on the Black Panthers and the attack on Black gangs was an attack on Black liberation," Freeman argued. "If all of us were getting together and getting along, that'd be a bigger threat than any one individual, ever, ain't it?"

On December 4, a special police task force raided the Black Panther Party apartment at 2337 West Monroe Street in Chicago. Police busted in and shot up the place, killing Hampton and another Panther, Mark Clark, while wounding four others. They claimed it was a shoot-out. That wasn't true.

That began a war that would stretch decades, devastate communities, target gangs, and pit us all against each other.

In Chicago, the mayor declared a "War on Gangs" shortly after the attack on the Panthers. It began a crackdown on Black gangs that would last decades. This escalated with the "War on Drugs." These two fronts made it virtually impossible to hold together any solidarity. The civil rights struggle and mass incarceration have been tied together from the beginning.

There are variations of this same story played out in Oakland and elsewhere. Tookie talks about how early incarnations of the Crips when first formed, looked to organize with the Panthers, but efforts at peace were actively derailed by law enforcement.

There are variations of this same story that played out almost everywhere, USA.

VIOLENCE PREVENTION AND RACIAL JUSTICE

One of the mistakes CeaseFire made early on that always haunted the program was not to embrace this political history. It was so focused, blindly, on the health aspect of the work that it neglected those broader political, social, and racial issues connected to violence. The analogy that got thrown around a lot was that a paramedic doesn't need to focus on all the other factors contributing to an illness; they just address immediate needs. They focus on clearing the airway, maintaining vitals, and so on.

I get it.

I understand.

I have often felt my work was more like a firefighter than anything else.

Yet, if it weren't for Shorty, I wouldn't have been exposed to much of this history. It would have been hidden and buried.

Freeman shared this history in a way that made the past real. It was personal, painful, and profound. That was part of his gift as a leader, perhaps, on account that it often felt he embodied that history himself. He made you feel connected to it.

Or, perhaps, it was on account that it felt, as often does with movements, that you are actually in the flow of history. As Shorty always put it, you can't know where you are going unless you know where you have been.

Before I formally joined CeaseFire, Shorty would make history personal, painful, and profound one more time by telling me what he knew about my father, ultimately bringing me into direct confrontation with one of his killers.

22

HEALING WOUNDS
Englewood, Chicago, 2017

In the weeks that follow Little Greg's memorial service, I check in with Wild Wild regularly. There are dark days. He won't get out of bed. I arrive to a dark, unkempt home. There are days he won't answer my calls. I show up to find him sitting in silence, lights off, surrounded by clutter. I help him straighten up, get things functional again. Bring food, clean up.

I get us conversing, stoke dialogue on just about anything to get him talking.

We talk about whatever is going on in his life. We talk sports, movies, music, or anything in the narrow terrain outside his grief. We talk a whole lot about nothing and everything. I try to speak without triggering his loss and recalling his pain.

I ask him to stream a track he's digging. We put on the game, sit and watch TV together. Experience normal for a spell. Little grooves of ordinary. In search of a return to a life before the loss.

We aren't avoiding the topic so much as we avoid dwelling in that pain. The kind of obsessiveness that isn't processing through so much as it is just sinking in. Drowning in the grief that often comes with sudden, violent death.

During this period, I ask him to stay sober.

"No judgment, brother," I begin. "You think you could go a few days without getting fucked up?"

Substances tend to distort. I'd seen Hennessy kick off a tailspin. Entire days could be lost smoking weed. Whatever it was that could get you numbed out of your head would just as easily stir things up.

"It helps me sleep, is the thing."

"I'm just worried it doesn't put you in the best head space."

"I been having dreams about Greg."

"What happens?"

"Usually, he tries to talk to me, but I can't really make out what he is saying. Sometimes he is the age he is now," Wild Wild says, "or, you know, the age he was before, and sometimes he is younger."

"Where are you at?"

"We in the gas station, where, you know," he answers. "Once we were in the house he grew up in, though. Another time, school. I wake up not remembering what he was saying."

"How you feeling when you wake up?"

"Angry," he says. "But really, I'm always angry."

Wild Wild eventually agrees to stay clean for a while.

These aren't formal therapy sessions. We don't have no clinical aims. I don't know how useful that'd be on its own anyway. They are informal meetings. Small windows of safe space removed from the outside world, where he don't have to feel some kind of way. There are no expectations to put up a brave front. He don't have to stay hard. There is no front or judgment. In this space, we mourn if we need to mourn. We laugh if we need to laugh. We sit if we need to sit.

"You want to know something crazy?" he asks me.

Bulls game on the flat screen. I look away from the TV to tune in.

"What's that?"

"The other day, I went to call him," he says. His voice dips into a sad, quiet lilt with a hint of fear.

"Who's that?" I ask, not following for a moment.

"Greg, man, Greg," he answers. "I went to call Greg. I think I'm losing my fucking mind."

"What happened?"

"I was thinking something, can't even tell you, now, what, and suddenly felt the need to tell him. I break out my phone and open contacts before it clicks."

"I think that is normal."

"Normal? I don't know, homie. Normal. I didn't get to dialing, but, for real, I had the phone in my hand, scrolling contacts to ring him before I realized what was up."

"I think it just means he's on your mind," I tell him, nodding. "That's all."

"Happen to you before?"

"Bro, I have been shopping and seen someone I know been gone a good minute walking down the street out front a store. I got to literally stop and stare. Then, I got to remind myself they gone—like, wait a minute, this can't be happening."

"For real?"

"You ain't crazy. You're not. It's just your mind trying to accept the fact he gone."

"Fucked-up way of accepting it."

"You just miss him."

"I do."

"Nothing wrong with that."

"It freaked me out, like, am I losing it, man?"

"You ain't losing it," I tell him. "Mind does all kinds of fucked-up things to process, I promise. This just that."

Our time together in those weeks focuses more on working through grief than mediation. I am not called upon as much to ask questions like *"What's it going to solve, you move on this guy?"* so much as I am *"How you holding up, homie?"*

I spend time acknowledging the loss and letting him know I care. It is as much a part of mediation as navigating any conflict. A lot of listening and reassurance that whatever it is he is feeling is normal. I make myself available. Running errands, picking up something to eat, whatever it takes to show support.

Meanwhile, the Englewood office works with his crew. A clique will swing back and forth in mindsets the same as any individual. We stay with them. Just the same as I am keeping in tune with Wild Wild, my team is checking in on his guys. They visit them at home. Call them up. Send texts. Take them out for lunch. They all grieving. They all experiencing rage, pain, and bereavement. Emotions on steady rotation. Everyone processing in their own way at their own pace in their own time at the same time.

Other times, it isn't so much processing as it is a crab mentality. If one of them makes progress on their grief, like a solo crab scaling the wall of a bucket to escape, the others come pull them back down metaphorically. It is a reflex, keeping all of them stuck at the bottom of the bin in their grief.

In between, we debrief with one another to stay on top of the crisis. We compare notes to sync up our strategy.

The dynamics of a group conflict require going back and forth with competing tensions. When everyone gathers in one place, the pressure to go along with social norms gets far stronger. Wild Wild is my responsibility. Out of earshot from his homies, I manage these conversations without much interference.

When plugged in with them, his guys express an urgency to get revenge that is overpowering. Grieving often creates a kind of desperation to do something, anything, to avoid the pain. If everyone is together, that "anything" fixes on taking out the shooter.

As a result, we keep tabs on everyone involved. We respond whenever someone is backsliding. For the most part, this is constructive.

At one point, Wild Wild even starts minding his friends. This is progress. He is not just checking in on them but also trying to get them off the revenge thinking. I hear from one of the guys in the office—other interrupters, not Wild Wild—that he is mellowing out his guys. They call on him, "When we going to do this thing?" and Wild Wild responds, "Just sit tight."

It is going this way for a minute, then it isn't.

"Fuck. This. Shit," Wild Wild exclaims, throwing his cell phone aside. "Fuck. This. Shit."

I am used to mood swings. They are part of the process. Emotions are predictably unpredictable. This outburst, though, flares up a little more intensely than anything I've seen in a while.

"What's going on?" I ask calmly, trying to bring the situation down a notch.

"They just saw dude at the jerk chicken joint."

Little Greg's killer has been in hiding for weeks. We'd manage to get the clique stable enough to keep from hunting. This is one of the tensions we'd been riding out, curbing these search parties. Overall, we are successful.

Now, the shooter resurfaces. The call had been random. The shooter had been spotted by an unaffiliated friend who figured Wild Wild would want to know. All these relationships we kept a pulse on for weeks, so much time and energy invested, controlling whatever we could control, now threatens to be undone by a chance encounter we couldn't have predicted.

"What you want to do?" I ask carefully.

Wild Wild is on his feet. He paces the floor. We are back to that first night in an instant. The rage returns. I can feel his anger, like a fever, radiating off him—movements, erratic and red hot.

"What do you want to do?" I repeat.

I can tell he isn't listening.

He is coming up with a battle plan.

He arms up.

"I need to do this thing."

He paces the floor. He loads his gun. He readies himself in front of me.

"Do you, though?"

Wild Wild pauses a moment.

"It has to be done," he says.

"Look," I tell him. "I know it feels like you got to do this thing right now, but let's play this out."

He hovers over the couch, wringing his hands. Stands and stares. A far-off, lost look in his eyes—vacant.

"Let's play this thing out a little, yeah?"

I get a nod in response. Wild Wild is too worked up to speak. Everything is at the surface.

"Let's say you all ride down on him right now. What is that going to solve?"

"I don't know if it is gonna solve shit, but he deserves what he has coming to him."

"I'm not arguing the point."

"Got to make this thing right," Wild Wild snarls.

"This gonna do that then?"

Wild Wild fixes his gaze on me.

"Meaning?"

"I am saying this to say, how is this going to make things better?"

I pose the questions to form a pause. A *"why?"* to buy time. A *"what is that going to do?"* to put something on his mind. These are asked, not for answers, as much as they are to widen the gap between thought and action.

Time won't reverse to unpull a trigger. However, it can be slowed enough for reflection so that the trigger don't get pulled in the first place. *"What are you trying to do?"* or *"What do you want?"* is a stopgap measure. In small increments, we ask not for answers but to borrow time and space in mind. We ask to create a moment so the hammer doesn't strike the primer.

I can't stop Wild Wild from storming out this house. I can't keep him from riding down on dude. I can't prevent him from calling his boys and asking them to do the same.

I can get him thinking about how his mama would feel if he were killed, too. I can get him thinking about keeping this thing from getting bigger. I can prompt him to consider the consequences.

"I hear you, homie, I do, but does this change anything?" I ask. "Didn't you tell me your mom was just about to have an asthma attack when she got the news about Little Greg?"

"That's right."

"How do you think she is going to respond if you get killed?"

"I got to do this thing, homie."

"What about your granny? What about your boys? What about me?" I ask, not expecting answers. "You want to put us through that again? So soon after, we all lost Greg?"

Wild Wild doesn't respond. He is not meant to, really. He settles slowly into his seat.

We talk through the moment.

He hears me.

We talk through the one after that.

He listens.

We talk through the next.

He nods.

"Never known justice to come from a courthouse," Wild Wild says.

Police got the shooter about a week after he resurfaced in the neighborhood.

"Truth," I reply. "But how you feeling?"

Even without the immediate threat of retaliation, my meetings with Wild Wild continue. I am in person or on Facetime with him almost daily. My engagement does not end with an arrest.

"Ain't nothing different," he shrugs.

"What would make it so?"

He gives this serious thought. Closing his eyes for a moment. He places his head in his hands as if in prayer.

"I don't know anything would," he says finally.

Without looking up, Wild Wild says, "I imagine sometimes how I'd feel if I'd gunned that motherfucker down. Play it over and over. I walk into that spot, firing, and don't stop till I've emptied my clip into him. I imagine how it be if that was how things went down."

His head remains hung as he speaks into his hands and falls silent.

"And?" I ask him.

"I don't think, if we were having this same conversation at that time, I'd be feeling any other way."

"Okay."

"I don't know anything would be different that way either, at least not as far as how I feel."

"I'm sorry," I say.

He looks up.

"It does get easier with time, though, the loss, I mean," I tell him.

"I know it."

"That's got to be something."

"It's something."

23

A NEW LIFE

Englewood, Chicago, 2002–2007

Freeman always had an alderman, a politician, a community organizer, or a church leader to meet. There were permits to pick up for peace marches. Masses to attend. Support groups for grieving parents. We'd distribute placards and window signs calling to "Stop the Shooting" to local businesses. Swing by a community halfway house to check in on a homie just out on parole, drop off a little cash to help them make ends meet, offer a handful of job leads.

We raced from one meeting to the next. This was more than on-the-job training. It moved us from who we were to who we were becoming. In community rec center basements with metal folding chairs that smelled of too-strong coffee and stale donuts, we organized a candlelight vigil. At clergy offices in ornate South Side cathedrals scented with sweet incense and melted candle wax, we spoke to assembled faith leaders. Storefront churches, community-based organizations, and a political group meeting in the back room of a secondhand shop.

"Some of ya'll know who I am," Shorty began, speaking to a group of community activists, "and some of ya'll know who I been."

In the assembly, there were grunts of affirmation and nods of acknowledgment. A sparse smattering of applause. Some leaned in as others leaned away.

"Yes."

"Yes."

"Go on."

"And some of ya'll don't know whether I'm worth believing," Freeman continued. "I get that. I do. I was part of the problem, but I am fixing to be part of the solution. That is going to take some convincing. That is going to take some time. It is going to take proof. I respect that. I got to earn that. I got to atone."

More applause. Shifting of chairs. Nods.

"Go on."

"Go on."

"Yes."

"Now, we are putting together this here demonstration for the tragic loss of a child killed by a bullet meant for someone else," Freeman continued. "I will join you the day of the demo. I will hold a candle. I will march."

Applause increases.

"Yessir."

"Yes."

"Yes."

"Because I am sick, like all ya'll, of the shooting. I am sick of the killing. I am sick of putting kids in caskets," Freeman continued. "I will march, but I ain't sure that will be enough. I am saying that when we got a kid with a gun get gunned down, we say they a 'mutual combatant.'"

Some shifting of chairs.

Clearing of throats.

Audible discomfort.

"We can't get no candlelight vigil for one of these little ones out there shooting, but losing that life is a tragedy, too. If we are gonna change this community, we gotta make it so any loss of life is unacceptable. We gotta make it so we won't stand for no killing no matter the child. Let's march for all the lives we lost, not just the lives of the innocent. That is all."

Freeman finished and found his way to his seat. A long silence, followed by a round of applause. It was easy to get the community behind the loss of innocent life, as Shorty pointed out, but harder to get activists and faith leaders to acknowledge the loss of someone seen contributing to the problem. It was important to Shorty to remind them that a *gangbanger* has got a mom, a granny, brothers, sisters, friends, and maybe, even a child of they own. Beyond that, though, it was important for Shorty to remind them even if they weren't somebody to someone, they were still somebody, anyhow. If we were to change the community's attitude around violence, we had to change its response to any loss of life.

"I am glad you are doing this with me, Cobe," Freeman told me as we climbed into the car after the meeting. "After everything we've been through and everything we done, it is good to be doing good for a change."

He sighed and reached across the seat to pat my shoulder.

"It's not just you doing all this with me, but how you are around Ty, too. It isn't easy for him, being in that chair, but you always looking out. You are a good friend. You're your brother's keeper. You are a good person, Cobe. I want you to know that."

"I'm working on it," I laughed. "I'm working on it."

I hadn't been a hundred percent when I first started. Contemplation to Preparation. It wasn't that I didn't want to make a change, but I had my doubts it was even possible. Preparation to Action. Trying to stay legit after release was challenging enough as bills came in and pressures mounted, but on top of these setbacks, there was easy money on offer. Action to Maintenance. Having Freeman so unwaveringly optimistic and supportive helped me shift my mindset.

Into this marathon of activities—mediations, conversations, meetings, and events—I officially joined CeaseFire. Money wasn't much. I quit the delivery job to dedicate myself full-time. To make ends meet, I was hustling cell phones out of the trunk of my blue Pontiac Sunfire. In those early days, the rush from helping those in need carried me through my own change. I was addicted to mediation work.

"Listen," Freeman continued. "I need to tell you something."

We were making our way out of the parking lot onto the street. I nodded.

"I hated it what happened to your daddy."

I wasn't expecting the conversation to go here. I nodded again.

"I was locked up when that decision was made, and I been sick about it ever since," he told me. "I wish I could have done something."

I drove down the street.

"I know it," I told him. "I know it. I appreciate you saying so, but I already know."

He nodded.

"I am sorry it happened to you."

"Thank you."

"It has been on my mind, Cobe. I know you want answers. You deserve that."

"Thank you."

"I just want you to know how hurt behind it I was, Cobe. You understand?"

I did. I told him. Then we didn't say anything more.

THE PHONE GUY

On the same corner where I used to hustle, I sold phones out of the trunk of my car. These were pay-as-you-go cells. They were much cheaper than buying a new phone with a plan at a mall kiosk. I was getting them in bulk. Moving them at a discount with prepaid cards from a gas station. It was a quick buck without doing anything shady.

This is how I met the woman I was destined to marry, Andrea. She pulled to the curb in a blue Pontiac Sunfire identical to my own. My first impulse was to show her all the features of the new-model Nokia plastic wrapped on the front seat.

"We got the same car," I called to her.

"That's probably why I keep getting pulled over," she quipped in a no-nonsense tone.

She wasn't joking, though. Police pulled her over constantly, thinking it was me. Still, we both laughed.

"I don't need a new phone."

"This one has everything on it," I told her. "You can make calls, send texts, check your e-mail. Everything. I'll show you how to set it up. It comes preprogrammed with my number."

"I'm not interested," she told me in a rapid-fire dismissal.

"In me or the phone?" I asked, holding up the box.

"I already have a phone."

"I'm Cobe."

Andrea and I were about as opposite as can attract. She worked in health care and was in school for nursing. She had three kids at home she was raising on her own and little patience for my sense of humor. She didn't need a new phone and probably had less need for me. The encounter would have ended right on the corner where it began, but we started running into one another around the neighborhood.

"You again," I bust out a few weeks later at the gas station.

"It's the phone guy."

"You don't remember my name? That hurts."

"It's not enough I recognize you."

She remembered.

"You need a new phone yet?"

"I don't."

Around this time, Ty was in rehab for his injuries. I visited the facility. Physical therapy for paraplegia involves a lot of range-of-motion exercises.

I would participate where I could, checking in on his progress. During passive exercise, someone else helps move your paralyzed limbs. The muscles still need motion. Most of the time, Ty could use his arms to manually exercise his legs. I would stand by the sidelines, rooting for him. I would step in whenever he couldn't.

"You eat yet?" I asked, calling him from a community event on my way back to the crib.

"Nurse supposed to bring something by in a bit."

"Fuck that. I'm bringing you a burger."

"I don't think she'll like that."

"Put her on," I reply.

"She is saying, 'No.'"

"What?"

"He wants to talk to you," I heard him saying in the background.

"She's shaking her head," he tells me.

"Ask what she wants on her burger."

"She says you're not supposed to bring in outside food."

"Let me talk to her."

I hear fumbling with the phone, and "Hello?" the nurse asks.

"I'm bringing you dinner," I tell her. "What you want on your burger?"

"You talking to me?" the nurse says, confused by the commotion of passed phones and burger orders.

"You. Nurse. I'm bringing you dinner. Maybe if there is something left over, my friend can eat, too."

"Why you want to buy me dinner?"

"You taking good care of my friend, right?" I tell her. "Let me say thanks."

When I show up with burgers, fries, and oversized drinks, it is Andrea, who is working the night shift.

"It's the girl from the block with my car," I laugh as I enter. I had not recognized her voice on the other line.

"You don't remember my name?" She asked coyly.

"Andrea," I respond.

"You can call me Angel."

"You remember mine?"

"Phone guy."

After that, my visits to Ty coincided with Angel's shifts.

CONFRONTATION

The man who killed my father was released from prison. I put together a meeting. Even while I was on something different, I needed to look the man in the eyes, and, if necessary, I would kill him.

"However you want this to go, it go," Freeman told me. He wasn't going to be involved. Still, he wanted me to know he understood whatever went down. "Just remember to ask yourself, what is it going to solve you do this thing?"

I stashed a piece, wrapped in fabric, in a drainpipe coming off the house in the gangway between buildings. It was a broken clay cylinder just below chest height, where I could slide my hand in the opening, positioning my grip over the gun without getting any notice.

I had my guys agree to meet me that day so I wasn't walking in solo. Just like old times, we formed a bottleneck. My soldiers made a choke point at the entrance and exit of a narrow corridor. My guys blocked the path casual-like so that he couldn't run in either direction.

I wanted him as boxed in, pinned down, and trapped as he had done my father decades before in the vestibule of that public housing complex. All it would take was a nod from me, and they would beat him down.

At this point, I had spent over a decade fantasizing about this moment. In my mind, I had not only seen but felt this moment more times than I could count. For some stretches, daily, I pictured it. I'd have gone to bed thinking of this moment and woken up feeling it.

I cultivated my rage in the way monks focus their calm. For years, I spent time every day pulling this man's picture up online from the Department of Corrections website and staring at it. There was a ritual to the activity. I would log on, enter the URL, and navigate to the page as sensations of rage would begin to activate. These were the days of modem dial-up. Slow load speeds. The squelch connection would trigger feelings throughout my body of roiling anger. The image was slow to load. His face materialized slowly in bands stacked one on the next until the picture resolved. Distorted with pixelation, a fuzzy patchwork of an image emerged. When it would finish, I could look into his eyes.

I imagined pulling my pistol and blasting him in the face. Every. Single. Day.

I imagined the blast would be at close enough range to feel the heat from the muzzle. I pictured pulling the trigger. Unloading every bullet from the fifteen in the clip. The hammer clicking dry on empty.

When the man who killed my father showed up that day, he was walked over to the drainpipe. The way you'd position a prisoner for execution on a firing line, we coolly moved him in place. I put my hand in and rested it on the piece. I wrapped my hand around the grip. Closed my fist over the handle, tight. I slid my finger over the trigger until it was resting on it.

"I just need to know what happened," I told him.

I could feel my whole body trembling. I couldn't tell you what I was looking for here exactly. My eyes burned into his, the same way I'd done hundreds of times looking at the DOC photo on my screen. It was different to see the fear looking back at me. I wondered how my father felt.

Now, the man in front of me spoke in a trembling voice. "We were jealous of your old man that he got things up and running so fast," he said. "Wasn't nothing more than jealousy. We didn't mean for it to go down like that. We were just meant to fuck him up a bit, is all. Never kill him. We were just trying to knock him down a peg. We went too hard."

I felt waves of anger from years of envisioning this moment sweeping over me. I rocked on my heels as if these waves were pounding the surf and me standing in their wake, separating them from the shore. There was so much anxious energy and adrenaline swirling through me inside, but on the outside, I was stone, cold, calm, leveling that gaze.

"What's it going to solve, you make this move?" Freeman echoed in my mind.

I couldn't answer that question, but I couldn't see how it could go any other way.

"We never meant for him to die," he replied.

My life seemed to flash before my eyes as if I were the one who was facing death. I watched those years pass, seeing what this man took from me. The pain he caused. The absence he left. The impact it had on my mother, my brother, my sister, and me, being without him all those years.

There is no single thought that sent me the other way. No revelation made me decide to open my sweat-slick palm from the grip. My finger eased off the trigger. I withdraw my hand from the drainpipe. I wish it had been something I'd said to myself to make those waves ebb. Every fiber in my being was primed to end this man before me. I'd rehearsed it almost every day for a decade.

Then, mercy.

It wasn't fear in his eyes let me put it to rest. It wasn't the apology or the appeal. Shorty's questions alone hadn't gotten me to rethink. Nor was it all the changes I had been making in my life over the years leading to this moment suddenly giving me peace. I wish it had been any one of those things or any one thing, period, that I could identify, though I suspect more likely it was all of them combined.

HAPPY FAMILY

It didn't take long after those initial visits to the facility for Angel and me to start dating. There were no real big discussions about it. It was just one day that we went out and then the next that we were together. Nothing was planned exactly; it was just overnight we were a big, happy family.

Her kids took to me immediately and, truth be told, I cannot really remember a time those three weren't mine. She had two boys, Quinn and Dre, and a baby girl, Nay Nay. I'd mess around that they were "bad" kids Angel stuck on me, but they had my heart from the beginning. We moved Latrell in just soon as we could. There was no stepbrother this or stepfather that which haunts other families. These all were my kids, and that is all there was to it. The house was full of love and laughter, even in rough spots.

Angel's mom, on the other hand, not so much. She took some time to warm up to me. She was cautious and skeptical of my intentions. Education was always important to Angel's family. While she went through some rough patches as a kid (Angel got a little gangster in her), she was always driven to get an education. Mom thought I was a distraction from classes at best. At worst, she thought I was bad news. She figured I was going to jam her daughter up. It took a lot of time for me to win her over. Mom's a big fan of mine now; at least, I tell her that all the time.

My family, on the other hand, adored Angel. She was an absolute blessing in my life. Mom and Granny saw Angel and the kids as being exactly the incentive I needed to turn things around for good. They saw her as intelligent, savvy, sharp, and no-bullshit—exactly the kind of woman to keep me in line. The family doted on those kids and smothered them with love.

We moved in together without much discussion, either. There was no heartfelt conversation at a kitchen table, holding hands and looking meaningfully into one another's eyes as we planned our next steps together. There was no ceremonial exchange of keys or a formal event where my furniture one day was moved into her home. Neither of us remembers even talking about it. It just seemed that one morning, it happened. I was getting my mail at one place, and the next, I had a forwarding address.

"If we are doing this, then I got to know you aren't going back to prison," she told me.

"I'm not going back."

NEW LIFE**   **223**

"You understand what I am telling you. For me. For the kids. I need you with this life one hundred percent."

"I know," I told her. "I am."

"I'm not risking my heart or their well-being on anything foolish."

There was no ultimatum. Not even a question, really. Angel, in a signature Angel fashion, just said this is the way it is from now on.

I agreed.

My schedule was flexible enough with CeaseFire that I could watch the kids while she focused on graduating from nursing school. Angel is a lifetime student. After her nursing degree, she would go on to become a nurse practitioner. She even inspired me to go back to get some schooling.

A short while later, we were married. This, too, happened without much discourse. There were no grand gestures, dropping to one knee with a huge diamond, while the Jumbotron pops the question in front of thousands of strangers. We knew we loved each other, and that was enough. We did go big on the wedding, though. There were some two hundred attendees. A lavish event. An amazing turnout.

We went to Jamaica for our honeymoon. Relaxed on sandy beaches. Watched wildly colored parrots fly through the lush green canopy beneath bold blue skies. For a man who spent most of his formative years in an eight-by-six cell, seeing the ocean for the first time, stretched out as far as the eye could see, was a miracle. As a kid, I never imagined much of anything too far off the block beyond getting sent downstate for a stint. This was truly paradise.

We bought our first home soon after, which we had built in the suburbs. We had rooms for each of the kids. We brought my nephew and namesake, Cobe, my sister's child, into the home to stay with us as well. Most fathers want to provide a better life for their kids—and I was given the opportunity to do that five times over.

IV

LOOKING UPSTREAM

㉔

GAME CHANGER
Englewood, Chicago, 2010–2015

"C'mere!" Boo shouted from across the lobby.

He had a bit of bulk on me but moved fast for his size. The thick chain around his neck, the width of a truck tire tread, glinted in the gelled light as he advanced, bouncing off his chest. He still had a bit of height on me as well and, with his stride, bound across the carpeted floor in quick motions.

When he reached me, he swallowed me up in his grip. He pinned my arms to my sides, wrapping around me like a boa constrictor, in a massive hug.

Then, he hefted me off the ground.

"I am soooo proud of you, baby brother!" he beamed, peppering me with kisses over my forehead and face while unleashing a giant booming laugh. Next to my mom, Boo was probably my number-one fan.

THE INTERRUPTERS

That year, 2011, was a game changer. Filmmakers Alex Kotlowitz and Steve James released *The Interrupters*, a feature-length documentary film profiling CeaseFire by following the mediation work of myself and other violence interrupters as we did our thing. Alex, Steve, and Zak Piper, a producer on the film, followed me, Eddie Bocanegra, and Ameena Matthews to mediations, funerals, interruptions, community events, office meetings, and strategy sessions. They spent a year with the three of us intervening throughout Englewood and Little Village. They interviewed my family— Angel, Uncle Phil, and Granny all made the final cut—with Granny's birthday party at the Lounge being one of the more memorable scenes in the film.

Alex is a journalist who became interested in violence when writing his first book, *There Are No Children Here*. In it, he follows two brothers, Lafeyette and Pharoah, growing up in the Henry Horner Housing Projects over on the West Side in the late 1980s. Violence is a theme throughout. It is the reason given for the book title and why the boys don't get no childhood.

I never met nobody asks questions the way Alex do. It is probably what makes him such a good reporter (or being a reporter is what made him so good at asking questions). In any case, he asks things most people wouldn't—*why you think he did that?*—and he keeps at it long after most would stop. Alex also never lets alone with one ask. He stays on the query with three or four follow-ups long after anybody else would have felt the topic exhausted.

So, after the book was published in 1991, Alex kept asking questions. He asked about the impact of community violence. He asked about trauma. He asked what might be done about it. In 2008, he came across an answer with CeaseFire that he wrote about in the *New York Times Magazine* in a piece called "Blocking the Transmission of Violence," which later became the inspiration for the film. In the article, he explored violence as a contagion transmitted through a community in the same way other epidemics passed from person to person.

He also looked at what many community groups had already known firsthand since the 1990s and early 2000s—in some cases, all the way back to the radical Black liberation movements in the 1960s and 1970s—that former gang members were "credible messengers" for addressing community violence.

His friend Steve directed *Hoop Dreams* in 1994. He had encountered similar experiences with violence following NBA hopefuls through impoverished inner-city neighborhoods, notably the Cabrini-Green housing project and West Garfield Park in Chicago. The two had been looking for a project together for some time. This seemed worth pursuing.

Kartemquin, a nonprofit company focused on "social inquiry," produced the film. Based on the North Side, they'd been doing social change movies since the 1960s. In a lot of ways, the company still had that same kind of vibe. They ran production out of a multifamily home built in the early 1900s that they'd turned into an office where they produced, edited, and promoted

movies. It would have been carved into apartments under other circumstances, with a crowded, creaky wooden staircase connecting units on the
first and second floors. Instead, each floor bustled with activities dedicated
to one of those functions. Editing in the basement. Promotion and outreach
on the first floor. Offices and admin upstairs. It had a community organizer
energy with a creative pulse. These digs became almost as much an office to
me after the film's release as my own office in Englewood.

The Interrupters put our work on a national platform. At that point, we'd
had a presence in Chicago, Baltimore, Kansas City, and New York, but
after years of trying, we still struggled to gain broader adoption. CeaseFire
had given a model for this approach borrowed from the discipline of public
health rather than criminology. An independent evaluation by reputable
criminologists from four universities spanning four years in the field, almost
in spite of themselves, deemed the work effective and collected the data to
prove it.

   In one story I heard, researchers who had been running the numbers on
the community data kept hitting the same astonishing results: "The recip-
rocals are disappearing!" they declared. Meaning the retaliations vanished
from the data set. No revenge killings. They would run it again and again,
getting the same results.

   Still, the science wasn't enough to gain political traction.

   Once the film got out there, former gang members turned violence prevention activists scattered coast-to-coast, grinding away at the problem in
their own backyards, were seeing themselves up there on the big screen.
That started opening doors for us. Cities that weren't giving us the time of
day for years started rolling out the red carpet.

Violence prevention in America is a messy morass of philosophies, method-
ologies, policies, and ideologies. There are obvious divides between hard-
line law and order and the abolitionist social justice movements. Between
these extremes, a schism of strategies and tactics: after-school programs,
slam poetry sessions, arts initiatives, sports camps, prayer groups, mentoring efforts, outreach, organizing, beautification, graffiti removal, mural
projects.

   They differ over where to begin interventions—Grade school? High
school? Teens? Twenties? At-risk? High-risk? Highest-risk?—to get the
best results. They argue about how to engage—outreach or community
center; you go to them, or they come to you—in order to be most effective.

They debate what resources to provide—activities, therapy, job training, job readiness—to have an impact.

Meanwhile, kids die.

It can be as contentious as any turf battle I fought when I was young.

The Interrupters premiered at the Sundance Film Festival in Park City, Utah. It is the largest independent film festival in the United States and acts as a showcase for new work. We traveled with the movie for its release. It was a full-scale Hollywood treatment. Press events and parties. Red carpet receptions. Getty Image photographers taking promotional pictures. Everywhere, film stars and filmmakers.

Danny Glover was there promoting *Black Power Mix-Tape*, which came out the same year. Jennifer Lawrence, not yet a star, just released *Winter's Bone*. Angel spotted Michael Moore from over a block away, who didn't have a movie that year but was just out showing support.

It was an exciting time, but I never lost sight of what was really important: making sure the work got seen.

CeaseFire rebranded as Cure Violence. The new identity leaned heavily into the health aspects of the work. Cure Violence was an umbrella organization linking community-based groups throughout the country. We weren't as focused on developing the model as we were promoting it. My own role shifted from the emphasis on street-level work to expanding the model across the country. I became a national community coordinator. This repositioning also allowed community organizations to learn from one another and build a movement.

The film was a great social change tool. I began to travel with it as it did the festival circuit, often on my own dime, and attend screenings at the Gene Siskel Film Center, an art house theater in Chicago, where it played. It got so that I had seen it so many times that I would mouth along with everyone in the movie. Everyone. Anyone who chanced a look over in my direction seated in the audience in that darkened theater would see my lips moving right along with Eddie, Doc, Mikey, Ameena, or any other subject speaking on the big screen, whether it was my scene or not.

To the credit of Alex, Steve, and the Kartemquin team, local community activist groups in cities where the film was shown were invited to attend. Often, we'd put together panel screenings after the show to make sure that the local groups got their due. We wanted the workers on the ground, whether they were Cure Violence or not, to get their props. It became a core organizing tool to bring people to the table.

In addition, *The Interrupters* wasn't just about opening doors or engaging partners. It also helped overcome some of the biggest challenges to adoption. Its run time of two hours and five minutes got mentioned by a lot of critics after its release, but from the perspective of getting a foothold in a new city, it spared us months. It was a shortcut through a marathon of phone calls, conversations, debates, discourse, panels, politicking, and intense meetings. For politicians and organizers who "couldn't picture *how* the model worked," it was now illuminated forty-five feet high by sixty-five feet wide.

Trying to change any system is often as hard as shifting a mindset. You are always going to have a group that wants to continue with the old way of doing things and innovators who see a different way forward. It don't matter what kind of system you are trying to change you are going to run into challenges. Systems often go out of their way to defend their dysfunction even when a better way forward is clear.

I can't think of anything more complicated than crime and justice. It is so tied up with people's sense of fear and anger. They see themselves at risk of becoming a victim, and they default to whatever they believe has traditionally kept them safe. It is tied up with centuries of unacknowledged racism, structural inequities, and disenfranchisement. It is tied up with a sense of morality, right and wrong, with punishment and rehabilitation.

For a change of this scale—at a national level, systemwide—you need more than one community, one city, or one state to try something new: you need a whole movement across the country, unified on the possibility of change and on a vision for what can be different.

The film helped show that vision.

At the height of the film's popularity, Shorty came to see it. I had watched the movie in venues around the country hundreds of times at this point as part of special screenings or festivals. Its theatrical release was shown in hundreds of theaters around the country. I was a mainstay at Chicago screenings downtown, bringing out coworkers, colleagues, family, and friends to participate in Q&As after the showing or just experience it with me. I'd given loads of interviews to serious journalists and cinephile film reviewers. I'd sat on a slew of panel discussions and private screenings. Despite all these viewings, I still wasn't sure how Shorty would respond.

He sat next to me. Lights went down. I minded myself so that I didn't get to lip-syncing my costars. That single stream of light fired out from the projector booth and beamed onto the screen. I watched in silence, occasionally throwing sneak peeks in Shorty's direction at parts I knew where audiences laughed, gasped, or let out some tears.

Shorty sat, inscrutable. The whole time the film played, I couldn't read his features. No obvious emotions. After the credits played, the lights came up. I was fidgeting. I wanted to hear his thoughts before they started setting up for the Q&A. Up front on the stage, you could hear the pop, crackle, and hiss of mics as they got ready to call me to the stage.

Shorty turned toward me. He reached across the seatback and placed a hand on my shoulder.

"I am proud of you, Cobe," he said softly. That meant everything.

SHORTY'S LEGACY

Shorty died only a few months later, in January 2012, at the age of sixty. He passed from natural causes. In the end, he was a family man who dedicated the last decade-plus of his remaining years to keeping peace. Working to heal the harm he caused the community.

It is in large part thanks to him that I became the man I am today. He helped me get my life together, kept me out of prison, and taught me violence prevention. During those early years, after I first got out, Shorty put me through the paces, keeping us both on the go morning, noon, and night dedicated to the cause. He still had a lot of doubters, especially in law enforcement, who felt he was running some kind of scam with his peacekeeping. By the time he was in the hospital, he had been involved in more than thirty conflict mediations and organized several gang summits to keep the peace in his violence prevention career. Facts!

On the night he passed, he called his daughter to come up to Ingalls Hospital. She knew he was dying, so she raced to his bedside. The hour was late. Shorty was having a tough time speaking as his health failed. His daughter leaned in close, her ear almost at his lips, to hear the final words from his deathbed.

In a hushed voice, near whisper, straining to be heard, Shorty gave instructions to resolve a mediation he had been working on that week.

25

THE NATIONAL PROGRAM

Englewood, Chicago, 2012–2017

Wheels up!

Takeoff!

Cure Violence scaled quickly. That small office on the tenth floor of the School of Public Health, on loan from the dean, where the model was first developed, now took over almost an entire floor. We had an admin team, leadership, a Chicago program, a hospital response, a school-based initiative, an innovation arm, a national effort, and an international program. There were two kitchens, a conference room, and a library.

I got my own office space for the first time in my career, which made me so proud that I showed up on a Saturday with cleaning supplies to tidy it myself (no disrespect to the maintenance staff). In retrospect, it was little more than a coat closet. There was a secondhand desk from basement storage with a drawer that jammed. The window looked out over the power generator for the hospital campus. To me, it may as well have been a corner suite overlooking the lakefront with a cocobolo desk. I decorated it with movie memorabilia from *The Interrupters* and a bookshelf of awards I'd won for my violence prevention work. By the time I started working for the national program, I set a record for fifty conflict mediations at Cure Violence, which, to this day, no other worker has matched.

Marcus McAllister and I worked in tandem to get the Cure Violence national program off the ground. We shared the space over the first couple of years. At the time, we were both national coordinators, so our responsibility on paper was training and technical assistance.

Every week, a new city, it seemed. New York. Baltimore. New Orleans. Camden. Oakland. San Antonio. St. Louis. Louisville. Jacksonville. Memphis. Milwaukee. Atlanta. Pittsburgh. Philadelphia. Kansas City. I don't know when it was that I first racked up fifty thousand frequent-flier miles to put me in an elite airline status, but I know it happened quickly.

In reality, it meant meeting with politicians in the mayor's office and those on the city council and in public health or public safety. Presenting on the model. Debating on its efficacy. Explaining in detail how it worked. A lot of time, we'd be in a conference room at a municipal office, setting up a laptop, before we'd even got to throw our bags at the hotel.

Then, out to the community. I'm not sure there is a hood in the continental United States that I haven't had the opportunity to walk. We'd meet with the community organization interested in running the program at their offices, then hit the streets. Only a few hours off the plane, we are on a guided tour of trap houses, open-air drug markets, alleyways, gangways, parks, and public housing.

We did this both east and west of the Mississippi, on each side of the Rockies, and in every one of the five regions that carve up the country. Meeting with gang members, community organizers, business leaders, and social work staff on street corners, sometimes into the early morning. Often, our bags were stacked back in a storage closet at the nonprofit while we walked the neighborhood. Still, ain't having seen the inside of a hotel yet at this point. We were on the move, always.

We would do site visits, program assessments, hiring panels, community forums, meetings, meetings, meetings, meetings, then outreach in the community of a new site, dinner with a new crew, back to the hotel to crash, and up the next morning to repeat.

Essentially, we built the national program from the ground up this way.

Marcus grew up in Los Angeles during the height of gang culture there in the 1980s and 1990s, which he brought to the table in meetings. Having representation from two of the most recognizable gang cities in the country added credibility when we were proposing to set up shop (eventually drawing on expertise from New York as well). As a kid, Marcus bounced between Chicago and California. He was infatuated with the lifestyle. Eventually, he caught a drug and gang conspiracy charge in southern Illinois at age eighteen. He served eight and a half years of a ten-year bit.

In 2005, Marcus joined CeaseFire as an interrupter and outreach worker. Eventually, he worked his way up to program manager, overseeing two sites in Illinois at the same time before joining the fledgling national team with me in 2011. Having that formal management background added a dimension to these conversations as well. Cities liked how our skills and experiences complemented one another when we were setting up shop somewhere.

From the start, a new city needs a few things in place to be successful. You need some form of political buy-in. It can be the Mayor's Office, city council, or someone higher up in state government. This has to be a champion bought in on the vision, willing to go to bat for the program.

Controversy follows these programs. There are times when a negative article hits the paper before we're even off the tarmac. We are doing damage control in the air. People don't like that we are "working with criminals," let alone that we are "employing them." Never mind it, everyone on the payroll already did their time. Never mind, everyone they work with, while still in the streets, is a human being first. They will criticize. If you don't have someone with a backbone who can debate these issues, the program is doomed from the start. I have seen elected officials full of conviction for the model fold under pressure when they are put on the hot seat, walking back support before anything formal can be put in place.

A new city is going to need access to shooting and homicide data. It has to be a source that shows the "hot spots" where violence is most likely to occur. This is how we decide *where* to start our efforts. If these data are blocked, which is often the case, you are going in blind. The more data sources, the better the coordination across systems, sectors, and institutions.

Also, a new city needs data to measure impact. Once a program gets started, you going to have to track progress. Critics love to play sleight of hand with stats. They will show increases in violence for places you haven't even been working to condemn the program. Juking the stats to make it seem like the violence is on the move rather than going down. Officials have blindsided me with skewed data, trying to discredit the program. Political buy-in is critical for getting that piece in place and keeping it, especially when the data needs to come from law enforcement.

Next, the city needs a community-based nonprofit with deep roots. A trusted organization with a history in the neighborhood. Ideally, they will have experience working with formerly incarcerated staff and understand that background. It helps, too, if the organization has other programs running besides the model so that they can help program participants get plugged into other resources.

That host organization, the nonprofit, should be networked into the surrounding community. Other community partners, faith leaders, activists, organizers, and organizations providing services. This is what Shorty and I spent all that time doing in the early days in Chicago between mediations. A new city needs a nonprofit that will put in the work to build those connections.

The program needs to be working with the right people. That is the trickiest part of the work. They need to hire people with influence on the street. It ain't just anybody with a record who can do this work. It needs to be *who* they know and *how* they know them that provides the credentials. These new hires need to know the highest-risk community members. They will need to know who is the person most likely to shoot or be shot. Ideally, they will need to know them by name and have their phone number. This new hire needs to be *somebody* to the people on the street they are trying to reach. That is the key.

And finally, they are going to need training—a lot of training.

R. Brent Decker, chief operating officer for Cure Violence Global, has the longest tenure of anyone on the team, starting in 2003 as employee number five. He has a master of public health degree in international public health and development and a master of social work degree in clinical social work from Tulane University. Decker, more than anyone else at Cure Violence, identified these criteria to adapt, train, and implement the model in contexts outside of Chicago.

The son of human rights activists, he grew up in Guatemala during the civil war there. His accent is so on point that I have seen Latino barbacks almost drop their bus bins in disbelief when they hear Spanish coming out of this tattoo-covered, bearded, biker-looking white boy as if he just performed a magic trick. Decker created the materials we use to this day to set up a program.

Touchdown.

This could be Omaha, Wilmington, or Chester, Pennsylvania. It could be Columbus, Georgia. Columbus, Ohio. Columbus, Alabama. It could be Greensboro, North Carolina. Grand Rapids, Michigan. The District of Columbia, Cleveland, Cincinnati, or Phoenix. Durham. Des Moines. Charlotte. Anywhere, USA, really.

We Uber from the airport to an oak-paneled conference room with an oversized matching table and high-back chairs. It smells of wood, leather, dusty books, and lemon furniture polish. When the seats swivel, they squeak out for WD-40. A half dozen politicians, staffers, and public health and justice workers pack the room. Politicians asking if we can be flexible about "sharing information with law enforcement."

"I know you say that you can't tell the police anything," says an official with a full Windsor knot taut at the neck, "but under what circumstances are you willing to disclose, say, the commission of a crime."

"Under no circumstances," Marcus responds. "We can't jeopardize the program by disclosing any information to the police. That is not our role."

"If we are giving information to the police, it will shut us down," I add.

"What about a murder?" asks a woman in a power pantsuit with high heels.

"No circumstances," Marcus says. "We are dealing with shootings and killings."

"Not even to prevent the commission of a crime?" the man asks incredulously.

"With all due respect, we *are* working on preventing the commission of a crime," I reply.

"Union will have our ass on that," another man retorts.

"You could stop something from happening?" the first man continues.

"We *are* stopping something from happening."

"Does it have to live in the public health department?" the woman asks. "Can't it be housed with the community policing team?"

"If it is based at a police station, it's the same as sharing information," I answer.

"So, you just going to go up to them and ask them not to shoot?"

"Basically, yes, that is how it works."

"And they are going to go along with it?"

"Depends on who it is doing the asking."

Marcus and I exercise patience, but the pressure is often intense. We explain the concept of "credible messengers" and the idea behind the violence contagion. It can sometimes feel like the city had us out for a dog and pony show. *"See, we entertained the program, but their demands were too unreasonable."* Other times, you might get a room divided. We'd field a few questions, but they'd have at it themselves. We don't even have to be in the room for these debates to occur.

There is almost always at least one detractor in the room who just "doesn't see how this could work." We are polite, honest, and assertive. We point out that it has worked repeatedly, in numerous cities, over and over again. It is never about selling a program. It is about setting it up for success.

Across town, a community organization in a ramshackle storefront opens its doors. It is a cramped space buzzing with activity. A mural is painted on the brick facade in bold, brilliant colors facing the alleyway. Halls wallpapered with motivational posters and kids' drawings covering coats of peeling paint. We enter looking for a bedraggled executive director, a former social worker/community organizer, running a hiring panel for interrupters to staff a brand-new Cure Violence program. In addition, they have a food pantry, counseling sessions, art classes, and a peace march planned at the same time. A kid in the corner, just out of juvie, creates a résumé on a loaned laptop.

"Seems busy around here," Marcus notes as we walk.

"Today? Nah." the ED answers, "You should've been here yesterday when the plumbing went out. It got nasty."

"Sorry to hear that."

"That's the glamorous life of a nonprofit executive director," the ED quips. "You land a $1.5 million grant in the morning and have to plunge out backed-up toilets all afternoon."

Recruitment is a big part of the job. Hiring panels are key. We will review résumés and interview candidates the same as most any gig, but the backgrounds explored are less about computer programs, communication skills, and customer service. Instead, we look for bona fides.

"What you do time for and where?"

"Who you know?"

"How you know them?"

These are some of the only gigs in the country where ex-offender status is a credential. In fact, without a rap sheet on your résumé, you can't even get through the door. Occasionally, a former probation officer, ex-cop, or an undercover operator will try to slip by posing as a candidate. This has happened more times than I can count. They charm or bully their way into an opening. Most of the time, we weed them out pretty quickly. The community has a way of exposing an informant. We'll be up on the panel along with other community contacts. Public health will be doing the interview alongside politicians, activists, organizers, other nonprofit staff, and Cure Violence representation.

This is only part one of the interview. The real test is going out in the community.

Dusk. We roll out. Six fresh recruits on the new crew with Marcus and me in tow. This is the *real* interview. In earlier sessions, we mapped the areas using shooting and homicide data. We are walking into "hot spots" that are radioactive. Blocks that are the most violent in the country. Our mission is to sync up with the highest risk. I'm watching my guys to see how they handle every exchange.

Alongside a lamp-lit park bench in the overgrown square of a public housing courtyard, a group of guys pass a bottle in a brown sack opposite a blunt. The joint rotates clockwise hand to hand while the bottle goes counter. A playlist streams a steady beat into the night air that rises with the smoke. They give nods of acknowledgment and a couple in recognition. This is a good sign.

Turns out one of our new workers was in the fed with one of the smoker's older brothers. Our new worker passes an outreach flyer we've made for the occasion. It lists phone numbers, resources, and the nonprofit address where we spent the day. Since this is a new program, it requires an explanation. Handing over some lit is taken as an offering, even if it was fresh off the copier hours earlier. There is an elevator pitch to promote peace with a loosely worded introduction, but I am scanning to see how it is received. Handshakes and laughter are a promising sign.

Another recruit served on drug charges and went away an addict. Recovery was a big part of his recovery. He earned his GED behind bars and enrolled in an addiction counseling certification program at the community college after he was released. At the nonprofit, he went from being in group therapy to running sessions. He considers himself a street social worker and plans to go back to school to earn a degree. When the spot opened for a violence prevention program at the nonprofit, leadership in the organization encouraged him to go for an interrupter position.

He is a gangly guy, swallowed into a too-big, gray-green sweatshirt that used to fit him when he went away. He's dropped so much weight since that it looks like he is wearing hand-me-downs. He is friendly, outgoing, and compassionate. I see why he makes such a good therapist, but after a few hours, I don't think he will make a good interrupter.

Streets have a long memory. Even with his drug days behind him, some of the guys we encounter give him the side-eye. They remember what he was like back in the day. He will have a tough time swaying a street dude to walk away. He never had the credibility or the influence, so I have to recommend that they don't move forward with him.

We spend the night walking on foot through the area. Then, dinner at a local joint. It is a late-night diner with booths and plastic tabletops. An orange hue to the fluorescent lights gives the area a glow from the sidewalk down the block. Inside, it is brightly lit and looks hospital-cafeteria-clean. It smells of grease and deep-fried deliciousness. We order burgers and fries, finding a space near the back where we can pull tables together to debrief the evening.

"This ain't no lick," I hammer from the front of the room the following day.

Training begins soon after the team is hired and vetted. For a lot of us, this is the first legit gig. As a result, we have to train the basics on how to navigate in a professional setting, alongside mediation skills, motivational interviewing, therapeutic techniques, and interruption tactics.

"If you see it as a lick and you just looking for cover while you get back to doing your thing, go work at Amazon down the block. They taking applications," I continue, getting some laughs.

"I'm serious, though. If you are in this, you are in it 100 percent, okay?" I rail, giving a variation of the talk Freeman once gave me. "No side hustles. No backpedaling. No one foot in and one foot out.

"Be loyal to the movement. Understand? If you still want to be dealing, that's fine, you do that, but you leave here today, okay? You do that somewhere else. Your loyalty to the movement is you go and do that business elsewhere.

"If you are on something bigger. If you are about being part of the solution for all the years, you were part of the problem. Then you are in the right place. Go out in history for being righteous. Be loyal to the movement."

Across the country, I fly hundreds of thousands of miles to train thousands of workers for more than one hundred sites in more than fifty cities in less than a decade. Cure Violence was scaling, yes, but it was part of something so much bigger. A movement that stretched back decades with the promise of liberation for the future.

26

ONE CITY, ONE GAME
Englewood, Chicago, 2011–2018

Joakim Noah, the center forward for the Chicago Bulls, was still settling into his adopted home a few seasons after being drafted. Chicago was different from the cosmopolitan upbringing he'd had in Manhattan with his Swedish mother and French African father. He'd been raised as a citizen of the world (holding citizenship in France, the United States, and Sweden), had gone to United Nations International in high school with kids from diverse global backgrounds, and traveled extensively. The racial divisions that separated the city came as a shock to the system.

His assistant passed along a copy of *The Interrupters* because she thought he'd like it. The movie was still getting national attention, which was pretty unusual for a documentary. It had a 99 percent on Rotten Tomatoes, the review aggregator, and started making the rounds on DVD. I knew it was big time when I pulled off the E-way and saw street vendors at the exit peddling bootleg copies. I imagine that is unprecedented in the history of documentary film.

When Jo watched it, he saw a Chicago removed from the one he was living in. Divided and divisive. He was taken with the movie and the cause. He posted something like, *"If you want to know what is really going on in Chicago, you should see this movie."* Meanwhile, at this time, I told anyone who would listen that it was my movie. Seriously, anyone: parking attendants, waitstaff, the smoothie maker at Jamba Juice. So, it seemed natural that when Joakim endorsed the film as a must-see on Twitter, I responded, *"Thanks for liking my movie!"*

Ironically, I was in New York, at the United Nations, when the tweet came through online. Friends were blowing me up: *"Are you really talking to Joakim Noah?"* and I was like, *"I think so, yeah!"* Jo and I started messing with each other back and forth, so I sent him my number online, not thinking anything of it.

I get this call a little while later. New York area code. Answer it. I don't realize it was him at first. I think it's a prank.

"I guess you don't know where I am from, huh?" Jo says, playing.

Now, I know I am busted.

"This really you?" I ask.

"I liked your movie, man," Jo told me. "We should meet."

I was going to be back in Chicago the next day. We met at a P.F. Chang's in the suburbs and hit it off right away. It was immediate. Development had wanted me to come up with a fund-raising ask. Friends wanted me to get his autograph. Film production studio hoped to leverage his endorsement. I was just honored to meet him. If it had ended with egg rolls, that probably would have been enough, but what started with that single tweet turned into more than a decade of collaboration.

We just started talking. There were no plans, no programs, no pitch decks, or ask. I invited him out to Englewood. I took him around the neighborhood. We met with different community organizations. I introduced him to some kids off the block and brought him to Granny's place. Most of the time, how these things go it is a photo op or an oversized check. A celebrity endorses some cause or an event. They show up at the appointed time in the designated place. Pictures are taken.

Jo wasn't about any of that. No fanfare.

He opened up the sixty-thousand-square-foot practice space for youngsters in the neighborhood to come down and play. From their perspective, these kids, who rarely, if ever, got off the block, this is everything. They might have a court at the park near home, but it ain't got no net. The rim is bent. The backboard busted. Here, it was bliss. Perfection. The sounds of squealing laughter echoing off the walls and the scuff of gym shoes on immaculate floors rang out joy.

Here, it is a state-of-art facility that was home to legends. It is a shimmering building of glass and steel with two gleaming courts. This is where the 1991, 1992, 1993, 1996, 1997, and 1998 championship teams honed their skills. This is the court where Scottie Pippen and Michael Jordan played.

Jo also made sure that there were always tickets set aside for our guys. He took care of outreach staff who wanted to bring a client to a game they might not have any way of seeing otherwise. He looked out for interrupters who welcomed the perk of getting out of the trenches for a game or two and just enjoyed themselves. We were all really grateful for his support.

A CITYWIDE PEACE TOURNAMENT

Asa Duce Powell is a serial entrepreneur and club promoter with the tall, sinewy build of a basketball player. I have known him forever. He is a little older than me, so we didn't hang out much as kids, but we were always cool. We grew up in the same group.

"What do you think about doing a citywide peace tournament?" he asked.

Duce splits his time between Vegas and Chicago, running a small entertainment empire. Hip-hop labels, party promotion companies, nightclubs, and businesses—all under his umbrella. He doesn't really get fame drunk the way some people do around celebrities, where they forget how to speak or act right. So, when he is speaking about bringing Jo in on something, it isn't just to blow himself up—the way it sometimes is with other people.

"Father Mike called," Duce said of Father Pfleger, the controversial activist priest at Saint Sabina, a Catholic church in Auburn Gresham who leads community organizing efforts.

"He is thinking of putting something together for the kids. Hosting a game or something."

Since I have known him, Duce has always remembered where he comes from. No matter his success, he always finds a way to give back. Motivational speaking gigs for guys in the joint, support for brothers who just got out, donating and investing his money, time, and resources to benefit the community.

Father Mike had been around as far back as when we were still tearing up the streets. Saint Sabina was a different kind of church under his leadership. He was a white pastor with a mostly Black congregation who always put himself out front of anti-violence, housing rights, and anti-poverty marches. After his adopted son was gunned down, violence prevention became his primary cause. He also was never shy about courting criticism—organizing alongside Jesse Jackson, Louis Farrakhan, and Al Sharpton—and painting a Black Jesus mural on the side of the church.

"What's he got in mind?"

"He wants to bring kids together to play at the church," Duce says. "I'm thinking we can go big, though, homie. Bring in kids from all over the city—the South Side, the West Side—to play a tournament. Do it up big. Talk to Jo about it. Get some players out."

Duce tends to think big. It is a large part of what got him where he was in the first place. For him, it was already more than just an event. He was thinking the NBA could mobilize. The press could come out. Make a big show of the thing, not to promote us but to promote the work.

I agreed to put together a meeting with Jo. We went to his place to pitch the idea. The three of us sat in a circle, running ideas past one another. Jo was reluctant to make it about anything other than the kids.

He didn't want his teammates, Derrick Rose, Todd Gibson, other players, or himself, pulling focus from what's important.

"This is not just a game," I told him cautiously. "We are trying to make a statement here."

"It is like a declaration, citywide," Duce said. "A declaration of peace. This is symbolic. Bringing these young men together in the same room, the same court, to play. That is important, but we also want to send a message."

"It's a gesture ya'll being there," I added. "It shows you care about the whole city."

Jo listens. He never comes in with an agenda. I will always credit him for that. There are a lot of times when money is the room, they think it means they have all the answers. I'm not just talking celebrities, either. I have seen funders do this, too.

The idea of doing this thing in a major way appealed. It was a way to use the Bulls platform to shed light on what was going on in the city. Most of the time, violence grabs headlines in a way that stokes fear and creates villains of children. Jo's involvement shifted the conversation from the same old story toward promoting a solution.

I was traveling a lot, so I had to coordinate from a distance. We arranged a series of games across the city. Saint Sabina hosted one. Community centers offered to open their gyms. A couple of neighborhood high schools opened their courts off-hours. The final game we wanted to culminate in a face-off at the United Center, the home of the Chicago Bulls and the largest NBA arena in the country.

Mikey Davis, who had appeared as my mentee in *The Interrupters* film, became indispensable to making these tournaments happen. Mikey had impressed audiences by taking it on himself to return to the barbershop he'd held up in a robbery to apologize (initially, he hadn't even wanted the cameras there). It was a real and raw demonstration of restorative justice in action. After the film, he threw himself into violence prevention work, splitting his time between the Becoming A Man (BAM) program and working to make these games go off without a hitch.

The venue was as important as anything else. It is a different kind of thing playing on an official court in an official game than a game of street ball in a public park. Real refs calling fouls. Buzzers sounding. Crowds cheering. A giant scoreboard with an actual score rather than your homie holding up fingers from a worn-out park bench with peeling green paint. These things have meaning.

When we first started talking about the United Center, people were saying, *"No way!"* It was too much of a liability bringing high-risk, gang-involved kids known to be violent into that space.

"Lower your expectations," we were warned.

"We'll get it," Jo told me. "We'll make it happen."

His guy, Matt Rosenberg, who manages his business interests and handles behind-the-scenes logistics on his career, made magic happen. He kept at it. Pulled strings. Had conversations. Exchanged favors. And made it happen. This was a big, big deal because it made things official. If we closed out our season with an event like that, playing a real game on a court defined by world-class legends, it incentivized kids to stick it out. They wanted their families as fans for a day in the seats of the United Center chanting their names. It helped kids stay with the program when they otherwise may have acted out and blown their chances under other circumstances.

I recruited Cure Violence staff to serve as coaches. I wanted to make sure that we aligned these games as closely to the model as possible. There has always existed tension between the Cure Violence and programs deemed early interventions. I think this came down from Doc, who felt that anything not on the model would be a distraction that diluted results. A lot of after-school programs, mentoring projects, leadership training programs, art, sports, and entrepreneurship efforts promote themselves as violence prevention. That is true, but they are a different kind of intervention, working with a different population. We needed guys who knew ball and mediation work, which itself is a special combination of skills.

This made sure we got out the right guys and worked with them in the right way. The coaches were so plugged in that they could connect what kids were learning on the court with what they did in the streets. We couldn't just bring in an off-duty high school coach to make that happen. It had to be someone able to balance all of those responsibilities.

Joakim paid for coaches' salaries and other expenses. I managed to recruit, coordinate, train, and hire this staff via texts and calls in hotel rooms
or on break between new site hiring panels. Mikey was on the ground im-
plementing these games out in the community and making sure everything
was working. A lot of times, I would touch down in Chicago after a week of
coordinating a new site and immediately drive to a school gymnasium from
the airport to check out the facilities.

"Basketball is part of the city," Jo affirmed after he'd been going back
and forth on it for a while. "If we can use it to reach these kids, actually get
through to them, why wouldn't we use it?"

"Does that mean you're in?" I asked.

"Let's do this, Cobe," Jo nodded. "Let's do it."

27

THE NEW YORK CITY CRISIS MANAGEMENT SYSTEM

New York City, 2012–2017

In New York, the program took off as fast as it had in Chicago. From four start-up sites working independently in relative isolation in 2009–2010 to twenty-two sites working in coordination through the health department. In only a couple of years, its growth skyrocketed. Marcus and I flew the 1,580-mile round trip almost monthly to recruit, hire, train, and retain staff in the Bronx, Brooklyn, Manhattan, Staten Island, and Queens.

This is especially significant given the law-and-order history of racist policing policies in the city. Stop and frisk, which sanctioned racial profiling, was born there.[1] This gave the New York Police Department the right to detain, question, and search citizens at random. Once the police stopped a civilian, they would "frisk" the external clothing for a weapon or "search" their belongings on sketchiest probable cause grounds. They were also allowed to use physical force if they thought it necessary. In 2009, Black and Latino people in New York were nine times as likely to be stopped by the police compared to white residents. It was later revealed that this was no statistical coincidence. Police had actively made Black people a target.

When activists began a campaign against the policy, marching on the mayor's office in protest, police escalated. They made the situation worse by declaring the protestors "professional agitators." Precinct headquarters were decorated with "wanted" posters singling out activists even though they had done nothing illegal.

Eventually, stop and frisk would be declared unconstitutional and ineffective. In the ten years spanning 2003–2013, nearly 90 percent of stops did not lead to a summons or arrest.

Zero-tolerance policing was also incubated in New York, allowing law enforcement to crack down on even the most minor of offenses.[2] These efforts, like stop and frisk, defined the law-and-order playbook. It focused on petty offenses like begging, graffiti, public drinking, vagrancy, or a dime bag of weed to "clean up" the city. Again, the policy was disproportionately focused on minority communities, with 87 percent of those arrested using zero tolerance being Black or Hispanic. Even low-level arrests led to extreme consequences beyond legal punishment, leading victims of the law to lose their jobs or be evicted.

Brothers Andre "AT" Mitchell and James Peterson with Man Up! were two of the Cure Violence early adopters in 2009. They'd been working as "credible messengers" for half a decade beforehand, intervening in conflicts, using street connections and influence.

Mitchell was impressed with the way the health model framed the intervention and fought hard to bring it to Brooklyn. They also blended community activism into their approach, cocreating the Crisis Management System (CMS), a systematic and comprehensive wraparound service model created to reduce gun violence that expanded the model by providing school-based interventions, employment services, therapeutic mental health resources, legal assistance, and a kind of violence prevention training program for neighborhood residents.

Man Up! has three locations in Brooklyn and is organized around the Kenyan tradition of *harambay*, which means "all pull together" in Kiswahili, referring to a communal sense of self-reliance.

"No one is coming to save us," Brother Petersen observed when he joined AT to get Man Up! off the ground. "We are going to have to do it for ourselves."

Harambay has everyone around the office space recognize one another as brother and sister, which is policy when you are at any location. There is mutual respect for everyone, no matter your background or where you are from originally. In addition to their violence prevention work, Man Up! provides youth and community development, music and art programs, a reentry project, and employment assistance.

The John Jay College of Criminal Justice Research and Evaluation Center conducted a comprehensive evaluation into the effectiveness of Man Up!'s Cure Violence replication in East New York. They found the organization responsible for a 50 percent decrease in gun injuries. Man Up! was also determined to be the best replication of the model in New York.

HUMAN JUSTICE

Around the same time in 2010, on the other end of Brooklyn, Jumaane D. Williams, a community activist designated by the police as a "professional agitator" among those in the gallery of "wanted" posters decorating the local precinct, would help to become another co-architect of the CMS. Jumaane would go from street activist to elected official, becoming first a city council member and, later, in 2019, a public advocate.

Jumaane had been an outspoken critic of racist policing practices like zero tolerance and stop and frisk, which connected the dots from resistance to these strategies to community-led public safety. Fundamentally, that is what the CMS hoped to accomplish: provide the community with the tools and resources to address violence on their own terms.

Jumaane collaborated with Community Capacity Development, which provided a "human justice" lens. The philosophy brought domestic human rights together with human development, which aims to reverse discriminatory economic policies that undermine the ability to generate intergenerational wealth. This helped make the violence prevention strategy further reaching, including wraparound support services that took aim at structural inequities and systemic racism.

CHALLENGES AND SETBACKS

Marcus gave the very first New York training back when the city had less than a handful of sites. This was in Crown Heights, with a program called Save Our Streets (S.O.S.) operated by the Center for Justice Innovation out of a storefront office. They'd been running a project there since 1998 focused on promoting community cohesion. Violence prevention seemed a natural extension of this work.

At this time, I was early in my national coordinator career. My position still straddled mediation and training, which was largely on account of leadership. I had just taken on oversight for Baltimore, where our first replication sites were based. In the early days of the program, Brent Decker moved there, spending months setting up the program while sharing an apartment with the public health professionals working to get it off the ground. That was how we operated in the early days.

Marcus was managing our New York efforts. We often trained together, but the day-to-day problem solving required to make these programs successful was often divvied up between us city by city.

Marcus talks about the work there as being in two distinct phases. The way you look at events sometimes as having a before and an after, but you can't pinpoint an exact moment everything shifted. The early phase was a bit messy. This would have been from 2009 to 2012, when Brent's relocating to get the program off the ground was standard operating procedure. Cure Violence was having to figure out how to operate outside Chicago yet. Other sites were having to understand and adapt the model. Programs that had a history of doing the work sometimes had a hard time adjusting to a new frame of doing things. Man Up! was an exception. They caught on immediately. Others, not so much.

Initially, Cure Violence wasn't necessarily providing "credible messengers" to give training. In Harlem, during an early site visit, one of our national training team was accused of being a cop by high-risk prospective clients. They literally run them out of the neighborhood. That was just one example, but it was one of many that were part of Cure Violence's growing pains. Things changed when the leadership realized they had to adopt the "credible messenger" approach 360, which was big for them.

Crown Heights, for its part, had a tough time early on identifying the highest risk. It had been working in the community for so long, providing social service programs, that they just moved a lot of the young men from one program to the other. This was right out of the gate, early in their implementation, so it is understandable. They knew the kids they worked with were at risk, so they figured there might be a little latitude on the criteria. There wasn't. I'm not trying to shade on anybody. These were just early struggles as everyone figured out what was what.

That second phase in New York, from 2012 to 2015, professionalized everything. This was the shift where our training materials, overall approach, and presentation skills shifted. It is also around that time that we got better at adapting the model. We figured out what were the nonnegotiables and the flexibles. There was a difference between where we had to stick to the science of implementation in terms of dosage and where we could adapt to the local context. We had to learn all of that.

And we had to learn it fast.

The first big infusion of money, $30 million, propelled us from ten sites to fifteen. New York exploded. Then, fifteen to twenty sites. Some of these were politically appointed. They weren't sites that made sense for the model at the time, but they received resources because of connections behind the scenes. We grew twenty to twenty-five, crossing almost into thirty. This was another part of our journey as an organization; we needed to really look critically at the model in detail so that we could start making distinctions.

Decker had come out of the world of public health. After he graduated, he spent years doing health and social justice projects in Central and South America, where he had spent much of his formative years. Traveling to Guatemala, Mexico, Ecuador, Bolivia, and Cuba. He was digging wells for drinking water, advocating human rights, and setting up programs.

He would eventually take over the International Program at Cure Violence before becoming the chief operating officer for the entire organization. At this time, however, as part of this second phase, he stepped in to overhaul all our training materials. He spent weeks shut off from the world, working around the clock, chronicling everything he'd learned from those early days onward. Codifying programmatic knowledge previously locked away in our heads. This was a large part of that professionalizing.

CREATING THE NATIONAL MODEL

New York has the largest network of violence prevention organizations in the country today. Operating across twenty-two communities citywide simultaneously with an explicit focus on neighborhoods significantly impacted by gun violence. No more backroom politics horse trading to get a low-key presence in a community where the response didn't make sense. More than fifty community-based organizations provide violence intervention and support services specifically to the highest risk.

I spent over a decade trekking back and forth to the city. I am so inspired by everything they've accomplished and proud to make my modest contributions. They deserve every success they've had and more.

From 2010 to 2019, there was a 40 percent reduction in shootings across all CMS areas. In the South Bronx, shootings went down by 63 percent. They went down 50 percent in East New York.

The Office to Prevent Gun Violence was launched out of this initiative to provide coordination and oversight in partnership with the New York Public Health Department. The city had changed the model through its engagement, expanding wraparound services to increase impact. They were poised to be the national model.

28

REAL CHICAGO
Englewood, Chicago, 2011–2018

"**T**his is Chicago-Chicago," Joakim joked, taking in the scene with awe. "Real Chicago."

Even when you knew what you were walking into, it was a sight to behold. Nation of Islam providing security at a once Irish Catholic church. NOI bow ties standing about the gothic-style, medieval-looking cathedral. Ornate skyscraping spires and gray castle-like bricks. Out of place in Auburn Gresham.

NBA stars, present and past, red scarf Muslims in brightly colored turbans, politicians, community leaders, congregants, and family members packed the South Side gym. It was a circus that first one. I will admit that. News vans and shuttle buses blocked the street. Outreach workers acting as coaches pace the floor. Kids from across the city, there to play. Stands packed. Scoreboards fired up.

Anywhere else, this thing would seem like an ordinary basketball camp. If you were coming in off the street, you might think it was a rec program. Kids rocking fresh uniforms, repping their neighborhoods, working off the pregame jitters, running drills, doing laps and layups.

Playing hard, same as under other circumstances. Same as they'd do for a homeschool team playing a cross-town rival. Save that, most of these kids have been forced out, kicked out, or plain left their schools. That, and, days earlier, they'd have been shooting at those cross-town rivals instead of shooting hoops against them.

"This is beautiful, man, beautiful," Jo continued in reverence.

"This cause of you, Big Homie," I told him.

"I can't take credit," he responded. "We did this together."

For our part, we played through that event without incident. The kids who participated honored the truce we'd established. No one brought a weapon. Everyone showed respect. There were some heated clashes in those early games. Our coaches pulled double duty to de-escalate. Occasionally, things might come to blows, but no one upped a piece in relation to the event. It wasn't nothing worse than some of the things that happened around any court in a high school or college game. NBA themselves have had to deal with worse on their own courts.

We used these blowouts as teaching moments.

"How many of ya'll lost someone to gun violence," I'd ask in a pregame huddle. "Show of hands."

Ain't no one in that space didn't have their hands up.

"How many of ya'll lost someone close to you?"

Only a few couple hands went down.

"How many of ya'll lost someone recently?" I asked. "In the last couple months or so?"

Almost all the same hands stayed raised.

"Take a look around," I instructed. "Ya'll have more in common, right, than what separates us?"

It wasn't just the kids we brought together who were learning and growing from this process. The organizations responsible for pulling this off were hosting debriefs following games to improve our approach. In the same way that Cure Violence programs would regroup after a conflict mediation to figure out how we needed to coordinate next steps, we tried to plan our response game to game.

We also made sure what happened on the street informed how we handled events on the court. It was the same way hospital response programs would sync up with community sites to make sure things happening in the neighborhood reflected what was happening in the waiting room. If we learned our power forward just saw his best friend killed two days before a game and knew that the group he was going up against on the court was responsible for the shooting, we provided extra attention.

Beyond these individual interventions, the debrief sessions contributed to two of the biggest changes in the program. We had, from the jump, squared neighborhood against neighborhood. Back of Yards versus North Lawndale, for example, or Humboldt Park up against Englewood/Auburn Gresham.

Sometimes, these brought rivals head-to-head in a game to resolve peaceably on the court what they would try to sort out through other means on the streets. Other times, they might not actually know the neighborhood they were going up against, but they were learning how bigger, broader, and more diverse the city was through these engagements.

Going into the tournaments in the second year, we changed things up. We formed teams from different, opposing cliques. Now, players had to rely on teammates they were shooting at only a few days earlier. In order to win the game, they legit had to pass to the enemy to shoot and score.

After a game, we would talk about team etiquette, skill building, sportsmanship, and relationship building. We would promote these positive attributes learned on the courts into their conduct on the streets. Translating these skills into their daily lives. A lot of these young men weren't ever likely to set foot in the same place, on the same street, ever, let alone play together on the same team.

Relationships began to form. Friendships outside the gym. Bonds began to influence interactions in the neighborhood. The players learned teamwork, collaboration, cooperation, and camaraderie through these exchanges.

"We using basketball to bring these kids in," I said in a debrief meeting, "but what we doing with them between games or between seasons is just as important if not more than what happens in the game on the court."

We began to develop programming that would keep these kids engaged in services once the tournament had ended. It was important to keep this momentum going. Father Mike started a program at Saint Sabina's in 2011 to keep working with program participants. Duce helped launch the Chicago Peace Organization to offer support services in the community to maintain consistency. Cure Violence workers had participants on their caseload, so they continued one-on-one interventions with individual program participants.

Mikey was working for Youth Guidance on the BAM program at this time through an introduction from Jo. He incorporated techniques for impulse control, emotional self-regulation, and other cognitive, behavioral, social, and emotional skills on and off the court in an informal way that he learned from that program.

That led to the second-biggest change: how to establish a binding truce citywide connecting teams that could carry over between seasons and transcend the tournaments themselves. That responsibility would fall to Jo's Noah's Arc Foundation and our next big initiative together.

A VEHICLE FOR CULTURAL CHANGE

From the beginning, Joakim and I saw basketball as the vehicle for cultural change. This was never about a single game, a single event, a single tournament, or even a series of tournaments. It was never even about basketball. It was about changing the conversation around violence.

The Cure Violence model promotes a public education component. In public health, it is referred to as social marketing. It uses promotional content as a health communication tool to change mindsets around violence. Everything from the bumper stickers, flyers, posters, and placards we distribute to CeaseFire's appearance on an episode of the hospital drama *ER* falls into that category. I'd never seen the organization do it right.

In fact, the most effective tool in our public education strategy to date came from *The Interrupters* movie, which the organization never fully embraced. The peace tournaments fit as a cultural change vehicle. They were an extension of the model, but ironically, the organization never saw their full potential. This may have been just biased against programs that were part of the broader violence prevention ecosystem. Cure Violence staff put in a lot of legwork in our off time to make it happen. It was only thanks to Jo that we pulled it off.

From our very first encounter, we connected. Jo dubbed me the big brother he never had. By the time we were rolling from our second season, we really were family, though. He'd come out to the house for the holidays. Angel and me set a place for him at the table during Thanksgiving. We were there for each other through special occasions, graduations, birthdays, and weddings. Joakim is one of the most generous people I have ever met. He always looked out for the family showing us kindness. I came to call his mother "Moms," and Granny always hosted when we were out in the neighborhood.

I was traveling almost nonstop, so I made it a goal to see a game at every stadium in the continental United States. There are thirty NBA teams in North America but only twenty-nine full-time arenas since the Lakers and the Clippers share one in Los Angeles. I would use my frequent-flier miles to tack an extra location on my trip after a week of training to catch a game. I'd fly in just to cross another stadium off my list. Having activities outside promoting the model helped me keep my sanity.

Wherever possible, Jo and I would coordinate schedules. When he was playing away games, we would grab dinner together. Often, conversation turned to building on the work and improving our tournaments.

"This has been one of the most powerful experiences I ever had in Chicago," Jo said as we ate dinner at a New York seafood joint.

"We've made quite an impact, homie."

"I've some ideas about keeping the momentum—the movement—going," Jo replied.

He laid out what became the Rock Your Drop campaign. Jo's mother, Cecilia Rodhe, the cofounder of the Noah's Arc Foundation, was an artist. She sculpted the *Drop of Consciousness* as a pendant. It was a teardrop-shaped metal bulb meant to symbolize the pain of losing someone to violence.

It was an icon intended to demonstrate to the city that violence was not just a problem for the South and West sides but a citywide problem. We included a pledge with the drop. This filled that gap we had been feeling between seasons, that we hoped would carry over the truce established throughout the season. It was a stopgap measure, but it was something we could put in place to keep the work going.

We filmed a public service announcement introducing the Rock Your Drop campaign, which included Spike Lee, Rhymefest, Matt Forte, FM Supreme, and other celebrities. Five years had passed since the release of *The Interrupters*, so we made a thing about getting the most prominent subjects of the film together for a reunion. The campaign was promoted on billboards, in magazines, on websites, and in media everywhere.

When I traveled, I threw fistfuls of rhodium, rose-gold, gold-plated, and silver drops with leather straps in my bag. We brought the pendant and the pledge city to city. I became a one-man ambassador for the campaign, distributing the jewelry everywhere I went. The foundation officially named me their community engagement director, which balanced the work I was already doing with Cure Violence. I saw these projects as interconnected initiatives for making a national change.

Meanwhile, Joakim's career took him from Chicago. He played for the New York Knicks, the Memphis Grizzlies, and the Los Angeles Clippers before retiring. These moves never derailed what we were building. In fact, Jo remained so committed that the work followed him from city to city. His support continued no matter where he played.

One night, over Chinese food in his Memphis digs, Jo turned to me and said, "When this basketball thing is through, Cobe, I am doing violence prevention with you full-time. You watch."

TAKING THE TOURNAMENTS NATIONWIDE

Over the next couple of seasons, we began replicating the basketball tournaments in other cities. In New York City, New Orleans, Philadelphia, and
Memphis, we repeated our successes. As with Chicago, we made sure that
the coaches were trained violence prevention experts. It was not just about
the game as much as it was leveraging the game to teach lessons that could
transfer to the street. These games resulted in dozens of peace treaties
between rival cliques around the country. Hundreds of young people were
introduced to conflict resolution and coping strategies.

Unfortunately, they did not take as well elsewhere as they had in Chicago, where we had seven seasons in succession. I suspect that's because
there was not as much on-the-ground support. After the 2011 peace tournament season in Chicago, other organizations popped up to provide the
year-round support. This kept the effort going. The other cities didn't mobilize the same kind of coverage. They hadn't set up the infrastructure. In
between seasons, whatever had been accomplished during the tournament
was often lost.

It was valuable to understand the contrast between these programs. It
demonstrates the value of the tournaments working in partnership with
a community-based effort. If we were to expand the peace tournaments
nationally, again, I would make sure we had resources in place to provide
year-round support even in the offseasons. I am still confident this can be
done at scale, but we'd have to replicate and amplify what we did in Chicago.

EXPANDING THE APPROACH

Matt Forte, running back for the Chicago Bears, connected with me during
the Rock Your Drop! campaign. We met at a Bulls game shortly after he
started his own foundation. Jo hosted. Matt had attended the event, interested in hearing what Jo was doing in the community and how he could help.

"You got to meet my man, Cobe," Jo told him. "This guy is the real deal.
He makes things happen."

"I've been fortunate, really fortunate." Matt said, "Not just playing pro,
but in my life in general. I feel it is my responsibility—an obligation—to
give back."

Matt just started throwing questions at me. He wanted to hear about
what I did as an interrupter mediating conflict, but also bigger picture, what
I thought needed to be done at a deeper level to address violence.

He liked what Jo and I were doing and thought there might be an opportunity to do the same with football. This was another element of leveraging sports to shift culture. We created a series of flag football games in parks around the city. This was often with younger kids and had a little different focus than the peace tournaments.

It was also important for Matt to show that there were opportunities beyond the NBA, NFL, or playing other pro sports. "I want to show these kids there are paths behind the scenes that offer plenty of opportunities without having to be in the spotlight," Matt told me. "You look at a show being made over at ESPN. Somebody working the camera, somebody working the mics, somebody running the soundboard, somebody doing graphics. It doesn't need to be about the guy behind the desk broadcasting or the player on the field catching a pass; there are hundreds of roles need to be filled to make something happen, but we don't recognize those as opportunities."

We hosted back-to-school drives. Stocked over four hundred backpacks with materials: notebooks, pens, pencils, markers, folders, art supplies, and whatever the kids needed. These givebacks were community events—BBQs with DJs in neighborhood parks—games, music, activities. At Matt's insistence, we went above and beyond. It wasn't just about meeting immediate needs but trying to give a little extra. We got $100 gift cards from Foot Locker so that the kids could buy themselves something special for their first day back they wouldn't be able to afford otherwise. New kicks, fresh looks, sharp threads. It went a long way for kids growing up with hand-me-downs to have even just one new shirt to start the year right.

TOWARD A CITYWIDE PEACE AGREEMENT

In 2015, we focused on our biggest effort in Chicago. We set out to develop a citywide peace agreement. Our aim was to extend beyond the season, covering the gap between tournaments. It would involve both program participants and their homies in the street alike from three gangs throughout the city. It would aim to keep peace year-round between the groups. The initiative was poised to be our biggest success—or our greatest failure.

29

GROUP MEDIATIONS
Englewood, Chicago, 2011–2018

As the peace tournament entered its fifth season, we'd figured out a lot. Our overall strategy had taken shape. We began to integrate everything happening on the streets with what we were doing on the court. The biggest challenge we faced was still the gap between seasons. During those months without a game, we didn't have the infrastructure in place to stay with all the players as they went back into the community.

Group mediation, especially when applied to large street organizations, requires a lot of care and feeding. It is a heavy lift, requiring a significant investment of time, energy, and effort. The arithmetic of an interruption requires a minimum of two parties. From a sheer numbers perspective, the arithmetic of a group mediation looks more like one of those complex equations Matt Damon has to figure out in *Good Will Hunting* that fill up a whole whiteboard. You are doing multiple one-on-one mediations, riding out emotional highs and lows, while simultaneously balancing the concerns of an entire organization. The gang may want more territory, for example, but the members who make it up may just be looking to let go of some of that pain. Managing a group mediation means managing all of this at the same time. We just didn't have the people in place to do this around the clock for the whole calendar year.

We had some success with the Rock Your Drop pledge. The campaign had been a national effort with a Chicago focus. It got a lot of attention. It was flashy, exciting, broad-reaching, and sincere. We sold or donated custom jewelry, the metal teardrop-shaped sculpture at the end of a chain (or leather strip), which was a visible symbol of your peace pledge. The same way a wedding band represents the vows taken between a couple. At one time, the whole street was rocking their drops.

Simultaneously, the Chicago Peace Organization, Cure Violence, Father Mike, and other organizations were doing the work on the ground. Even with all these groups, our resources were stretched thin, and we weren't all on the same model for community intervention. Cure Violence had succeeded nationally, getting everyone across the country to move from the same playbook, but with the peace tournaments, we didn't have a centralized model. That made it difficult to have any kind of formal follow-through. We could get players in the door to work with them all season, but there needed to be a plan for ongoing work after a team exited the tournament and following the conclusion of a season after an all-out winner was declared.

Another challenge we had was more organizational. At the time, Cure Violence leadership, with the exception of Decker, looked at the tournaments the same way they had the documentary, as a distraction from the work. It was a lack of imagination and a failure to understand Black culture that they didn't see how what we were doing was an extension of the model. In ideal circumstances, these projects would have been combined formally. If resourced correctly, it could have an even deeper impact.

Mikey and I split the workload. Cure Violence promoted me to director of national programs. I hired Mikey to be a national trainer and took a position at Noah's Arc Foundation as a community engagement director, with Mikey serving as a community engagement specialist. It was double duty to balance these responsibilities. I'd fly in from New York, Baltimore, Philadelphia, or Kansas City and head out into the neighborhood on the South or West side to check on a game.

When Jo was out of town, he opened his condo in the city to give us a place to crash. It was a sprawling penthouse overlooking the Loop with wraparound windows from shiny wood floors to high ceilings with exposed ductwork, all open between rooms. In the center of the hallway sat a temple-sized stone Buddha with flower garlands around his neck and an incense dish at the base. The location was only a few minutes from my office on the University campus, so I could sit in on a few games back-to-back before heading there to crash.

Mikey had been a youngster when I was still running the streets. He'd seen me at my worst, and I took some responsibility when he'd cliqued up himself becoming a stickup man. After he'd gotten out, around the time of the documentary, I'd taken him under my wing. It was the same kind of apprenticeship that Freeman provided me with the same rocky beginnings.

We'd be riding down to mediate between GD and BD sets with Mikey going, "Why the fuck you want to get with them, huh? You know what they are into?" This after he'd already come so far to make amends. Meaning even when he got it, there was still a lot of the streets in him that he had a hard time letting go.

By the time we did the tournaments, though, he was already an exceptional trainer, taking charge of aspects of the movement. Mikey and I balanced schedules so that he could hold it down in Chicago, overseeing tournaments while I was traveling. Then, when he was on the road, I stepped in to fill the gaps. He'd also gotten tight with Jo, seeing him the same way as Jo looked at me, a big brother, so they would spend a lot of time hanging out.

"I don't think it is about 'raising awareness,'" Mikey said over a container of fried rice. Chinese takeout had become a staple of our planning sessions each season. "People are aware of the issue. It is about changing they thinking on it."

We were eating in Jo's living room. The conversation focused on how we could have a greater impact with the resources we had in place. We three—Jo, Mikey, and I—regularly discussed what we could do to have a deeper cultural impact. On this occasion, Mikey and I wanted to go big. We wanted these games to be game changers.

"What was brilliant about the drop was having that pledge be a part of it," he continued, referring to a nonviolence pledge that we had included as a part of the Rock Your Drop campaign. "It made the commitment real. We need a gesture like that, which makes it actionable. It makes the pledge actionable."

"What if we bring together the players and their crews for a summit?" I respond. "We focus on establishing a citywide peace treaty between groups by the end of this season. We already connected to these guys, so that piece won't be difficult."

"The players act as ambassadors," Mikey added. "They bring everybody to the table. It recognizes their role."

We talked like this for hours. Finishing our meal and making our way out onto the landing. The evening air was brisk. Lights from the high-rises to the east separating River North from the lakefront shimmered like stars. The whole city stretched out before us in all directions. Set against this backdrop, we began to plan our most ambitious effort yet: a citywide peace treaty.

264   INTERRUPTING VIOLENCE

THE MOST SUCCESSFUL GANG TRUCE IN HISTORY

The most successful gang truce in history was in April 1992 in Watts, just a few days before the Los Angeles uprising that followed the verdict in the Rodney King beating.[1] It involved four street organizations (the Grape Street Crips, PJ Watts Crips, Bounty Hunter Bloods, and Hacienda Village Bloods) from four housing projects (the Jordan Downs Projects, the Imperial Courts, the Nickerson Gardens, and Hacienda Village) to get results. Six war-weary leaders (Aqeela and Daude Sherrills, Twilight Bey, Anthony Perry, Dewayne Holmes, and Tony Bogard) from two gang factions (the Crips and the Bloods). Police, it was agreed, not only weren't going to do nothing to stop the violence, but they also often fanned the flames. Anywhere USA police would be taking gang members into rival territory, making them fend for themselves, as they had done me back in the day. Peace was going to be up to the gangs themselves. These gang leaders turned activists exercised shuttle diplomacy for years before it was brokered.

This treaty should be taught in history classes. Its architects should have gotten a Nobel Peace Prize. It laid the foundation for so much of the community violence intervention movement in this country. Instead, like much of the Chicago history that Shorty spent years educating me on, it still remains mostly hidden.

On April 26, 1992, the peace treaty was signed at a Muslim mosque in Watts, modeled after the 1949 Armistice Agreement between Israel and Egypt. It was tested almost immediately. The Los Angeles uprising began three days later, on April 29. The whole city up in flames would have provided an easy cover to violate the terms of their agreement, but the truce held throughout the chaos. It held, in fact, for more than a decade. In the first two years of the agreement, police data indicated a 44 percent reduction in shootings and killings.

Academics debate whether these agreements work, the same as they have debated community violence intervention programs since their inception, for some of the same reasons. They argue that this approach, establishing a truce, recognizes the gang as an authority. It legitimizes them as a social entity. It makes them politically stronger.

Yeah, okay. The thing is, they should be looked at as a legit social entity, at least in these roles. In Chicago, Lords–Stones–Disciples became a political force when there was no other way for the community to have a voice, advocating for jobs and promoting self-reliance. They are also often the only ones who have influence over the outcomes. As a popular mural in the Nickerson Gardens housing projects once read, "Nobody can stop this war but us."

This was Los Angeles, but it could have been true for Anywhere, USA.

CITYWIDE PEACE SUMMIT CONVERSATIONS
ON PAIN AND LOSS

That fifth season, then, we put everything into building a peace treaty between three warring groups. It was dedicated to putting this agreement in place. The focus of the tournament became about bringing these guys together to hash out any grievances. The pressure was on. It was one of the largest gang truces in my career, involving well over a hundred young men.

One of the things Shorty had been really good at in his career was coordinating peace summits. These were big gatherings of members from several groups across the city to have these large-scale, deep-processing conversations. The first time I had ever seen it done was when a large gathering of young men was asked to raise their hands if they lost someone to gang violence; it was Shorty leading a peace summit.

That recognition that everyone in the room had experienced some kind of loss was a powerful thing to behold. They recognized in that moment their shared pain. It is hard to hate someone when you truly understand them. Harder still to hate when you share that understanding, feeling much the same way yourself. I repeated this exercise in group huddles since the first season we hosted. It had become a regular part of the program.

As we pressed toward a new goal of signing a peace treaty across the membership, it was essential to bring in gang members who weren't even participating in the program. We needed to broaden our reach beyond just the guys we were working with directly. We recognized that we would have to find a way of bringing together entire groups. We organized peace summit–type conversations. We would bring out guys in the same group— Gangster Disciples, for example, whether they were actively in the peace tournaments, lost out for the season, or had never been part of the game in the first place—and sit them down together.

We started with groups of thirty. We would gather these guys together for a kind of informal group counseling. These didn't follow therapeutic models. We didn't do cognitive behavioral therapy with participants or anything like that. We just got them talking about the pain of loss and grief. We encouraged them to be vulnerable and to share openly with each other.

We began to run these in and around tournament games.

One group. Thirty guys at a time. A two-and-a-half to three-hour session. Deep work.

Building toward that citywide agreement.

FLASH POINT

Mid-season, during a tournament game, we hit a flash point. Everything we'd been working on threatened to come undone. That night, three guys from one of the groups, who hadn't even been involved in the tournaments, showed up to watch their guy play. They were all out fans at first. Cheering their guy on. Then, after watching a bit, they realized one of the team members was opposition. Suddenly, the whole vibe shifted.

It was like, *"How you going to play alongside someone who killed our guy?"* It messed with their heads. They weren't there to cause trouble, but went into some kind of shock seeing their guy friendly with someone that may have been involved in killing one of their own.

They started talking shit from the bleachers. First, among themselves, loud enough so we could hear them. Then, outright booing their own guy. Same team they'd come to see.

Cure Violence workers were doing security at the time. They pulled the guys aside to try and cool them out. One of them left out in a rage, shouting through his exit. Slamming the door behind him. So, now we have to worry where he might be going. Wondering if he is going to round up more guys to ride down on them in the parking lot after the game. Concerned he is going to get a piece.

The other two hung out for the rest of the game. They stayed cool. By then, the damage was done. The team that got heckled lost. They were in their feelings over it. Hurt and salty over the drama. Angry at the teammate that brought them out. It was a mess.

Everything that we had been working on for five years and four weeks now seemed on the verge of unraveling thanks to some static between friends over the very thing that the tournament was designed to do.

We went into high alert in the lot afterward. Hung back to make sure everyone had cleared out without incident. The event was treated the same as any mediation where a chance encounter might trigger a potential conflict. After the guys emptied out, we continued talking with the team to make sure none of those hard feelings lingered. We had a track record for keeping anything that happened on the court from spilling out into the streets. We had been pretty good throughout all five seasons at keeping whatever happened on the streets from creeping onto the court.

Now, as we were in the midst of our biggest undertaking, those separations threatened to dissolve.

DOING THE REAL WORK

Throughout the season, we'd meet with one group to discuss then another. Individually, one-on-one, a guy is more real with you. He'll fess up to being scared. He'll share his fears. He'll tell you about his pain, grief, and loss. He'll confide in you the sense of overwhelming hopelessness that consumes his life.

In a group setting, this is much harder.

Participants feed off each other from the jump. They are afraid of being vulnerable. They come with jokes or speak as statues, depending on disposition, with little in between. You have to accept that is part of the process, meet them where they are at, and, sometimes, come with jokes, too.

Our goal in those initial meetings is to get each group to agree to sit down together. That's it. As simple and straightforward as it sounds, that is all we are working toward. Period. Get each group in a room, at a table, together, to talk.

In a group mediation, you are like a conductor, directing energy rather than music. Let the pushback have its place. Those expressions of resistance are intended to clear the air more than anything. It is the space between the notes where the music happens, they say. Discharge that nervous energy by giving it nothing to push against.

Then the real work can begin.

You have to get everything out on the table. In the beginning, this is about processing. There are moments where this is the first time these young men have expressed themselves. Some have not shared feelings like this since they were a child, especially in public. The emotions are real and intense. The experience is honest and raw.

Part of the reason we go there is to get consensus among the group. *"Ya'll tired of this shooting and killing, ain't it?"* As we build trust, we move into a discussion on what they want to get out of these negotiations. This isn't about making demands. It is about coming to some common ground. Creating an empathetic space. Finding an understanding that all three parties can agree on.

After meeting with individual groups for weeks, we were making progress. Not only were the groups willing to sit with each other and open up, but they were also willing to sit with their enemy. Progress.

PLAYBOOK FOR A PEACE SUMMIT

In a peace summit, when you are bringing together conflicting groups, neutral ground is key. Downtown offers good locations. It is far enough off the block that no one could claim it as their territory. There was an added wrinkle in doing them around the peace tournaments. We don't want the summits associated with the games. If the negotiations fall apart on the summits, then we risk losing everything we've built with the tournaments.

We find a spot downtown. On a Saturday morning, the participants are bussed in. The meeting time doesn't compete with the games. Our coaches are in attendance. We also mobilize other violence interrupters and outreach workers. All hands on deck. The staff leading negotiations are even more neutral than the ground they walk. It is important that none of our guys were seen as playing favorites or taking sides.

At this point, we've spent months running back and forth between all three groups. We held one-on-one sessions with almost every member of all three organizations. Then, group sessions with each organization individually to get them ready to sit down together. Coaches met with their teams. Cure Violence staff bring their clients. Other organizations bring out their participants.

On the day of the summit, we bring everyone together. We lay out ground rules. Everyone is to show respect for one another. No cutting someone off. No talking over one another. No shouting each other down. No finger pointing. Everyone gets a chance to say their piece. If things get heated and the rules are violated, we take a break.

I say a few words to open the meeting. Pacing the front of the room with a long-tail mic. "I want to thank y'all for coming," I tell them, wrapping the cord a bit around my arm and elbow so I could move more freely. "You have a choice in being here today, so just showing means something."

There was no pressure to participate. We didn't tell them they'd be booted from the program if they didn't attend. It was unlikely any agreement would be reached if participants felt forced.

Cure Violence staff stand, arms folded across their chest, about the room. Most of the youth sit at round tables, the kind put out for a wedding banquet with folding chairs. They did their best to look distant. Fronting they couldn't care less what is happening here. That isn't true though. I can see it.

"We've heard from all y'all in the past several months. We've heard how every one of you lost somebody at some point to violence. Go ahead. Look around. Look at each other. We are all feeling it."

They eye one another, eye the opposition. Every one of them scan the table, then the room in succession. Chairs shift uncomfortably against the tiled floors. The metal legs groan as participants fidgeted, followed by scraping sounds.

"We're here to come to some kind of agreement today so that we can all get a little relief. That we can stop losing friends."

We begin letting each of the three groups speak. Each table has a representative. We express some of the concerns to the group at large. Then the small groups discuss and debate, bringing that back to a bigger discussion. The representative stands up and reports out to the gathering. They take turns explaining where they are coming from on a given topic.

Some of the topics up for debate are pretty straightforward. Group A wants to be allowed to go to a store at the intersection near Group B's territory without incident. They debate terms. For our part, it is important not to sway the conversation. We don't want to put solutions out there for them. Speak for them. We want participants to express solutions for themselves.

If we put something forward, *"We want y'all in Group A to do this for Group C,"* like a mandate or a dictate, it is far less likely that anyone would abide. If someone in Group A suggests it, though, it is more likely that all the groups, including Group C, would adopt the decision. Our only role, record everything. We sit back and write it out.

There is a tendency for mediators, myself included, to want to push an agenda. We can see a way forward, so we think, *"If we put this out there, it'll make sense."* Better though to hold back. Listen. Encourage. Affirm. We shouldn't take over the conversation.

We spent all day going at it back and forth. There were a few calls for breaks. Things got heated. Mostly, though, we kept the conversation going. Nobody storming out in a huff. No name-calling or threats. Once each group expressed itself, we read back the points of agreement, everything each of the three groups put forward.

I would read out loud the agreed-on point. Then, the representatives from each group would confirm. We are as slow and meticulous as a legal proceeding. By the end of the day, we had a written peace agreement that would last well beyond the season and for a few years beyond.

I don't know exactly how many lives were saved over the seven-year span we did the basketball program. A lot of kids walking around today wouldn't be here if it weren't for the program. Fact! It took all five seasons of the tournaments to reach this point. All of those games, conversations, support, and energy contributed to the positive outcome. In the season we reached this agreement, there were as many back-and-forth meetings, conversations, negotiations, and arrangements with each group as there had been games throughout the tournament.

30

RIGHTING THE
UPSIDE-DOWN WORLD

Englewood, Chicago, Present

Uncle Phil had a saying for every occasion, enough so he could fill a book this length with his wisdom. He was a smooth, charismatic, and comedic bartender for much of his life. His "Phil"-osophies were funny, clever, and playful, but they were also, often, powerful and poetic. One of his favorites, which I often think about, was "Life is a beautiful thing once you learn to live it."

Phil had learned to live it. He took every day on his own terms with courage, humor, and a personality larger than life. Phil made a memorable and lasting impression on everyone he encountered, which was his philosophy of change in the world—and his secret to making great tips as a bartender.

In July 2019, Uncle Phil passed from cancer. In his last days, I shuttled him back and forth between his home and the hospital for treatments. There were bad days when he had difficulty getting off the couch and good days when he was his old self joking around. Mostly, though, he bravely took whatever came at him in stride. We spent his last night together in the hospital before he passed.

Phil was a model for how I live my own time.

This loss was months before the world would flip upside down for everyone. The COVID-19 pandemic hit hard in January 2020. Communities of color were disproportionately impacted. In the United States, during the first year of the outbreak, Black, Native American, and Latino people experienced three times as many cases as whites. We also encountered five times as many hospitalizations and two times as many deaths.

Behind bars, incarcerated individuals were affected by COVID at four times the rate of the general population because of cramped, crowded living conditions and poor health care policies. Racial injustice in the system means this disproportionately impacted Black men who were locked up.

Racism, it was often said, was the *real* pandemic.

Interrupters were declared "essential workers." Suddenly, we had to contend with the intersection of three pandemics in our communities: violence, racism, and COVID-19. Given our access to the community and the fact that we were still out and about in the streets, we quickly adapted our role. We moved from solely focusing on violence prevention to serving as community health workers—as if overnight. We checked in on the elderly, delivering food, providing resources, distributing masks, and leveraging the relationships we built over the years.

This was true in Chicago, Baltimore, New York, Philadelphia, and New Orleans. This helped shift the public perception of us at the time as well. We also launched a public education campaign for the most vulnerable, highest-risk population of all three epidemics. Even while most of the country was shut in, we took to the streets to do the work.

The virus would expose those other two in a painfully public way, forcing a reckoning for this country and pushing racial injustice to center stage.

My work was mostly grounded as air traffic shut down. We moved whatever we could online. Some of the workshops and training could be done through teleconference, so like so many industries in America, we made that shift.

Other aspects of the work require being in person. Moving around in the neighborhood with people, watching body language, witnessing how they receive and are received. In response, I would log thousands of miles behind the wheel to keep the movement going. Zigzagging ghost highways, empty of traffic, across the Midwest, South, and East Coast. I loaded a box of cleaning products and personal protective equipment that went with me everywhere, along with luggage and training materials. People often messed with me that I had a wipe for every doorknob and a bottle of sanitizer whenever I got on the other side, but I managed to make it through these times without getting sick.

Shortly after the loss of Uncle Phil, my brother, Michael (Boo), and my mom, Alfreda, were taken from me. These losses came in quick succession, one after another, in the next two years. My brother had a heart attack, and my mom passed from COVID-related complications.

While Boo and I had our differences, he was always there for me. He was my big brother and cared for me as a big brother should. Whenever it came to having to make a decision between loyalties, Boo always chose me, chose family, over any other tie.

Immediately after prison, when I chose peace, I had concerns about how my brother might look at me. They were misplaced. When Boo knew that I was on this path for real, for real, he showed me nothing but pride and affection. There were times when I had to talk him down from situations later in life. He listened to and respected what I had to say by then and knew he could count on me to point him in the right direction. In the second half of our lives together, the only time I had to push him off me was when he was showering me with kisses. I miss my brother every day.

My mother passed away in August 2021. We made accommodations for her to come to live with us once she got out of the intensive care unit. No sooner did we have things set up did we get word that COVID claimed her. It was a tragic loss for the family and our community. I took it hard.

She had a huge, all-encompassing heart, just like her mama. She gave generously down to her last dollar without reservation. She took in people who didn't have anywhere else to stay, often letting folks stay rent-free until they were good for it. Her door was always open, and her laughter filled the home, beckoning you to come in and join her at the kitchen table.

I have shared in this book some of the hardships she encountered after losing my father. When she got clear of these experiences and found herself again, she led with a generosity that still inspires me. Mom was a home health aide later in life. She would do in-house care until health complications of her own made it too difficult to get around. Mom loved her job, but she lived for her family. That was her purpose in life, she would say, her family. Especially the grandkids, which she loved in the way only a grandmother could. *They are my reason for being*, she'd say.

I feel blessed that I could make all of them—Phil, Boo, Mom—proud of me before they left this life. I feel her loss every single day, but I know she is still with me.

In 2020, the murder of George Floyd ignited something in our community. Those pent-up frustrations exploded. It had been building for some time and was unleashed. I had been in Baltimore after the loss of Freddie Gray and in Chicago after the murder of Laquan McDonald by police. My work had taken me from Ferguson to Flatbush, but this instantly felt different.

American cities erupted in rage. It was the broadest uprising in U.S. history. Nothing in my lifetime came close. Protests around the country focused on police brutality, racism, inequities, and inequality. The conversation around public safety and police was forced into the national spotlight. The racist history of law enforcement in the United States and the reality of police as an occupying force in communities nationwide were suddenly thrust into public consciousness.

The community violence intervention model, which I had been promoting for over a decade, reached new prominence. Activists I'd been with in the trenches, including many I trained, were now going to Washington. It was a huge honor to see my colleagues go to the White House to get a community-based model, which had its roots in decades of street activism, get formally adopted. President Biden pledged $19.4 billion over ten years to community-based crime prevention strategies.

Eddie Bocanegra, who appeared with me in *The Interrupters*, joined the Department of Justice as a senior adviser to community violence intervention. Eddie has been pioneering new violence prevention innovations since he left Cure Violence, which has only continued to improve on these approaches and expand the model. He started the Urban Warriors program when he was with the YMCA, which connected gang-involved youth with military veteran mentors.

Eddie also has done more to incorporate mental health strategies into street-level work, training outreach workers and interrupters in cognitive behavioral therapy and other short-term approaches than anyone else I know in the field. In his role at READI Chicago, which is now a national model, Eddie added an employment component, especially for those reentering the community. This is an essential part of the work.

When the White House wanted to learn about successful violence prevention models in 2022, they focused their observations on New York sites. President Biden visited New York to learn how all the moving pieces of racial and economic justice combined with violence prevention could come together.

Jumaane D. Williams, the activist turned city council member who was instrumental in getting the New York CMS model off the ground, became a New York City public advocate in 2019. He has since set his sights on governor.

In 2022, AT Mitchell, featured throughout this book, who led one of the first sites in New York to adopt the Cure Violence model, was named gun violence prevention czar and cochair of the Gun Violence Prevention Task Force.

In Chicago, Norman Kerr, who cocreated the very first CeaseFire model, became the first gun violence prevention czar in Chicago around the same time. Marcus McAllister, who traveled with me across the country and back for years, launched his own consultancy in public safety.

In 2023, Cure Violence Global got a new doc at the helm. Dr. Monique Williams (no relation) was hired as the executive director of the organization. She is a strong sister who ran community violence intervention work in Louisville. She did her dissertation looking at the violence prevention health model within the context of a broader social/racial justice ecosystem.

I went back to school, earning a BA at Northeastern Illinois University through the University Without Walls program to address what I felt were some of the gaps in the Cure Violence model, specifically the racial justice aspects of the work that the health model often neglects. Dr. Williams has been a mentor and an inspiration to me in this work, so it will be an honor to work more closely in the future (I'm not just saying that because she is my boss now). As of this writing, I am working on completing my master's in social work.

I believe that the future of violence prevention as a field, the future of the work, and the future of my people will benefit from this broader, more comprehensive approach. It is an honor to have her help lead us there.

Joakim Noah retired from the Los Angeles Clippers in 2020. True to his word, Jo made good on the promise he made over a decade earlier: *"When I am done with basketball, you and I are going to be in this violence prevention thing together."* Jo has dedicated much of his personal focus and resources of the Noah's Arc Foundation to these efforts. On October 28, 2021, the Chicago Bulls hosted a "Joakim Noah Night" in his honor and named him a community ambassador for the team.

In July 2022, Angel and I traveled to Trancoso, Brazil, for his marriage to Lais Ribeiro. We danced all night in a giant tent just off the beaches of Bahia.

In May 2023, the Noah's Arc Foundation launched the One City program, formalizing the peace tournaments into a citywide initiative that brings together nearly thirty violence prevention programs and three hundred kids throughout Chicago to play in seasonal tournaments. We've added basketball clinics and community supports, including financial literacy, entrepreneurial training, and mental health interventions so as not to repeat the challenges we faced in the past. We received state funding for our efforts in the city and have begun to look at replicating this more sophisticated design in other cities around the country.

I still maintain my position at the Noah's Arc Foundation and Cure Violence as well as launching a nonprofit of my own, Transform Justice, which looks to enhance the cultural aspects of the work to support the community violence intervention ecosystem. I also have three new reasons for being, inspiring me to keep working toward a better future. Latrell had a baby girl, Nova Marie Williams, who, for obvious reasons, we've named "NoNo," Quinn had a son, Quintus Pascal Collins, Jr., whom we call "Peanut," and my daughter, Nay Nay, just gave birth to her first little one, which she fittingly named Miracle. My grandbabies are pure joy.

When I look ahead, I see hope and possibility in the future. It has been a struggle to get this work the kind of recognition that it deserves. It is going to be even more of a struggle to get these programs to be where they will need to be in the future, but I am confident and optimistic.

EPILOGUE

Anywhere, USA: The Future

Violence as we know it has ended. In Black and brown communities across America, community violence intervention programs are fully funded at scale. A New York CMS–like system is implemented nationwide. In the same way, emergency response networks are coordinated city by city, state by state in sync. Rather than fire, ambulance, or police dispatched, these crisis hubs coordinate violence interruption, outreach, social service resources, or mental health provisions.

Conflict mediators walk a beat, once "hot spots," now cooled. They gauge the temperature in the community through casual conversations. Chill with the guys on the porch, some. Help an elderly resident up the stairs with her groceries. There is still conflict because, of course, there is still conflict. This is a reality, not some utopian fantasy. Conflict is resolved through communication. Basic needs are expressed and met. Food, shelter, compassion, and clothing are provided.

Peace councils, similar to what was set up in Austin, made of community, give hearings to settle up debts. Matters are resolved for the good of the community with the community in mind. Forums are organized to clarify miscommunications. Spaces are created for honest, authentic, transparent expression. They operate with mutual respect.

Restorative justice circles work not to punish but to make amends for the individuals harmed and the community at large. Harmful behaviors are addressed in an open way. Emotional injuries from the harm are expressed and discussed. Accountability is taken. Things are made right. More complicated emotional or mental health issues are referred out, with specialists providing clinical oversight.

Ordinary citizens are trained in de-escalation techniques. Teachers, store owners, the counter guy at the chicken shack, and the bartender at the club know basic conflict resolution skills. They are the first line of defense. When a shoulder bump results in a spilled drink, no one pulls a gun. *"It doesn't need to get crazy in here,"* everyone agrees. It doesn't even have to come to blows. General empathy prevails. That is the new norm.

Institutions operate trauma-informed. Everyone exercises a certain level of compassion. On the streets, a *harambay* philosophy for all, the way Brother Mitchell and Brother Petersen from Man Up! practice the Kenyan tradition of everyone pulling together in a show of mutual respect in Brooklyn. Everyone is equally invested in the well-being of the community. We make decisions on behalf of the collective rather than on our individual motives in a given moment.

We look out for our neighbors. We take care of one another. We meet each other's needs.

This future is more realistic than flying cars. We have the technology. We just need the will to get there.

Over a decade ago, Michelle Alexander and Bryan Stevenson, both civil rights lawyers, began a public dialogue about mass incarceration. Alexander with *The New Jim Crow: Mass Incarceration in the Age of Colorblindness* and Stevenson with *Just Mercy: A Story of Justice and Redemption*. They took a long, hard look at the justice system, raising some painful, powerful questions on the structural, systemic racism embedded within it.

They each presented a compelling argument that mass incarceration in America contributes to the cycle of poverty. Each of them helped set the stage for debates around civil rights, voters' rights, the "war on drugs," poverty, systemic racism, punishment, and rehabilitation in this country. As a result, they contributed to a lot of justice reform in that period.

It is time to reimagine the justice system in its entirety. Humbly, I hope that this book can help feed a conversation focused further upstream. Interrupting violence often occurs before contact with the justice system has taken place. It looks at community conflict at the street level, which leads to incarceration, injury, or death. It presents a new model for how these conflicts can be handled in a way that doesn't result in more trauma and pain. It is designed in many ways to end the cycle of violence.

Michelle Alexander identified that one of the key challenges to the contemporary civil rights movement is the resistance of activists to associate with criminalized populations. In my own experience, this has begun to change. I am seeing new generations of activists willing to cross that divide. It is inspiring. It gives me hope.

Throughout this book, in sharing my story, I have also tried to share encounters I've had with various systems that pushed me toward a fate as an incarcerated gang member. This is not to dismiss any of my own personal responsibility but rather to point out that the systemic racism embedded in institutions, the system itself, owns some of the responsibility for the culture that has been created. I believe that we can change these things to invent the future we want.

It used to be that when I was asked what I think is required to turn things around in our communities, I'd shrug, *"That is above my pay grade."* I would tell you how to create a community violence intervention from the ground up, but asking me what the community needs is like asking a paramedic about surgery, I would quip.

My go-to answer was always, *"My job is laser-focused on stopping the shooting and killing. Period. Hard stop."*

I was wrong on that. When I would circle up with some of the guys—other interrupters in conversation later—we did have answers. We had seen enough, experienced enough, and lived enough to have solutions. We'd compare notes, sharing stories and experiences as patterns emerged. I began to see systemic themes play out from Kansas City to Louisville, Kentucky, connecting dots well beyond the model. There are so many touch points, little moments of inflection, in an individual life and the life of a community that can send it in the opposite direction.

Violence prevention isn't just about cops, courts, judges, and jails. It involves education, health care, housing, economics, employment, mental health services, and an entire ecosystem that can keep youth from making decisions that can't be undone.

Economic and entrepreneurial training, alongside microloan business investing, can help reverse the generations of wealth stolen from Black families through redlining and racist banking practices, as can access to employment opportunities, job training, and job readiness programs, especially for formerly incarcerated individuals and youth.

School-based programs, conflict resolution, de-escalation training in the classroom, and trauma-informed care strategies in the community can help to disrupt the school-to-prison pipeline. I shared my experiences from grade school through high school, where I ultimately abandoned my education, considering what could have helped spare me from my fate. I also believe that additional resources, training, and support for educators are necessary to help shift their role away from policing behavior to focus on teaching.

Similarly, the role of the police, courts, prison, and probation are often deeply marred by corruption. I was framed for a crime I didn't commit because the police couldn't catch me up on anything I was doing. I share these experiences to show how, often, without transparency and accountability, justice is treated more like a game than an ethical principle in action.

Law-and-order thinking, in my experience, condemns the person rather than punishes the crime. This includes policing policies like zero tolerance, stop and frisk, and so on. They don't make things safer but rather target Black and Brown citizens and collectively punish already wounded communities.

Reentry, in particular, is a perfect example of this skewed logic. More often, probation of the recently released is an extension of state control. Rather than providing support and services, the state usually treats these as barriers. The formerly incarcerated are rarely set up for success on the outside. In my case, if it was not for the love of my family, a strong support network, and the compassion of Shorty Freeman and others, I may have ended up back behind bars.

Housing, health care, social support services, job training, continuing education, and so on should not be left to informal networks. They improve someone's chances of successfully staying out of prison, so if that is the goal, shouldn't providing them be the standard operating procedure?

Most of these observations on various touch points in the criminal justice ecosystem are based on personal experience and observation. I have seen how they make situations worse or help transform someone on the verge of change. My hope is that some reading this will be inspired to go deeper than these observations and find ways to improve these aspects of the system in the future.

NOTES

CHAPTER I

1. Stuart Schrader, "Yes, American Police Act Like Occupying Armies. They Literally Studied Their Tactics," *The Guardian*, June 8, 2020, https://www.theguardian.com/commentisfree/2020/jun/08/yes-american-police-act-like-occupying-armies-they-literally-studied-their-tactics.
2. Elijah Anderson, *Code of the Street: Decency, Violence, and the Moral Life of the Inner City* (New York: Norton, 1999).

CHAPTER 2

1. Andrew J. Diamond, *Chicago on the Make: Power and Inequality in a Modern City* (Berkeley: University of California Press, 2017).
2. Natalie Y. Moore, *The South Side: A Portrait of Chicago and American Segregation* (New York: Picador, 2017).
3. Thomas P. Bonczar, "Prevalence of Imprisonment in the U.S. Population, 1974–2001," Bureau of Justice Statistics, August 2003, https://bjs.ojp.gov/library/publications/prevalence-imprisonment-us-population-1974-2001, accessed June 23, 2021.
4. Ruth Delaney, Ram Subramanian, Alison Shames, and Nicholas Turner, "Reimagining Prison Web Report: American History, Race, and Prison," *Vera*, April 2016, https://www.vera.org/reimagining-prison-web-report/american-history-race-and-prison, accessed June 23, 2021.

5. Isabel Wilkerson, *The Warmth of Other Suns: The Epic Story of America's Great Migration* (New York: Vintage Books, 2011).

CHAPTER 3

1. G. Robert Blakely and Brian Gettings, "Racketeer Influenced and Corrupt Organizations (RICO): Basic Concepts—Criminal and Civil Remedies," *Temple Law Quarterly* 53, no. 1009 (1980), https://scholarship.law.nd.edu/law_faculty _scholarship/603, accessed June 23, 2021.

2. Nicholas D. Kristof and Sheryl WuDunn, *A Path Appears: Transforming Lives, Creating Opportunity* (New York: Knopf, 2014).

3. Everytown Research & Policy, "Gun Violence in America," January 2022, https://everytownresearch.org/report/gun-violence-in-america, accessed June 23, 2021.

4. Educational Fund to Stop Gun Violence and Coalition to Stop Gun Violence, "A Public Health Crisis Decades in the Making: A Review of 2019 CDC Gun Mortality Data," 2021, http://efsgv.org/2019CDCdata, accessed June 23, 2021.

5. Lakeidra Chavis, "The Problems with Chicago's Gang-Centric Narrative of Gun Violence," *The Trace*, August 31, 2021, https://www.thetrace.org/2021/08 /chicago-mayor-police-gang-database-shooting, accessed April 13, 2022.

6. Dawn Delfin McDaniel, "Risk and Protective Factors Associated with Gang Affiliation among High-Risk Youth: A Public Health Approach," *Injury Prevention* 18 (2012): 253–58, https://injuryprevention.bmj.com/content/18/4/253, accessed June 23, 2021.

7. Abby Rogers, "How Chicago Became the Deadliest City in America," *Insider*, November 23, 2012, https://www.businessinsider.com/how-chicago-became-the -deadliest-city-in-america-2012-11, accessed June 23, 2021.

CHAPTER 4

1. A. C. McFarlane, "The Long-Term Costs of Traumatic Stress: Intertwined Physical and Psychological Consequences," *World Psychiatry* 9, no. 1 (2010): 3–10.

2. Catherine Y. Kim, Daniel J. Losen, and Damon T. Hewitt, *The School-to-Prison Pipeline: Structuring Legal Reform* (New York: New York University Press, 2010).

CHAPTER 6

1. Tom Skilling, "Ask Tom: How Cold Was Dec. 24, 1983?," *Chicago Tribune*, February 19, 2016, https://www.chicagotribune.com/weather/ct-wea-0220-asktom -20160219-column.html, accessed June 23, 2021.

2. Linnet Myers, "Confession Recanted; Man Found Innocent," *Chicago Tribune*, June 1, 1987, https://www.chicagotribune.com/news/ct-xpm-1987-06-02-8702100591-story.html, accessed June 23, 2021.

CHAPTER 7

1. National Institute of Justice, "Children Exposed to Violence," September 21, 2016, https://nij.ojp.gov/topics/articles/children-exposed-violence, accessed June 23, 2021.

2. Nicholas Turner, "We Spend $296 Billion Each Year on a Justice System That Doesn't Make Us Safer," *Forbes EQ*, July 1, 2021, https://www.forbes.com/sites/forbeseq/2021/07/01/we-spend-296-billion-each-year-on-a-justice-system-that-doesnt-make-us-safer/?sh=4630e96e7070, accessed July 27, 2021.

3. Shelly S. Hyland, "Justice Expenditure and Employment Extracts, 2016," Bureau of Justice Statistics, November 2019, https://bjs.ojp.gov/library/publications/justice-expenditure-and-employment-extracts-2016-preliminary, accessed June 23, 2021.

4. Nazish Dholakia and Daniela Gilbert, "Community Violence Intervention Programs, Explained," *Vera*, September 1, 2021, https://www.vera.org/community-violence-intervention-programs-explained#, accessed April 13, 2022.

5. Alex S. Vitale, "The Police Are Not Here to Protect You," *Vice*, June 1, 2020, https://www.vice.com/en/article/7kpvnb/end-of-policing-book-extract, accessed April 13, 2022.

6. David Bayley, *Police for the Future* (Oxford: Oxford University Press, 1996).

7. Roge Karma, "We Train Police to Be Warriors—And Then Send Them Out to Be Social Workers," *Vox*, July 30, 2020, https://www.vox.com/2020/7/31/21334190/what-police-do-defund-abolish-police-reform-training, accessed April 13, 2022.

8. "Hundreds Rally for Human Justice during Walk from Brooklyn to Long Island City," News 12, The Bronx, October 10, 2022.

9. Tandy Lau, "K. Bain Brings New York City Gun Violence Interruption to the Highest Office," *New York Amsterdam News*, August 25, 2022.

10. Lau, "K. Bain Brings New York City Gun Violence Interruption to the Highest Office."

CHAPTER 8

1. Libby Nelson and Dara Lind, "The School-to-Prison Pipeline, Explained: Police Officers in Classrooms Are Just the Tip of the Iceberg," *Vox*, 2015, https://www.vox.com/2015/2/24/8101289/school-discipline-race, accessed April 13, 2022.

2. Marilyn Elias, "The School-to-Prison Pipeline," *Teaching Tolerance Magazine*, Spring 2013, https://www.learningforjustice.org/magazine/spring-2013, accessed April 13, 2022.

3. Janet E. Rosenbaum, "Educational and Criminal Justice Outcomes 12 Years after School Suspension," *Youth & Society* 52, no. 4 (2020): 515–47, https://www.ncbi.nlm.nih.gov/pmc/articles/PMC7288849, accessed April 13, 2022.

4. Tandy Lau, "K. Bain Brings New York City Gun Violence Interruption to the Highest Office," *New York Amsterdam News*, August 25, 2022.

5. Ira Glass, "487: Harper High School—Part One," *This American Life*, February 15, 2015, https://www.thisamericanlife.org/487/harper-high-school-part-one.

CHAPTER 13

1. W. R. Miller and S. Rollnick, *Motivational Interviewing: Preparing People for Change*, 2nd ed. (New York: Guilford Press, 2002).

2. Miller and Rollnick, *Motivational Interviewing*.

3. Terrell Thomas and Rachel Eisenberg, "Centering Youth in Community Violence Interventions as Part of a Comprehensive Approach to Countering Gun Violence," Center for American Progress, October 2022, https://www.americanprogress.org/article/centering-youth-in-community-violence-interventions-as-part-of-a-comprehensive-approach-to-countering-gun-violence, accessed June 12, 2022.

4. Cure Violence Global, "The Evidence for Effectiveness," September 16, 2021, https://cvg.org/wp-content/uploads/2022/09/Cure-Violence-Evidence-Summary.pdf, accessed June 12, 2022.

5. Tom Kutsch, "Evaluating a Top Violence Prevention Program in Chicago," April 25, 2022, https://www.thetrace.org/newsletter/chicago-readi-community-intervention-gun-violence-shooting, accessed April 27, 2022.

6. Thomas and Eisenberg, "Centering Youth in Community Violence Interventions as Part of a Comprehensive Approach to Countering Gun Violence."

7. Megan Cahill et al., "Evaluation of the Los Angeles Gang Reduction and Youth Development Program," September 2015, https://www.urban.org/sites/default/files/publication/77956/2000622-Evaluation-of-the-Los-Angeles-Gang-Reduction-and-Youth-Development-Program-Year-4-Evaluation-Report.pdf, accessed June 12, 2022.

CHAPTER 16

1. Douglass Starr, "This Psychologist Explains Why People Confess to Crimes They Didn't Commit," June 13, 2019, https://www.science.org/content/article/psychologist-explains-why-people-confess-crimes-they-didn-t-commit, accessed June 23, 2021.

2. Starr, "This Psychologist Explains Why People Confess to Crimes They Didn't Commit."

CHAPTER 17

1. W. R. Miller and S. Rollnick, *Motivational Interviewing: Preparing People for Change*, 2nd ed. (New York: Guilford Press, 2002).
2. Nancy R. Gibbs, "Murder in Miniature," *Time*, September 19, 1994, https://web.archive.org/web/20070428135038/http:/www.time.com/time/magazine /article/0,9171,981460,00.html, accessed June 12, 2022.

CHAPTER 19

1. Annelies Goger, David J. Harding, and Howard Henderson, "A Better Path Forward for Criminal Justice: Prisoner Reentry," April 2021, https://www.brook ings.edu/research/a-better-path-forward-for-criminal-justice-prisoner-reentry, accessed June 12, 2022.

CHAPTER 21

1. Tony Thompson, "Stanley 'Tookie' Williams: One of the Last Men to Be Executed in California," *The Guardian*, March 13, 2019, https://www.theguardian.com /books/2004/nov/28/biography.tonythompson, accessed June 12, 2022.

CHAPTER 27

1. New York Civil Liberties Union, "A Closer Look at Stop-and-Frisk in NYC," December 2021, https://www.nyclu.org/en/stop-and-frisk-data, accessed June 23, 2021.
2. RAND Corporation, "Zero Tolerance and Aggressive Policing (and Why to Avoid It) in Depth," 2018, https://www.rand.org/pubs/tools/TL261/better-policing -toolkit.html, accessed June 23, 2021.

CHAPTER 29

1. William J. Aceves, "The Watts Gang Treaty: Hidden History and the Power of Social Movements," *Harvard Civil Rights–Civil Liberties Law Review* 57 (2022), https://harvardcrcl.org/wp-content/uploads/sites/10/2022/09/WattsGangTreaty.pdf, accessed January 23, 2022.

BIBLIOGRAPHY

Abdullah, Sadar. Interview. Conducted by Josh Gryniewicz. February 22, 2022.

Anderson, Elijah. *Code of the Street: Decency, Violence, and the Moral Life of the Inner City*. New York: Norton, 1999.

Bain, K. Interview. Conducted by Josh Gryniewicz. March 3, 2021.

Bayley, David. *Police for the Future*. Oxford: Oxford University Press, 1996.

Bernard, Shirley. Interview. Conducted by Josh Gryniewicz. January 24, 2022.

Blakely, Robert, et al. "Racketeer Influenced and Corrupt Organizations (RICO): Basic Concepts—Criminal and Civil Remedies." *Temple Law Quarterly* 53, no. 1009 (1980). https://scholarship.law.nd.edu/law_faculty_scholarship/603. Accessed June 23, 2021.

Bonczar, Thomas P. "Prevalence of Imprisonment in the U.S. Population, 1974–2001." Bureau of Justice Statistics. August 2003. https://bjs.ojp.gov/library/publications/prevalence-imprisonment-us-population-1974-2001. Accessed June 23, 2021.

Bryant, Hilda. Interview. Conducted by Josh Gryniewicz. January 24, 2022.

Chavis, Lakeidra. "The Problems with Chicago's Gang-Centric Narrative of Gun Violence." https://www.thetrace.org/2021/08/chicago-mayor-police-gang-database-shooting. Accessed June 23, 2021.

Cure Violence Global. "The Evidence for Effectiveness." September 16, 2021. https://cvg.org/wp-content/uploads/2022/09/Cure-Violence-Evidence-Summary.pdf. Accessed June 12, 2022.

Decker, Brent. Interview. Conducted by Josh Gryniewicz. December 9, 2021.

Delaney, Ruth, et al. "Reimagining Prison Web Report: American History, Race, and Prison." April 2016. https://www.vera.org/reimagining-prison-web-report /american-history-race-and-prison. Accessed June 23, 2021.

Dholakia, Nazish, and Daniela Gilert. "Community Violence Intervention Programs, Explained." September 1, 2021. https://www.vera.org/community-vio lence-intervention-programs-explained#. Accessed April 13, 2022.

Diamond, Andrew. *Chicago on the Make: Power & Inequality in a Modern City.* Berkeley: University of California Press, 2017.

Educational Fund to Stop Gun Violence and Coalition to Stop Gun Violence. "A Public Health Crisis Decades in the Making: A Review of 2019 CDC Gun Mortality Data." 2021. http://efsgv.org/2019CDCdata. Accessed February 15, 2022.

Elias, Marilyn. "The School-to-Prison Pipeline." Spring 2013. https://www.learning forjustice.org/magazine/spring-2013. Accessed April 13, 2022.

Everytown Research & Policy. "Gun Violence in America." January 26, 2022. https://everytownresearch.org/report/gun-violence-in-america. Accessed February 15, 2022.

Gibbs, Nancy R. "Murder in Miniature." September 19, 1994. https://web .archive.org/web/20070428135038/http:/www.time.com/time/magazine/arti cle/0,9171981460,00.html. Accessed June 12, 2022.

Glass, Ira, host. "487: Harper High School—Part One." February 15, 2015. https:// www.thisamericanlife.org/487/harper-high-school-part-one.

———. "488: Harper High School—Part Two." February 22, 2015. https://www .thisamericanlife.org/488/harper-high-school-part-two.

Goger, Annelies, David J. Harding, and Howard Henderson. "A Better Path Forward for Criminal Justice: Prisoner Reentry." April 2021. https://www.brookings .edu/research/a-better-path-forward-for-criminal-justice-prisoner-reentry. Accessed June 12, 2022.

Hyland, Shelly S. "Justice Expenditure and Employment Extracts, 2016." November 2019. https://bjs.ojp.gov/library/publications/justice-expenditure-and -employment-extracts-2016-preliminary. Accessed June 23, 2021.

Johnson, Cookie. Interview. Conducted by Josh Gryniewicz. January 24, 2022.

Karma, Roge. "We Train Police to Be Warriors—and Then Send Them Out to Be Social Workers." July 30, 2020. https://www.vox.com/2020/7/31/21334190/what -police-do-defund-abolish-police-reform-training. Accessed April 13, 2022.

Kim, Catherine Y., Daniel J. Losen, and Damon T. Hewitt. *The School-to-Prison Pipeline: Structuring Legal Reform.* New York: New York University Press, 2010.

Kristof, Nicholas, and Sheryl WuDunn. *A Path Appears: Transforming Lives, Creating Opportunity.* New York: Knopf, 2014.

Kutsch, Tom. "Evaluating a Top Violence Prevention Program in Chicago." April 25, 2022. https://www.thetrace.org/newsletter/chicago-readi-community-inter vention-gun-violence-shooting. Accessed April 27, 2022.

McAllister, Marcus. Interview. Conducted by Josh Gryniewicz. March 8, 2022.

McDaniel, D. D. "Risk and Protective Factors Associated with Gang Affiliation among High-Risk Youth: A Public Health Approach." *Injury Prevention*,
2012;18:253-258.

McFarlane, A. C. "The Long-Term Costs of Traumatic Stress: Intertwined
Physical and Psychological Consequences." *World Psychiatry*, 9 (2020): 3–10.
doi:10.1002/j.2051-5545.2010.tb00254.x.

Miller, W. R., and S. Rollnick. *Motivational Interviewing. Preparing People for
Change.* 2nd ed. New York: Guilford Press, 2002.

Mitchell, Andre "AT." Interview. Conducted by Josh Gryniewicz. February 25,
2022.

Moore, Natalie. *The South Side: A Portrait of Chicago and American Segregation.*
New York: Picador, 2017.

Myers, Linnet. "Confession Recanted; Man Found Innocent." June 1, 1987. https://
www.chicagotribune.com/news/ct-xpm-1987-06-02-8702100591-story.html. Accessed June 23, 2021.

National Institute of Justice. "Children Exposed to Violence." September 21, 2016.
https://nij.ojp.gov/topics/articles/children-exposed-violence. Accessed June 23,
2021.

Nelson, Libby, and Dara Lind. "The School-to-Prison Pipeline, Explained: Police
Officers in Classrooms Are Just the Tip of the Iceberg." 2015. https://www.vox
.com/2015/2/24/8101289/school-discipline-race. Accessed April 13, 2022.

New York Civil Liberties Union. "A Closer Look at Stop-And-Frisk in NYC."
December 2021. https://www.nyclu.org/en/stop-and-frisk-data. Accessed June
23, 2021.

Noah, Joakim. Interview. Conducted by Josh Gryniewicz. November 8, 2022.

Parker, Charlie. Interview. Conducted by Josh Gryniewicz. November 15, 2021.

Patrick, Willem, and Criminal Justice Reform Initiative. "The Justice Ecosystem:
It's More Than Police, Courts, and Jails." June 22, 2022.https://www.aspeninsti
tute.org/blog-posts/the-justice-ecosystem-its-more-than-police-courts-and-jails.
Accessed June 25, 2022.

Peterson, James. Interview. Conducted by Josh Gryniewicz. February 25, 2022.

RAND Corporation. "Zero Tolerance and Aggressive Policing (and Why to Avoid
It) in Depth." 2018. https://www.rand.org/pubs/tools/TL261/better-policing
-toolkit.html. Accessed June 23, 2021.

Rogers, Abby. "How Chicago Became the Deadliest City in America." November
23, 2012. https://www.businessinsider.com/how-chicago-became-the-deadliest
-city-in-america-2012-11. Accessed June 23, 2021.

Rosenbaum, Janet E. "Educational and Criminal Justice Outcomes 12 Years after
School Suspension." *Youth & Society* 52, no. 4 (May 2020): 515–47. https://www
.ncbi.nlm.nih.gov/pmc/articles/PMC7288849. Accessed April 13, 2022.

Schrader, Stuart. "Yes, American Police Act Like Occupying Armies: They Literally
Studied Their Tactics." June 8, 2020. https://www.theguardian.com/comment

isfree/2020/jun/08/yes-american-police-act-like-occupying-armies-they-literally
-studied-their-tactics.

Skilling, Tom. "Ask Tom: How Cold Was Dec. 24, 1983?" February 19, 2016.
https://www.chicagotribune.com/weather/ct-wea-0220-asktom-20160219
-column.html. Accessed June 23, 2021.

Starr, Douglass. "This Psychologist Explains Why People Confess to Crimes
They Didn't Commit." June 13, 2019. https://www.science.org/content/article
/psychologist-explains-why-people-confess-crimes-they-didn-t-commit. Accessed June 23, 2021.

Thomas, Terrell, and Rachel Eisenberg. "Centering Youth in Community Violence Interventions as Part of a Comprehensive Approach to Countering Gun
Violence." October 2022. https://www.americanprogress.org/article/centering
-youth-in-community-violence-interventions-as-part-of-a-comprehensive
-approach-to-countering-gun-violence. Accessed June 12, 2022.

Turner, Nicholas. "We Spend $296 Billion Each Year on a Justice System
That Doesn't Make Us Safer." July 1, 2021. https://www.forbes.com/sites
/forbeseq/2021/07/01/we-spend-296-billion-each-year-on-a-justice-system-that
-doesnt-make-us-safer/?sh=4630e96e7070. Accessed July 27, 2021.

Vitale, Alex. "The Police Are Not Here to Protect You." June 1, 2020. https://www
.vice.com/en/article/7kpvnb/end-of-policing-book-extract. Accessed April 13,
2022.

Wilkerson, Isabel. *The Warmth of Other Suns: The Epic Story of America's Great
Migration.* New York: Vintage Books, 2011.

Williams, Andrea (Angel). Interview. Conducted by Josh Gryniewicz. December
6, 2021.

Williams, Latrell. Interview. Conducted by Josh Gryniewicz. November 12, 2021.

Williams, Mildred (Granny). Interview. Conducted by Josh Gryniewicz. November
2, 2021.

Williams, Mildred (Trice, sister). Interview. Conducted by Josh Gryniewicz.
December 6, 2021.

Williams, Ray. Interview. Conducted by Josh Gryniewicz. November 15, 2021.

INDEX

ABOUT THE AUTHORS

Cobe Williams is the director of national programs for Cure Violence Global (CVG), where he trained more than five thousand workers in violence prevention. He appeared in the film *The Interrupters* and in *People*, *Vice*, *Ebony*, and the *New Yorker*. He received a standing ovation at his TEDx event. He serves as a community ambassador for basketball star Joakim Noah's foundation. Cobe earned a BA at Northeastern Illinois University and is pursuing a master's in social work. He lives in a Chicago suburb with his wife, Andrea, and their four children.

Josh Gryniewicz is an author, storyteller, comic book writer, and health communicator. He was a contributing author to *Beyond Suppression: Global Perspectives on Youth Violence* and *Crime & Society* and a regular columnist with *PopMatters*. In 2018, he founded Odd Duck, a storytelling-for-social-change creative consultancy, advising nonprofits, foundations, and health care organizations throughout the country. He is the former communication director for Cure Violence.